FIFTY CENTS AND A BOX TOP

SOUNDING APPALACHIA

Travis D. Stimeling, Series Editor

FIFTY CENTS AND A BOX TOP

The Creative Life
of Nashville Session Musician
Charlie McCoy

CHARLIE McCOY

with Travis D. Stimeling

WEST VIRGINIA UNIVERSITY PRESS
MORGANTOWN • 2017

First edition published 2017 by West Virginia University Press
Printed in the United States of America

ISBN:
paper   978-1-943665-71-6
epub   978-1-943665-72-3
pdf   978-1-943665-73-0

Library of Congress Cataloging-in-Publication Data is available
from the Library of Congress.

Cover design by Than Saffel. Cover photograph courtesy of the
author. Photographer unknown. All other photographs courtesy
of the author unless noted otherwise.

CONTENTS

Foreword / *Travis D. Stimeling* / vii

Acknowledgments / xi

1. West Virginia Days / 1

2. Rock-and-Roll Charlie / 7

3. The Road to Nashville / 19

4. College and the Return to Nashville / 26

5. Music City Opportunities / 42

6. The Studio Scene / 54

7. The Artists / 70

8. The Recording Artist / 87

9. *Hee Haw* and Other Television Appearances / 109

10. An Artist Overseas / 123

11. The Harmonica and Me / 144

Conclusion: Reflections on a Good Life / 153

A Note on Sources / *Travis D. Stimeling* / 167

Appendix A: The Nashville Number System / *Charlie McCoy* / 171

Appendix B: Charlie McCoy Album Discography / 175

Notes / 217

About the Authors / 219

Index / 221

FOREWORD

Travis D. Stimeling

In late October 2015, as the leaves on the oaks and maples and poplars that cover the slopes of the Allegheny Plateau revealed their brilliant autumnal colors, the New River Valley town of Fayetteville, West Virginia, prepared for a celebration in honor of one of its native sons. In this sleepy town of around three thousand residents, several hundred people filled the seats of the historic Fayette Theatre in recognition of Charles Ray "Charlie" McCoy, born in nearby Oak Hill more than seven decades earlier, and fellow West Virginia Music Hall of Fame member John Ellison. In this theater, where young Charlie watched singing cowboy stars Roy Rogers and Gene Autry sing their way through community conflict, Fayetteville mayor Dennis Hanson read proclamations from West Virginia governor Earl Ray Tomblin and the Fayetteville town council in honor of Charlie's nearly six-decade career as one of the most-recorded session musicians in the history of American popular music. Standing on the same stage where his interest in music was first piqued, McCoy humbly accepted these proclamations and proceeded to play a relatively brief set of country standards, pop hits, and Irish folk songs with accompaniment from guitarist Richard Kiser. A steadfast sideman, McCoy's brilliance at the harmonica shines as he plays clean runs of parallel thirds, slowly and carefully bends the pitch of single notes, and brings the house down with his show-stopping finale, "Orange Blossom Special." Were it not for a twist of fate that found him as a first-call Nashville session musician instead of a rock-and-roll star, it is quite possible that most people would have never heard McCoy's multi-instrumental talents. Thankfully, Charlie found his way to Nashville at a moment when the city's musicians were producing hits that reached both the country and pop charts, and he was at the center of that community. From Ann-Margret to George Jones and Simon and Garfunkel to Bob Dylan, Charlie McCoy has exerted an indelible influence on the sound of popular music in the United States and abroad.

This book recounts Charlie McCoy's remarkable journey from a small southern West Virginia town to the Country Music Hall of Fame. During this journey, he has played with hundreds of legendary recording artists, joined forces with dozens of top session musicians, come into homes around the United States through his work on the television program *Hee Haw*, and played music on three continents. Yet, while some people might use such an impressive professional resumé as an excuse to remain far from the madding crowd, Charlie remains a genuine and kindhearted individual who is more likely to ask people about their lives than to brag about his own accomplishments. Many of the people I have met in my musical travels around West Virginia and Nashville point to his kindness and encouragement, just as he spoke gently with an aspiring young harmonica player after his performance in Fayetteville. Like his baseball hero Stan Musial, McCoy quietly but commandingly built a hall of fame career and became a leader among his peers while never losing the common touch.

I witnessed this common touch firsthand in May 2015, when Charlie invited me to join him for a recording session during one of my research trips to Nashville. That day, he was recording overdubs and vocals for a song that he had written with a longtime collaborator. As I entered the studio, he greeted me with a warm handshake and a smile and offered to get me a cup of coffee. He talked to the engineers (who appeared to be in their twenties), joking around while also gently communicating his needs for the session. As session musicians entered to play and sing their parts, Charlie did not micromanage them, but instead allowed them to play what they thought the track needed. And, when he entered the vocal booth to cut the lead vocals, he even let me offer a suggestion to improve the phrasing of a particular line. This has been the key to his success as a session musician and recording artist: allowing people to be themselves and finding ways to help them perform at their best.

This approach is precisely how McCoy became a leading member of the so-called Nashville A-Team. As a harmonica player, his bright tone shines clearly through nearly every recording he has contributed to, and his plaintive bends and wails are as iconic as the vocal performances he has accompanied. And, when a harmonica was not called for, he drew upon his experiences as a music education major to play nearly every instrument available to him. Among his recording credits, one finds that Charlie has committed his guitar, bass, trumpet, saxophone, vibraphone, and organ playing to tape. He is, in the estimation of his peers, a musician's musician.

ACKNOWLEDGMENTS

Charlie

As I wrote this book, I spent a great deal of time reflecting on the many people who have supported me as I have built a life in music. I have been blessed in so many ways, and I am grateful for everyone who has shown me kindness, who has mentored me, and who has given me an opportunity. It would be nearly impossible to list everyone who has played an important role in my life, but a few people deserve special recognition.

First, I am grateful for God and his son Jesus Christ, who has forgiven a messed-up man like me and paid the price for eternity. I know that he has another gig for me after this life is over.

My wife Pat loves me despite my music addiction, and she has shared my dream of spreading music to the world. She has brought order to my life and has accomplished the impossible task of understanding me. I'm also grateful that she helped me with the first draft of this memoir.

My parents always did what was right for me, even when it was inconvenient or painful. Although it must have been tough for them to make things work after the divorce, they never let it get in the way of loving me.

My kids, Ginger and Charlie Jr., are both successful parents and have great careers. Thanks also for giving me five super grandchildren. They are pretty super kids themselves!

My first wife Susan was the best mother that Ginger and Charlie Jr. could ever have.

Thanks to my brother Buddy, who has been everything that a big brother should be.

My extended family has provided so much support over the years. I am grateful for Jackie Kelley Dyer and J. B. Dyer, Judy Vinto Learmonth, Carol Jane Learmonth, Jennifer Learmonth Kincaid, Sue Cooper Garrett, Carol Maguire Campbell, Sherrie Garrett Fries, Steve Fries, Christina Fries, Stephanie Fries, Jerrie Bennett Shepherd, Karen McCluskey Carter, Suzanne McCluskey Hogan, Ken Jordan, Debi Newbill McCoy, Chris Clark and Linda Garrett Clark, Dean Cheek and Lana Garrett Cheek, Terry Hardin and Linda Greer Hardin, Wes Hardin, and Charles and Alice Garrett.

Many people have played key roles in my career. Thanks to Elon Kealoha, Margaret DeSola, Shirley Vineyard, Doris Ludder, Mme. Renée Longy, Happy Harold, Mel Tillis, Jim Denny, Archie Bleyer, Fred Foster, Tex Davis, Kent Westberry, Snuffy Smith, Wayne Gray, Wayne Moss, Ted Fuller, Eric Paul, Ray Pennington, Andrew Heller, Greg Howard, Sam Lovullo, Eddy Mitchell, Jean-Yves Lozac'h, Philippe "Guzze" and Francine Kulczak, Frédéric Leibovitz, Helen Bank, Calle Nielsen, Nils Tuxen, Jodle Birge, Mogens Villadsen, Kenji Nagatomi, Mari Nagatomi, Pat Conway, Laney Smallwood Hicks, The Charlie McCoy Band, The United, The Tomboola Band, Robert Křest'an and Druhá Tráva, The Tennessee Five, and Bruno Tillander, Randy Smith, Sam Bumpus, Gary Sharp, and Steve Horrell. Thanks also to the Nashville Association of Musicians and Nashville AFTRA. Thanks also to Jo and Bob Meador.

Thanks as well to all the musicians who have asked me to play on their records over the years. You all made my career possible.

Thanks also to Jay Orr, Adrienne Innis, Jonathan Merkh, and Eddie Stubbs for their help during the early work on this book.

Of course, a life of professional success would mean nothing without great friends to share life with. Thanks to all the people who have shown me friendship and hospitality over the year: the Isbell family, Shirley and Louise Humphrey, Roy and June Burcher and their family, Whit and Peggy Parks, Ron and Mavis Taylor, Vince Hatfield and his family, Jimmy Nall and his family, Joe and Irene Clark, Weldon and

Judi Myrick, Vickie Vipperman, Holly Hicks Singleton and Lindsay Hicks Gipe, Teresa Hicks, Jerri Moss, Christy Moss, Connie Moss, Lynda and Don Smith, Delores Buttrey Rhoten, Martina Tuxen, Bodle Schmidt Nielsen and Christina Nielsen, Bernadette Molenaar, Yvonne Rooda, Irene DeRooij, Patricia Lozac'h, Aurelie Bourgeois, Annabel Peyrard, Alain and Annie Valadon, Jean-Marc and Anny Versini, Nils and Tove Hedeman-Hansen, Kim and Lotte Lisbygd, Benny and Janna Pedersen, Anni Filt and Dorte Johansen, Ole Berthelsen, Luboš and Marketa Malina and their neighbor Jana Betlamová, Robert Krestan, Petr Kuklik, Dave and Linda Gordon, Mike and Diane Purvis, Dick and Peggy O'Bitts, Chris and Dottie Reed, and George and Patience Humphrey. And thanks also to all the people at the Gathering and our friends at the Landings.

Travis

As someone who grew up watching Charlie McCoy on *Hee Haw* and listening to his work with so many of the country legends on my parents' stereo, the opportunity to play a role in telling his story has been humbling. I am deeply grateful to Charlie for granting me the opportunity to work on this project, for answering the many questions that I sent his way, and for helping me understand his vision for this book. I am also very thankful for all the wonderful music that Charlie has brought into my life over the years. In many ways, my decision to become a country music scholar was shaped at an early age by the profound emotional experiences I had while listening to his work.

I would also like to thank several people who have provided assistance with this project along the way. First, I would like to extend my gratitude to Pat McCoy, who shaped the initial draft of this book manuscript and provided an excellent text from which to build this book. Sean Wilentz, Jeff Rosen, Parker Fishel, and David Beal provided valuable access to session tapes for Bob Dylan's *Blonde on Blonde* album. Paul Laird pointed me to useful sources dealing with Mme. Renée Longy and her relationship with Leonard Bernstein. Several colleagues and mentors have also been instrumental in providing moral and intellectual support throughout this project, including Evan MacCarthy, Jada Watson, Rich Kienzle, Curt Ellison, Henry Carrigan, Burgin Mathews, Nathan Gibson, and Greg Reish. At West Virginia University Press, Derek Krissoff, Heather Lundine, and Abby Freeland were immediately enthusiastic about this project and gave me the courage to pursue this new kind of writing.

CHAPTER I

—

WEST VIRGINIA DAYS

Oak Hill, West Virginia, is a small town located in the middle of what was once one of the largest coal-producing regions in the state. Home to only a couple of thousand people, it was a big town compared to some of the coal camps that were in the surrounding hollows. In the 1930s, just a few years before I was born, some travel writers came to Oak Hill as part of Franklin Roosevelt's New Deal, and they described it as "a merchant's town with well-stocked stores, strong banks, active civic enterprises, and an unusually large number of places of entertainment." On payday, folks came from all around to shop, take in movies, and talk about what was going on in the surrounding communities. The rest of the time, it was a fairly quiet, small coalfield town.

These days, Oak Hill is probably most famous for being the place where the great country singer and songwriter Hank Williams was found dead in the backseat of his car. He was passing through Oak Hill on his way to a New Year's Day show in Canton, Ohio, as 1952 gave way to 1953. It is also the place where, in March 1941, I was born to Opal Winona Kelley and Ray Hampton McCoy.

My parents divorced when I was two years old. My mother, who wanted to stay near her family, remained in Oak Hill to take care of me. My dad, on the other hand, set out for Miami.

Oak Hill had a radio station, WOAY, that featured live musical acts. One of them, a fellow named Elmer Hickman, lived across the street from us. He called himself "the Blue Mountain Yodeler" and would sing and play by himself for fifteen minutes every weekday morning. He always opened his show with Eddy Arnold's "Cattle Call." One day, when I was about five years old, he invited me over and let me strum on his guitar. It was my introduction to playing music.

Later that year, my mother took a job as a legal secretary and, as a consequence, needed to move us to the county seat, Fayetteville. Although it was only six miles north of Oak Hill, it was almost a different world. Just a short distance from the majestic New River Gorge, Fayetteville was a sleepy little town with lots of beautiful trees and big old houses. Those same writers who visited Oak Hill described my new home as a town "without bustle and hurry," and it was a great place to be a kid. There was always a lot to explore, and on the weekends, there were opportunities to go down to the theater and watch movies with my friends.

In first grade, I developed anemia and had to spend seventeen days in the hospital. The doctors recommended a move to a warmer climate to avoid the harsh West Virginia winters. By the time I reached second grade, my dad was settled in Miami and had a good job there, so my parents decided that I would need to leave my friends at Fayetteville Elementary School that October to spend West Virginia's cold months in the tropical Miami air. I am sure that this was a tough decision for my mother, but she loved me enough to let me go to Florida during the school year.

In Miami, we lived in a room that my dad had rented from the Pollard family, a couple who had moved to Miami from Michigan, and I attended Gladeview Elementary School in the northwest part of the city. My first year of school in Miami was a hard one because I missed my friends in West Virginia so much. At the end of the school year, my mother traveled to Miami to take me back to Fayetteville for the summer. I couldn't wait to get back there to see all my old buddies again!

That summer, I was introduced to the instrument that would end up being my main musical outlet: the harmonica. Like a lot of boys in 1949, I read comic books, and I saw an ad in the back of one of them announcing: "You can play harmonica in seven days or your money back. Just fifty cents and a box top." Well, I convinced my mother that I just had to have one, and she sent off the two quarters and the required box top. I waited for what seemed like an eternity, but one day, it showed up in the mail. I was overjoyed as I opened the package, and no sooner did the harmonica find my mouth than I was running around the house making all sorts of noise on it. Before long, my mother had heard about all she could stand and banished me to the porch. That was bad news for the neighborhood dogs and cats.

It didn't take long for me to grow tired of huffing and puffing and not making any sounds that resembled music. I took out the box the harmonica came in and peeked inside to find a piece of paper with instructions. I brought the paper to my mother, who patiently explained that when it said "blow," I needed to exhale, and when it said "draw," I was supposed to inhale. She also showed me how the numbers they provided corresponded to the holes on the harp. Using this newfound information, I started to work my way through the four songs that were printed on the instruction sheet: "Suwannee River," "Oh, Susanna," "My Country 'Tis of Thee," and "Polly Wolly Doodle." But, despite my initial interest, I soon forgot about the harmonica because baseball season was in full swing.

At the end of the summer, it was time for me to pack up and move back to Miami, but I protested. I didn't want to move away from my friends. I begged my mother and dad to let me stay in West Virginia, and, despite concerns about my health, they relented and allowed me to stay.

Third grade was the year that I decided I wanted to be the next Gene Autry or Roy Rogers. Like most kids in small-town America, I spent many of my Saturday afternoons watching western movies with my friends. You could go to the movies and have a soft drink and pop-corn for twenty-five cents, a perfectly reasonable price. Gene Autry and Roy Rogers, the "singing cowboys," were two of the biggest stars of the day, appearing in dozens of great western films. Their movies included a lot of great musical numbers and had plenty of action scenes to keep our interest. Many of my friends thought that Autry and Rogers were sissies because they played the guitar and sang, but I didn't really care.

I didn't have an opinion on the singing, but, thinking back to my visit with Elmer Hickman, I was hooked on the guitars they played.

That Christmas, I drew a picture of a cowboy with a guitar and told my mother that I wanted to be another Gene or Roy. To my delight, a beautiful Harmony guitar from Montgomery Ward appeared under the tree on Christmas morning. (I still have it today.) On Christmas day, I took my new treasure to my grandparents' house, where my uncle, Keith Kelley, surprised me by picking it up and playing it. He showed me some chords, and I was on my way to learning the guitar. Soon, I could play the chords while singing "Home on the Range." My mother thought it was amazing and cute that her son could actually do this.

She was so proud, in fact, that she volunteered for me to play and sing between the acts of a school play at Fayetteville Elementary School. When she broke the news to me, I was petrified. There was no way that I was going to play in front of all my friends, and singing was absolutely out of the question! I tried to beg off, but my mother was firm. "No way," she said. "You *can* do this, and you *are going* to do this."

She may have been adamant, but I had a plan to get out of it. About fifteen minutes before it was time to leave for the play, I went to the tool drawer, found the wire pliers, and snipped each of the six strings. My mother was livid, and I got a much-deserved spanking as a result. But the spanking didn't hurt nearly as much as going without guitar strings for the rest of the school year and all of the next summer.

My mother remarried, and we moved in with my stepfather, Robert J. Thrift Jr. He was a successful lawyer and was elected to be the circuit court judge. Married life had its ups and downs for my mother. The relationship was stormy at best. My half-brother, William A. "Buddy" Learmouth, was seven years my senior and had already moved out to live with his uncle. My stepfather was not terribly supportive of my music either. He didn't care much for my harmonica or my guitar, with or without its strings.

As things got worse at home, my mother once more proved her love for me. She called my dad and asked him to come up to West Virginia and take me back to Florida so that I wouldn't have to live in this bad situation. I was crushed. Although I loved my dad, I didn't want to leave my friends in West Virginia again. Even worse, it seemed that there was little doubt that I could ever return.

When we arrived in Miami, my dad helped me unpack my suitcase, and he found my harmonica. "Where did you get this?" he asked. I told him about the box top and fifty cents. To my surprise, he picked it up and began to play "Home Sweet Home," both the melody and his own rhythmic accompaniment. I was mesmerized.

"How do you do that?" I asked, eager for new knowledge about the instrument I'd been playing around with. He showed me how to play the rhythm and melody at the same time, a skill that served me quite well when I didn't have other people to play with.

Once again, I enrolled at Gladeview Elementary School, a school at least five times the size of Fayetteville Elementary. I grew more confident in my musical abilities and began to want to play for an audience. So, less than one year after cutting the strings off my guitar, I volunteered to play harmonica at a school assembly, and I was permitted to play the four songs that I had learned with the original harmonica instructions.

During my fourth grade year, my mother and stepfather worked out some of their problems, which made it safe for me to return to West Virginia for the summer holiday. From that point, I split my year between the South Florida coast and the West Virginia mountains. This compromise proved to be a blessing in disguise, thanks especially to South Florida's superior school system.

My West Virginia summers presented the opportunity for lots of boyhood fun, and, as my friends and I became even more serious about our music, we started to play music together. One summer, I entered a talent contest with two of my West Virginia buddies—John Absalom and Buddy Lively—in nearby Ansted. Buddy played a little bit of piano, John played the ukulele and sang, and I played guitar and sang. We must have done okay because we walked away with around $5 in prize money.

Although it was difficult being away from my friends and family during the school year, being away allowed me to treasure my Mountain State summers. To this day, I still consider West Virginia to be my home, and I'm honored to be a member of the West Virginia Music Hall of Fame and to be the recipient of an honorary doctorate from West Virginia University. But it was in Miami that the music bug bit me hard, sending me on a lifelong search for opportunities to create new and interesting music.

CHAPTER 2

—

ROCK-AND-ROLL CHARLIE

When I was fifteen, Dad came home from work one night and asked, "How would you like to have an electric guitar?" As a kid who was excited about music and was getting turned on to rock and roll, Dad's question was like offering a steak to a hungry wolf. He must have seen how my eyes lit up at the suggestion.

"There is one catch, though," he warned. "If I buy this electric guitar, you have to take lessons." There was no question in my mind. Of course, I would take lessons!

As soon as I got my hands on the Gibson electric guitar and the small amplifier that came with it, I went to the studio of Elon Kealoha, a native Hawaiian musician who had relocated to Miami. His main instrument was the Hawaiian steel guitar, but he also played and taught ukulele, mandolin, and guitar. Kealoha taught several kids in my neighborhood, including Bob Frick, whose parents bought him a baritone ukulele after he showed interest in my guitar, and Jimmy Slichter, who played Hawaiian steel guitar.

During my first lesson, I learned how to play the popular theme from the 1949 film *The Third Man*. I must have shown some promise because it wasn't long before Kealoha asked me to join him and Jimmy Slichter for a gig at the Dade County Home Show. We played Hawaiian songs, which, while Kealoha's favorite, were not mine. It was fun playing in a group, but I just didn't have an appreciation for Hawaiian music at the time. Instead, I was a typical child of the 1950s who was

7

far more interested in the rock-and-roll music that was dominating radio airplay at the time. At home, I preferred playing along to the music of Elvis Presley, Carl Perkins, and Fats Domino to practicing the music that Kealoha wanted me to learn.

Jimmy told me that he knew a guy who could play the piano just like Fats Domino. I was a big fan of Domino's music. Elvis was quickly becoming the king of the musical universe, but I loved Domino's rhythm and blues sound. Jimmy introduced me to Harold Saive, who knocked my socks off by playing the introduction to "Blueberry Hill." As soon as I heard him, I had a brilliant idea: I wanted to start a rock-and-roll band.

I mentioned my idea to Kealoha, who promptly shot down the idea. I'm sure that he was getting tired of seeing all his students playing rock and roll, which didn't require the kind of technical skills that he was teaching. Rock and roll was probably cutting into his bottom line, and he warned me that it wasn't wise to spend too much time working on it. To him, rock and roll was a passing fad that wouldn't help me make a living as a musician. "You can play all the rock and roll you want," he said, "but 'Society Swing' is where the real money is. If you can play the 'Businessman's Bounce,' you can always work."

Despite his warnings, I was undeterred and quickly formed a band to play at a school assembly. I knew a guy at school named Paul Hooper, who played acoustic bass and would be an ideal partner to recreate the rockabilly music that was filling the airwaves. Jimmy Slichter didn't seem to be interested in rock and roll, so Paul, Harold, Bob, and I formed a band with an old buddy of mine, Rick Haley, who told me that he could play drums. Expecting a full rock-and-roll drum set, I was disappointed when Rick showed up at the assembly with only a snare and a pair of brushes, which didn't give us the kind of energy I had hoped for. To open our show, I chose to sing Fats Domino's "I'm in Love Again," which he made famous in 1956. Rick wanted to sing with the group, too, so I said, "Why not?" He sang an Elvis song, which was met with the screams of the girls in the audience. The local radio stations that the kids listened to played a lot more of Elvis's music than the rhythm and blues that I liked, so I wasn't surprised that the audience seemed to enjoy Rick's singing more than mine. Unfortunately, the band faded from existence fairly soon after that because we didn't have any more gigs.

During the 1950s, many different kinds of businesses experimented with live music as a way to draw customers to their establishments. One night, I was at a drive-in restaurant, watching a country singer named Kent Westberry and his band. I wasn't much of a country music fan at the time. In fact, as a sixteen-year-old rock-and-roller, I didn't allow myself to enjoy country music.

While I was watching Westberry and his group, a guy I'd never met before walked up to me and asked, "Is your name Charlie McCoy?"

"Yes," I said.

"My name is Jim Yelvington," he informed me, "and I understand that you have a band."

"I used to," I replied.

"Me, too," he said. "Why don't you bring your guitar and come with me one day to meet my drummer?" I was a little leery of this guy because I wasn't used to people being so forward. Later, I would find such forwardness to be a very important part of the music business.

One Saturday, he showed up at my house in his mother's Buick and told me to get in the car. My dad was working, so I called him and asked his permission to go, and he told me that I could as long as I was home by the time he got home from work. I hopped into the car, unsure of what awaited me. Jim drove like a maniac, and I thought I was in a James Dean movie. Surely, my end was near!

Luckily, we arrived safely in front of a big house with a swimming pool. I figured that anyone who had a pool must be filthy rich. We went into the house, where Jim introduced me to his drummer friend, Jim Isbell. I don't think he was too impressed with me at first, since I came from the sticks of West Miami. But when we started playing music, any differences between us were quickly erased. It was an immediate mutual admiration society. I had never heard anyone play drums like he did.

Over the years, I became very close with Isbell's family. His sister Susan was a real babe, and I had quite a crush on her. Unfortunately, I was too young for her. Jason, his father, was one of those guys who could do anything. His mother, Dottie, even included me in her memoirs, and I am proud to be included. In June 2008, we traveled to Boone, North Carolina, to celebrate her ninetieth birthday, and, even as she approached the century mark, she remains sharp as a tack. Jim's family has always been very dear to me, just like my own family, and he and I have been friends for life.

From that afternoon jam session, we decided to form a band. I played guitar, Isbell played drums, and Yelvington got a bass. A fellow named Charlie Fye played the saxophone, which was essential for much of the rock and roll and rhythm and blues that we were interested in playing. Rounding out the group was Kenny Stevenson, a guy we met who played the accordion. Although I didn't think much of the accordion, he had found a way to amplify his so that it sounded like an organ. Together, we had everything we needed for success in the South Florida rock-and-roll scene.

We started playing dances every Friday night in Hollywood, Florida, and every Saturday night in Fort Lauderdale. The top disc jockey in Miami, Bob Green, served as the emcee and promoter for these events. At first, we didn't have a name for the band, and it wasn't really a problem because people were coming to the dances because of Green's promotions rather than to hear a specific band. But we knew that we were going to need one if we wanted to build a brand and develop a reputation around the region. One night, a local record distributor named Henry Stone stopped by one of the dances and offered to record us on his label, Agenda Records. As part of the deal, he wanted to name the group Charlie McCoy and the Agendas.

As far as I was concerned, this was the kind of break that we were looking for. My friend Steve Alaimo, whom I had met at one of the dances, had taken Stone up on his offer, and his group, the Red Coats, was having great success with a record that Bob Green played over and over. Still naive about the record and radio business, I thought that Steve must have had a national hit on his hands because I kept hearing him on the radio. Unfortunately for Steve (who went on to be a star of the Dick Clark show, *Where the Action Is*), the record was being played only in Miami. I desperately wanted to sign the contract, but my dad didn't trust Henry Stone. He wouldn't let me sign, much to my dismay. I was crushed for a little while, but, soon after, Agenda Records folded, proving that my dad was right. Although the label closed, the group's name stuck, and Charlie McCoy and the Agendas was born.

Like a lot of kids of my generation, I spent a lot of my spare time listening to the radio, trying to take in all the sounds that I could. Radio in those days was still segregated, with black radio stations specializing in rhythm and blues music and white stations playing Top 40 and country music. Most of my friends listened to Top 40, and, when I was with them, I listened, too. But when I was alone, I would slowly scan the radio dial in search of the rhythm and blues music that I loved. For the most part, I was interested in the ways that the rhythm and blues musicians sang and played the guitar, the instrument that had become my entire musical world. That all changed when, during one of my dial-scanning sessions, I heard the haunting harmonica of Chicago blues musician Jimmy Reed. Although it had started me down my musical path, I pulled out my harmonica only on rare occasions, blowing a lick or two and then setting it aside to collect dust. But upon hearing Reed's wailing blues harmonica, I became obsessed with it and decided to dedicate more time to mastering the blues harp.

One of the most important resources at my disposal in this quest was a Nashville radio station, WLAC, which I found while searching the radio late one night. WLAC was a "clear-channel" station, which meant that no other stations could broadcast on its frequency of 1510 KHz. As a consequence, the signal—especially on a cloudless night—was clear and strong. WLAC played all the great blues harmonica players: Sonny Boy Williamson, Slim Harpo, Little Walter, and all the Jimmy Reed records that you could want. The signal was best late at night, and I wanted to stay up very late listening. Unfortunately, my dad, who was not a fan of rhythm and blues, didn't want me keeping the radio on at such late hours. Luckily, while hanging out with my neighborhood friend Luis Rodriguez, I found a solution that would allow me to continue listening to my favorite music while also keeping my dad at bay. Luis's dad was a ham radio operator, and he was very skilled with electronics. He told me that he could put an earphone jack in my clock radio so I could listen while the speaker was bypassed. To his dying day, my dad never knew about the earphone jack in the back of the radio and the many nights that I listened to WLAC to learn harp licks.

Listening to WLAC may have inspired me to learn to play the blues, but it wasn't the most useful tool for someone who wanted to focus on the details. Like radio broadcasts today, a song might be played once and then not heard again for hours, days, or even weeks. And, in the days before taping was affordable, it was impossible to play a recording over and over again. Thankfully, most of WLAC's programs were sponsored by record shops, including Ernie's, Randy's, and Buckley's. They conducted brisk mail-order business, shipping packages of five or six records to rhythm and blues fans all across the South. I ordered several of these packages so I could dig into the music in greater depth. Although I ran the risk of getting in trouble with my dad, I worked out the timing of the deliveries to ensure that he would never find out. Dad worked late, and the mailman came in the middle of the afternoon. That meant that I could get home from school and hide my treasures before Dad got home. As far as I know, my growing record collection was as hidden as my late-night listening habits.

Although my dad wasn't a fan of some of the music I was playing, he wasn't opposed to my deep interest in music. In fact, he helped launch one of the most important musical performances of my fledgling career. One night, my dad was having a drink at a local club called the Tropicopa. When the band that was playing that night took a break, he overheard them having a discussion with their manager about a possible tour with several stars from the popular television program *American Bandstand*. Unfortunately, they didn't have a rock-and-roll guitarist and were in desperate need. With enough beer to take away his inhibitions, my dad boldly proclaimed, "Hey, my kid plays the hell out of rock-and-roll guitar!" They tried to brush him off, probably thinking he was just another rowdy drunk patron, but he was relentless. Finally, they decided to make him put his money where his mouth was. "Look," one of them said, "we have a rehearsal here on Sunday afternoon. Bring your boy here at two o'clock." They probably thought that was the last they would ever see of him.

Over breakfast the next morning, my dad looked across the table and said, "I think I put my foot in my mouth last night." He explained the situation. "I hate to make you do this," he said, "but, if you don't, I'll never be able to show my face in that place again." Far from being upset with him for putting me in this situation, I was thrilled at the opportunity. On Sunday, we went to the Tropicopa, my guitar and amplifier in hand. When we walked in, they gave me the once-over, surely taking stock of the fact that I was just a kid.

The band was called the Rockin' Maniacs, and they were led by a fellow named Reggie Perkins. It seemed like the band had been a lounge act, but they were changing their focus to rock and roll so they could work more. Most of their rock-and-roll songs were tunes like "Route 66" and "The House of Blue Lights," and they probably did a lot of Louis Prima's music before changing tastes forced them to adapt.

"What do you want to play, kid?" Reggie asked.

"Just play some of your regular songs, and I'll fill in," I replied confidently.

The sax player, Angelo Gillotti, called up "Honky Tonk." As good luck would have it, I had just learned it note for note. Angelo played a couple of choruses and then looked over and said, "Take it, kid." I played it just like the record, and I watched as all the guys started to smile.

"Call our manager," Reggie said. "Tell him we've found a guitar player." The piano player, Chuck Yarborough, and the drummer, Roy LeCroix, were grinning from ear to ear.

"We have to talk to our manager," Reggie warned, "but I'm sure this is a go. We'll call you as soon as we hear from them." I think that my dad was really beginning to regret his inebriated enthusiasm, and he was concerned that the tour would be a long and grueling one for a seventeen-year-old kid. Fortunately, they didn't give him too much time to worry because, even though the wait felt like an eternity to me, they called the very next night to offer me the job.

The tour started just a short time after. We were hired to back up Danny and the Juniors, Dicky Doo and the Don'ts, Jody Reynolds, and Connie Francis on a tour of Jacksonville, Orlando, Tampa, Fort Myers, Miami, and Savannah, Georgia. Also on the tour was the Champs, which was a self-contained group, and my guitar idol Chuck Berry was added to the roster in Savannah. A lot of kids from my school were in the audience when we played Miami, so I returned to school as something of a hero when the summer was over.

I had one very important advantage over Reggie and the boys: I listened to rock and roll all the time. So while they were more experienced musicians overall, I had a deep understanding of the music that was selling at the time. This knowledge came in handy when we were rehearsing with Connie Francis, who had landed a big hit with "Who's Sorry Now?" She was the first "star" I'd ever worked with, and I was a little nervous as we started rehearsal. Her manager passed around the charts for her set, and mine just had chord symbols on it. I remembered that a teacher had told me once to just play the rhythm part when you see a chart like that, so I did what I thought I was supposed to do. As we rehearsed her big hit, Connie kept saying, "It doesn't sound right." After a few more times through with no changes, she asked us to play our parts individually so she could hear where the problem was. When it was my turn, she found the problem. Although I knew the guitar part from the record, the chart made me think that I was supposed to chunk along on the chords. Wanting to redeem myself, I asked her if we could play it again.

"I don't see what good it will do," she said, "but okay." We started to play, and just a little way into the tune, she stopped us. "Let's all congratulate the kid," she exclaimed. "He's finally learned to read music!" Reggie and the boys were relieved that we could live to play another day.

The opening act on this tour was Dicky Doo and the Don't's, who were touring in support of their current hit, "Click, Clack." The recording began with a guitar lick, which meant that I had to play the very first notes that anyone would hear during each show. At one performance, I was preparing to go out on stage to get the show started when I saw a guy moving around the back of the stage. Just as the emcee introduced Dicky Doo, the guy tripped over the power cord to my amplifier, but I was focused on making those opening notes sound great and didn't notice. I played the introduction, but no sound came out of the amplifiers. There I was, just standing there with the entire show hanging in the balance. To keep the audience from getting too restless as we determined the cause of the problem, Dicky danced around with a huge grin, but every once in a while, he would look back and cuss at me for holding up the show (even if it wasn't my fault!). After what felt like a lifetime, someone finally reconnected the amplifier to the power, and the show went on without a hitch.

The real highlight of the tour for me was getting to play with Chuck Berry. He had revolutionized the guitar and made it one of the most significant instruments in a rock-and-roll group. I was in love with his music, and I hoped to soak up some of his expertise in our brief encounter. In rehearsal, I asked, "Mr. Berry, what do you want me to do?" He smiled and said, "Just be careful, son." When the emcee introduced him, he came onstage with his trademark "duck walk," guitar cable in hand. As he moved past his Fender amplifier, he stuck the jack right in the hole without even looking. I was blown away! I kept looking at the other guys in the band to see if anyone else had seen what I had, but they were too busy playing.

Just as I was filling my spare time with music at home, I did everything I could to fill my school hours with music-making as well. Although my head was mostly in music, I did quite well in all my classes, graduating forty-third in a class of 458 students. But I don't think that would have been the case if it hadn't been for the musical opportunities that kept my mind engaged. My first involvement in school music came during my seventh-grade year at Ponce De Leon

Junior High School in Coral Gables. Every day, I took a very long bus ride to school, where some of the Coral Gables kids treated us like country bumpkins. At first, I was put off by their snobbery, but when I learned that the school offered chorus, I decided that I could stick it out. The chorus teacher was a very likable woman named Doris Ludder. She was interested in getting the students involved in the entire chorus experience, even teaching us how to conduct and letting some of us try our hand at leading our classmates in a song. Toward the end of the school year, Mrs. Ludder left for maternity leave, and Margaret DeSola took over as her substitute. Mrs. DeSola ended up being my chorus teacher all the way through high school, moving with me to the new West Miami Junior High when I was in eighth grade and Southwest Miami Senior High when I reached tenth grade. Mrs. DeSola was a very important mentor to me. She chose me to be the student director, and she did everything that she could to expand my musical education. She was a great musician and a wonderful teacher, as was her husband, who, as the band director at Miami Jackson Senior High School, led one of the very best student bands in the city. One of his students, Larrie London, went on to become a great studio drummer in Detroit and Nashville.

During my senior year of high school, I was the beneficiary of a new experiment in the Florida schools: music theory instruction. The course was taught by Shirley Vineyard, who came to Southwest Miami to teach orchestra in the middle of my junior year. As soon as the state approved the theory curriculum, the school sent notice for anyone who was interested in the course to meet with Ms. Vineyard after school. We took a little placement test to determine which course of study we would be permitted to take. If you knew anything at all about music (which I did), you were put in the advanced class.

There were only fifteen students in my class, which made use of the laboratory model of music instruction that was popular at the time. We learned about part writing and voice leading and worked on exercises to teach us how chords related to one another. Then, once a week, a student ensemble would come to class to play our exercises. Sometimes it was a string quartet, other times a brass quartet or a group of woodwind players. We wrote the exercises on the board, and the musicians played exactly what we wrote down. Of course, we could hear some of our mistakes immediately, but Ms. Vineyard would show us others and make us correct them in front of the class. Then the group would play the improved work, helping us hear and understand the techniques aurally as well as logically. One thing that didn't improve, though, was my penmanship, which would have made a doctor proud. On the last day of school, Ms. Vineyard told me, "I think you have really got a handle on this subject, but unless you learn to write better, no one will ever know." She also gave me an important pearl of wisdom that has helped me throughout the years, reminding me, "Now you know all the rules. Forget them, and be creative."

Music theory class only confirmed an idea that I had begun playing with by the end of my junior year: I wanted to study music in college, focusing particularly on music education. There was only one problem. Music schools required that their students have a primary instrument to major in, and guitar and harmonica didn't count in a world dominated by orchestra and band musicians. Mrs. DeSola and Ms. Vineyard put their heads together and decided that the easiest instrument for me to learn in a short time was the double bass. Because I wasn't going to spend the summer in West Virginia, Ms. Vineyard allowed me to take one of the school's basses home for a summer of intensive study. By senior year, I was almost ready for orchestra, but only once I had taken out a pencil to draw fret markers on the neck of the bass. As a guitarist who was accustomed to being able to just put my fingers near the frets to get the right notes, this technique helped me immensely with intonation. It took much longer to get a decent sound with the bow, but my old buddy Paul Hooper, who was the principal bassist in the school orchestra, helped me out a lot.

By the time I graduated from high school, I had built a musical resumé that had prepared me for a wide variety of professional musical experiences. I had a working understanding of the basics of music theory and could read written musical notation. I had spent hours and hours trying to cop licks from my favorite recordings and working to incorporate them into my playing. I could play a few instruments (some better than others), and, as I had learned from the bass, I knew that it wouldn't take me long to play a passable part on an unfamiliar instrument. And I had been on the road, working with nationally known recording artists and holding my own. The only question that remained was what the next phase of my young career would look like.

—

CHAPTER 3

THE ROAD TO NASHVILLE

Although I was a fan of the singing cowboy movies when I was a kid, I hadn't really given much thought to country music since the rock-and-roll bug bit me. I had plenty of work with the Agendas, and I was doing everything I could to become the next big thing. But my attitude began to change when Jim Yelvington convinced me to go to the Old South Jamboree with him one Saturday night.

We pulled into the Dade County Armory and found a parking lot that was filled to the point of overflowing. We paid our admission and walked into the middle of a big square dance. To my amazement, every person there was dancing around in a big circle and having a good time. Compared to the audiences that I was used to playing for, though, these folks seemed to be the absolute opposite of cool. As I stood there staring at what I thought was just a dumb redneck ritual, Jim slipped away without explanation.

When the dance was finished, the bass player announced, "We're going to take a break now, and when we come back, we have a great surprise for you. Charlie McCoy is here tonight, and hopefully he'll do a couple of songs." I was stunned. I didn't know the bass player, and I certainly hadn't announced my visit in advance. As I stood there bewildered, Jim returned, sporting a suspicious grin. He had gone backstage to set me up, knowing full well that I didn't play country music.

I was upset to say the least. "What have you gotten me into?" I asked. "I can't play with this country band!"

He just laughed. "You have to," he chuckled. "They've already announced you."

"I won't do it," I said, becoming more and more perturbed.

"Look, just go talk to them. It can't hurt," Jim said.

"Well, okay," I relented, "but you owe me a big one."

I went backstage to meet the bandleader and steel guitarist, Bill Johnson. I didn't know many country songs, so when he asked me what I wanted to play, I went to the music I was most familiar with.

"How about 'Johnny B. Goode'?" I asked, hoping he would say no. To my surprise, he replied, "Great! What key?"

"A," I said, "but I don't have a guitar."

"No problem," he replied. "You can use one of ours."

We played "Johnny B. Goode," and the crowd went crazy and began to demand another. Digging deep into my Chuck Berry bag, I called "Roll Over Beethoven," which got the same reaction as the first tune. I was surprised by their response, and it was beginning to become clear that I had initially misjudged the crowd. "Maybe playing for teenagers all the time isn't all it's cracked up to be," I wondered. "These people were really genuine in their reaction and everyone was so nice."

The bandleader at the Old South Jamboree was "Happy" Harold Thaxton. After my guest spot, he came up to thank me for playing and asked if I would be interested in playing every week. Like so many establishments in the middle of the 1950s, he was trying to attract a younger clientele, and he thought that I might do the trick. He offered me a fifteen-minute slot during each hour of the Old South Jamboree, and he would pay me $20 each night. That was big money for a seventeen-year-old, and I was excited to play for such an appreciative audience, so I gladly accepted his offer. I went on to play the Old South Jamboree for more than a year, but unfortunately, the show ended because of declining attendance. The neighborhood started to get rough, and people just didn't want to continue going there.

The Old South turned out to be a breeding ground for a lot of young talent, and many of the band members went on to successful careers in Nashville. The lead singer, Bill Phillips, recorded for Columbia and was the opening act for Kitty Wells and Johnny Wright for many years. The bass player, Donnie Young, had a successful stint singing harmony with Faron Young. Later, he changed his name to Johnny Paycheck and had a good run of hit records. The fiddle player, Charlie Justice, toured with George Jones and Tammy Wynette for a long time. Bill Johnson later achieved fame as a songwriter with the classic "A Wound Time Can't Erase." Wayne Gray, who was a regular visitor to the Old South, played guitar with Tex Ritter for quite some time. And it was at the Old South where I again encountered Kent Westberry, who went on to become a great Nashville songwriter that I would cross paths with for many years to come.

The Old South is where my journey to Music City would begin, as well. The Dade County Auditorium often hosted a big country music show, and the stars would come by the Old South after their performance. One Saturday night, Mel Tillis dropped in. Although *Billboard* reported that country disc jockeys considered him one of the "most promising male artists" in 1958, I wasn't familiar with him or his music.[1] When I asked Happy about him, he explained that Mel was a very successful Nashville songwriter and an up-and-coming recording artist. By the end of 1959, he would have his first major success when honky-tonk star Webb Pierce recorded Mel's song "I Ain't Never" for Decca and took it to number 24 on the *Billboard* "Hot 100" chart, which measured crossover success.

After my little set that evening, Mel came to me and said, "Boy, you need to come to Nashville, I can get you on Decca tomorrow." I figured that he might have had had a beer or two, and even though I was flattered, I didn't put much stock in that remark. Afterward, I talked to Happy about Mel's comment. Happy said, "I wouldn't take it too lightly. I don't think he can get you on Decca, but he does have important connections in Nashville." At that point, the seeds had been planted. I needed to get to Nashville as quickly as possible.

The contestants lined up for their chance to win the grand prize, a trip for two to the Bahamas. Although I was just there to play the guitar for all the musical acts, a number of my fans from the Old South were in the audience and decided to start shouting, "Let Charlie do a song!" I didn't think I should enter the contest, but the audience was certain that I should. The judges heard their pleas and told me that it would be just fine. I knew exactly what the Old South crowd wanted to hear, so I pulled out an old Chuck Berry song called "No Money Down." The audience went wild, which was lucky for me, because they voted by applause, helping me win the contest.

With Mel Tillis's invitation on my mind, I had no interest in the grand prize trip to the Bahamas, so I asked the contest organizers if I could have the cash to make a trip to Nashville. They agreed, and I began making preparations to leave town. I had just graduated from high school, and, with nothing in my way, I was chomping at the bit to leave. Happy volunteered to drive me, so we loaded up his Cadillac and took off for Nashville with Happy's girlfriend (and future wife) Anna, who came along for the ride.

When we arrived in Nashville, we went directly to Cedarwood Publishing Company, where Mel was based as a writer. The owner of Cedarwood, Jim Denny, greeted us, and when we told him that Mel had invited me up for a visit, he told us that Mel was still on the road and wouldn't be back to Nashville for quite some time. I was surprised, though, when Denny told me that Mel had mentioned me after his last trip to Miami. Happy told him that Mel thought he could get me a contract at Decca, but, even without hearing me, Denny thought that Mel had been a bit too optimistic. Fortunately, though, he agreed to help me get some auditions.

The next morning, Denny called to let me know that he had been true to his word and had arranged auditions with Chet Atkins at RCA Victor and Owen Bradley at Decca. I auditioned for Atkins first, playing "Johnny B. Goode" through my Fender Bassman amp. Later, I played for Bradley, who told Denny, "I think he's pretty good, but I wouldn't know what to do with him." I was crushed, but I would later learn that Nashville simply didn't know how to handle rock and roll in 1959. But, at eighteen, I thought I knew everything and defensively dismissed these rejections as little more than small-town backwardness.

"What do these people in this small town know?" I thought. "I'm pretty big in Miami, and Miami is much bigger than Nashville."

As I was processing this second rejection, Bradley said, "I'm doing a session on Brenda Lee this afternoon. Do you think Charlie would like to come watch?" I didn't know what a session was. Denny looked at me and asked, "How about it?" Still dejected, I agreed. After all, I didn't have anything else to do.

That afternoon, Happy drove me to Jim Denny's office and dropped me off so he and Anna could go shopping. Denny took me to Bradley's studio on 16th Avenue South, a Quonset hut building that was attached to an old house in the heart of the developing Music Row neighborhood. Bradley, a dance bandleader in Nashville and a very talented pianist, had opened the studio with his brother Harold just a few years earlier and had quickly turned it into one of the premiere recording facilities in the South. It was even outfitted for film production. At one end of the enormous studio was a set of stairs, and at the other was a state-of-the-art control room.

As the musicians gathered in studio, Bradley had me sit on the stairs, where I would have a great view of the proceedings. As I climbed onto my perch, the musicians milled around, set up their equipment, and talked easily to one another. They all looked like old guys to me, but most of them were just a few years older than I was at the time. Of course, when you're eighteen, everyone looks old.

Before long, the artist—thirteen-year-old Brenda Lee—entered the studio. I couldn't imagine why anyone would make a record with such a young girl, and I had little hope that the session would be worth sticking around for. Unfortunately, Denny had left me at the studio, so I was stranded for the next three hours. Absorbed in my disappointment, I decided to try to make the best of it.

As the session began, Bradley came into the studio and put a disc on a small turntable. The musicians listened to the recording, a demo of a song by Ronnie Self called "Sweet Nothin's." As the musicians listened carefully to this rough recording, I was surprised to notice that they didn't have any written music in front of them. With my band and music theory background, I couldn't imagine that professional musicians could work without sheet music. The guitar player, who seemed to be in charge, said a couple of things to the assembled musicians, and they began to run through the song. The band was a large one, consisting of a piano, bass, drums, three guitars, and a saxophone, along with a vocal group of two women and two men. They played through the song twice, and then Bradley said, "Okay, guys. Let's make one!"

Just a couple of minutes later, the musicians listened to the playback of the recording they just made. To my amazement, it sounded like a finished record! All of a sudden, the session had my attention as the session musicians' exceptional musicianship drew me into their work. They decided to do two more takes of the song, but I couldn't understand why. The first one sounded great to me.

When Denny returned at the session's end, he introduced me to the band. Floyd Cramer, who would have a hit recording with "Last Date" the next year, was the pianist, and Boots Randolph was the saxophonist. Bassist Bob Moore and drummer Buddy Harman held down the rhythm section, while Grady Martin, Harold Bradley, and Ray Edenton provided a layered guitar accompaniment. The Anita Kerr Singers—Kerr, Dottie Dillard, Gil Wright, and Louis Nunley—provided the background vocals. These musicians had played on hundreds of recordings that received airplay on the country and pop charts, and the recording of "Sweet Nothin's" that I watched them make would be met with similar success, helping to launch Brenda Lee's long and storied career.

The rest of the day and night, I dreamed about that session. All of a sudden, being a star wasn't so important to me. If there was any way possible, some day, somehow, I wanted to be a part of what I had just seen in that studio. I probably wore Happy and Anna out that evening over supper talking about the session. That night, Denny called the hotel and told Happy that there was another session the following morning that we could attend if we wanted. We had planned to leave for Miami that morning, but Happy was willing to wait.

We returned to Bradley's Quonset Hut studio for a session with Carl Butler, who was recording for Columbia with Don Law producing.

Many of the musicians who had played in Brenda Lee's session the previous day were there again, although Joe Zinkan had replaced Bob Moore on bass. The surprising versatility of Nashville's session musicians became apparent as soon as I saw Boots Randolph, whom I had seen playing the saxophone the previous day, with a valve trombone in his hand. And, as a rock-and-roll fan, I was excited to see that the Jordanaires were providing the backing vocals, the very same Jordanaires who sang on all of Elvis's records. After the session, which yielded the single "Remember the Alamo," Denny introduced me to Neal Matthews, their second tenor and arranger, who was kind enough to show me the shorthand notation that they were using to build the arrangements.

After this second session, I was really fired up. What I had witnessed in the recording studio those two days was absolutely amazing. I had never been around musicians who were so good. And not only that, they were kind and easygoing people to boot. My head was swimming with visions of Nashville's Music Row all the way back to Miami.

—

CHAPTER 4

COLLEGE AND THE RETURN TO NASHVILLE

Compared to my experiences in Nashville's recording studios, Miami seemed unbearably dull. But since my auditions in Nashville hadn't produced a recording contract, I needed to find something to keep myself occupied and moving toward my ultimate goal: to be a professional musician. My dad, who never had the opportunity to go to college, wanted me to give it a shot. With his encouragement, I decided to enroll as a music education major at the University of Miami in nearby Coral Gables, which had an excellent music program, and Dad took on the heavy financial burden of paying my college tuition on his blue-collar salary.

Between my return from Nashville and the beginning of the school year, I had an entire summer to continue building my chops around Miami. My gig at the Old South kept me busy on the weekends, and I spent a lot of my free time at home practicing the bass to prepare for my freshman year. Toward the end of the summer, one of Happy Harold's friends called me to substitute for his guitar player, who needed to be away for a month, at a club in downtown Miami called Club 17. To play there, I had to get a union card, but I wasn't old enough to work a union gig. That wasn't a problem for them because they gave me a fake union card and a fake ID card so I could start working.

I didn't know much about Club 17 when I agreed to play there, and it didn't take long for me to regret taking the gig in the first place. Club 17 was what we called a "skull orchard," a rough-and-tumble place where people came to drink, fight, and fall in love. Lots of musicians started their careers in places like Club 17, and they were great places to learn how to gauge an audience's mood and choose songs that could keep the fights to a minimum. But for a teenaged kid who was used to playing for the nice people who came to the Old South for its family environment, Club 17 was an uncomfortable shock.

After two weeks at Club 17, the piano player went on vacation, so they brought a substitute in for him. His name was Bobby Braddock, and he had come to Miami from a town on Tampa Bay. Our paths would cross several times over the years, as he became one of Nashville's most successful songwriters, scoring hit after hit for more than four decades. He cowrote one of country music's all-time classics, "He Stopped Loving Her Today," which I played on with George Jones in 1980. And, in 2003, he produced Blake Shelton's first number-one hit, "The Baby," which I also played on. Braddock is one of those rare folks who can write, play, and produce with equal skill, and that's why he's been inducted into the Nashville Songwriters Hall of Fame and the Country Music Hall of Fame.

The Club 17 gig came to an end, and in September 1959, I officially enrolled at the University of Miami. It was a private school, and many of the kids who went there came from a wealthier background than I did. When I parked in the student union lot, my old 1937 DeSoto stood out like a sore thumb among all the sports cars that my peers were driving around. At least my car was always easy to find!

One of the first things that new music students were expected to do was take a placement test for music theory. Since I had taken a great music theory course in high school, the faculty placed me in the sophomore class and allowed me to skip the first four semesters that students usually took. There was only one other freshman in the class, and she had taken summer courses at the prestigious Juilliard School. When I went to class the first day, the professor tried to figure out how I had learned so much music theory, so he asked me if I had been to music school or a conservatory.

"No, just high school," I replied.

He asked, "Where did you go to high school?"

"Southwest Miami," I said.

"Who was your teacher?"

"Shirley Vineyard."

"Oh," he said, "that explains it." The high school music theory experiment had paid off.

The rest of my schedule included English, freshman orientation, ROTC, music history, solfeggio, class piano, and private bass lessons.

Although I had already been playing bass for a while, my bass teacher was clearly depressed when I went to my first lesson. When he saw me play, he asked me where I learned to play. When I told him that I was self-taught, he said unhappily, "I was afraid of that. Let's forget everything that you don't know and start from scratch." He also made his musical priorities clear from the start, adding, "Our goal here is to enable you to play in the symphony, and I'm afraid we have a very long way to go." As a rock-and-roll and country musician, the symphony was the last thing on my mind, but I would have to focus on it if I wanted to be successful in school.

Class piano wasn't much more friendly to a musician who had developed most of his skills on the bandstand. My good ear got me in trouble regularly because, when someone would play a lesson, I was able to hear it and play it back. Unfortunately, I played it with all the wrong fingerings, which didn't let me learn the proper technique for playing the piano. The professor told me to stop relying on one of my greatest strengths and "read the music."

My ear came in handy in solfeggio class, which was the best part of my college experience. Solfeggio is a tool that helps you sing and play musical notation from sight and to write down and reproduce music that is played for you. My teacher was an elderly French woman named Mme. Renée Longy-Miquelle, whom we all called Mme. Longy. Before she came to the University of Miami's Conservatory of Music, she had served as head of the Longy School of Music in Boston, which her father had founded in 1915, and been on the faculty of the Curtis Institute of Music and Juilliard. Mme. Longy was a legend around the University of Miami Conservatory of Music. Rumor had it that she had once failed the great composer and conductor Leonard Bernstein—the famous conductor of the New York Philharmonic—because, although he was a prodigy, he was goofing off in class and she wanted to get his attention. Later in life, I learned that he had actually done quite well in her classes, but I'm glad that the story helped me stay ahead of my studies.

Mme. Longy sat at a piano instead of a desk, and, although there were about twenty students in the class, she never took roll call and still knew who was absent. As she sat down on the first day, she played an A on the piano, holding the piano's sustain pedal down until the note finally died away. She did this every day for the first week, letting it ring even while she was talking. Everyone in the class was curious about why she did this every day. Was this just a quirky habit of hers, or did it have some pedagogical purpose?

By the second week, we found out. Mme. Longy started class just as she always did, holding the sustain pedal to let the A ring. Then, without warning, she looked at one of my classmates and demanded, "Mr. Green, sing a perfect fifth to my piano note." At that point, she had everyone's undivided attention. From that day forward, she would see who wasn't concentrating on their work and would nail them every time.

Mme. Longy's pedagogy was very rigorous and used techniques that were common in the best European conservatories. To learn how to read in the different clefs, we sang from a book of chorales by Johann Sebastian Bach, reciting the names of the notes as we sang each piece. As we turned the page, she would often call on a student to continue singing as a soloist. Hopefully, the student was paying attention because Mme. Longy would make a mental note of every mistake. We also took daily melodic, harmonic, and rhythmic dictation exercises, which required us to write down what we heard using musical notation. When the year was over, I think I could have written down the music that the birds on the telephone wires were singing.

Mme. Longy's class was the highlight of my college experience. Not only was I learning so many valuable things about music, I also didn't have to worry about getting behind in my homework. We did all the work in class, but the skills that I was learning transferred over to everything I was doing in my music studies.

The rest of the college experience was quite difficult for me, though. I had been a good student in high school, but I didn't spend much time reading my lessons then because my eyesight wasn't good and I never told my dad that I needed glasses. (I often wondered later why the school hadn't sent a note home to inform my dad about this.) Throughout high school, I would listen to the lessons in class and, using my nearly photographic memory as an aid, learn enough to do my lessons. College lessons, on the other hand, required far more reading than I was used to doing, sometimes forcing me to work through a hundred pages or more for a single assignment. It was far more difficult than I could handle, even after I started wearing glasses, because I hadn't learned how to read long assignments.

Although I was thoroughly enjoying Mme. Longy's class and was spending my spare minutes trying to cram in as much music theory study as I could, I was also beginning to learn that music schools—at least at that time—placed far more value on classical music than on other forms of music-making. This all came to light when I was summoned to the dean's office for a meeting with the dean of music, John Bitter. A flutist and orchestra conductor who graduated from the Curtis Institute of Music in Philadelphia and had even been a guest conductor of the Berlin Philharmonic before coming to the University of Miami in 1950, Dean Bitter had called me to his office to investigate a rumor about me that he had heard circulating around the Conservatory.

"I understand that you play rock and roll and even *country music*," he said.

I answered proudly, "Yes, I do!"

Clearly, that wasn't the answer he was looking for. "We think that, in order to better your serious music education," he said, "you should give up these lower forms of music."

His attitude hit me the wrong way because he clearly didn't understand how important those forms of music were to me, both musically and financially.

"I'm sorry you feel that way, sir," I said. "This school is a big financial load for my dad, and I am earning money for school by playing on the weekends. The only way I could quit is if you gave me a scholarship."

"You haven't advanced enough on your major instrument," he replied. Of course, I was doing the best I could, but I was struggling to stay afloat as I balanced a heavy course load, the challenge of relearning an orchestral instrument, and sitting on a bandstand every weekend.

"I'm sorry, sir," I said, "but I must work to buy gas to get to school."

Financial need wasn't enough to convince him. Unmoved, he dismissed me, saying, "Very well, but think about it long and hard."

To say the least, this meeting left me discouraged and disgusted. I knew that I needed to practice more to continue improving on the bass, but I needed financial support to help me buy the practice time. And I was also frustrated that so many of my teachers, whom I respected immensely, looked down their noses at the music that I enjoyed playing so much.

Later that day, I went to solfeggio class, where Mme. Longy presided over another challenging lesson. As I was leaving class, she asked me to stay behind for a minute. After my encounter with Dean Bitter, my mind was racing with reasons that she might want to talk with me.

"I understand that you were called to the dean's office today," she said with a comforting tone in her voice. "He wants you to quit playing rock and roll and country music."

"Yes," I replied, "but I tried explaining to him that I need to work so I can help my father with my college expenses."

To my surprise, she said defiantly, "I don't care why you play this music. Are you any good at it? If not, practice more or quit!" Unlike the dean, who condemned me for embracing many different kinds of music, Mme. Longy was open-minded, hewing only to her high standards of musical excellence. Her kindness and encouragement helped to sustain me as I tried to make my way in an environment where I felt increasingly out of place.

I was also beginning to question my interest in music education. Through my accordion-playing buddy Kenny Stevenson, I got a part-time job teaching guitar students at a local music store. It didn't take much of that to show me that I hated teaching. All the young students wanted to play like rockabilly star Duane Eddy, and the college-aged students wanted to play Kingston Trio songs. There wasn't much variety there, and it wasn't long before I burned out on the entire experience. It wasn't just that guitarists had limited interests either, as I learned one Saturday when I helped the guys at the store host an accordion recital. There were twenty accordion students, and at least twelve of them played "Lady of Spain." These experiences led me to wonder, every now and then, why I was studying music education in the first place.

Despite my worries, teaching at the store did have one significant benefit: access to great instruments at a discounted price. That's how I bought a brand new Gibson Les Paul Custom guitar, also known as "the Fretless Wonder." It was only the second one in the city of Miami, and I was so proud to be its owner.

After making it through the first semester at the university, I enrolled for the second, but I was having serious misgivings. I wanted to study music, but I continued to struggle with the reading that was required for my non-music classes, and the amount of time I had to spend on them was taking away from my time to practice the bass and study for my music courses. And memories of my summer visit to Nashville weren't far away either, serving as a constant distraction. This second semester was even harder than the first, and I was trying hard to hang on because I knew that my dad was very proud that I was going to college. But as I was driving to school one day, the stress became too much. I pulled my car to the side of the road and asked myself aloud, "What am I doing? I don't want to teach music. I want to play."

In April, I received a phone call from Kent Westberry, who had recently gone to Nashville. He moved there with a friend named Snuffy Smith, who was the first bass player I'd ever known who could play both a left-handed and a right-handed bass. As "Kent and Snuffy," they had landed a record deal with MGM—the same label that Hank Williams had been on—and had just released a song called "Bye, Bye Buddy." To promote the single, they were preparing to go on the road with another MGM artist named Johnny Ferguson, who was promoting his new single, "Angela Jones," written by John D. Loudermilk.

Ferguson had two weeks booked in Toronto, Kent told me, but he needed a guitar player, and Kent had recommended me for the job. I was stunned! It was a chance for me to get back to Nashville, but I also knew that if I quit school, my dad would be crushed (if he would even let me go in the first place).

"Kent," I said. "I want to do it, but I need to work out a couple of things. When do you need to know?"

Kent said, "We need to know right away, and we'll even come down and drive you to Nashville."

Now I was at a crossroads. On the one hand, here was an opportunity for me to fulfill my dream of returning to Music City to start a career as a professional musician, but on the other, I didn't want to let my dad down. After weighing my options, I decided it was time to take the leap and leave my college career behind. It took me a week to build up the courage to tell my dad about this opportunity and my decision because I was worried about how upset he would be. His reaction was even worse than I imagined it would be. He was always a caring father, but I could see his emotions shifting between anger, hurt, disgust, and worry.

"You'll get up there," he admonished, "lose your job and be back here in no time at all. Without this college degree, what are you going to fall back on?"

The only thing I could do to convince him was show him how passionate I was about my music and how determined I was to be successful. So I explained to him that I hated teaching and that all I really wanted to do was play. And, channeling Mme. Longy's advice, I made it very clear that I knew how hard it would be to make a living as a working musician and that I was willing to put in the long hours to get good enough to make it. Although he was obviously disappointed that I wasn't going to become a college graduate, he eventually relented and gave me his blessing. Later, I realized that, even though he seemed angry, all he was really doing was trying to help me be sure of my decision, just like any good parent would do.

I loaded into a car with Kent and Snuffy and drove all night to Nashville. There were no interstate highways then, so it was a long hard trip along the two-lane roads that connected small southern towns to one another. I was so excited, though, that I couldn't sleep. Visions of Nashville ran through my head, and I began to imagine what it would be like to work with the many talented musicians who called Music City their home. I felt like a bird released from its cage, and I was ready to fly as far and wide as my newly discovered wings would take me. I did, however, think about Mme. Longy, whose encouragement had meant so much to me, and whom I was leaving behind to pursue a career playing the rock and roll and country music that Dean Bitter had looked down his nose at. But one thing was certain: I wouldn't miss anything about teaching guitar students.

We arrived at Kent's house in the morning. His wife cooked breakfast, and we left shortly after to go to the first rehearsal with Johnny Ferguson. I hadn't been able to sleep all night, but I was ready to get started. Upon arriving at the rehearsal, Kent introduced me to Johnny, who shook my hand and then turned back to Kent.

"I didn't hear from you, so I hired another guitar player," he told Kent.

My heart began to race as my dad's admonishments ran through my head. I had quit school to pursue a job that wasn't even there in the first place. Exhausted from the long drive and crestfallen by the news that Johnny Ferguson didn't need me to play guitar, I was ready to give Kent an earful for leading me into this situation. Just as I was about to open my mouth, Johnny intervened.

"What else do you play?" he asked, clearly feeling sorry for me.

"I play harmonica," I said. He looked at me and shook his head.

"We don't need a harmonica. Can you play drums?"

It was at this moment that I learned a lesson that would serve me well over the years. Even in my emotional and sleepless state, I knew that if I said no, my Nashville days would be finished before they ever started. Although I had played around on the drums at Jim Isbell's house, my skills were very limited. But, with foolish confidence, I responded firmly, "Yes, but I don't have any."

"That's okay," he said. "We'll get some for you." We went down to Hewgley's Music Shop, a regional music store chain, where Johnny cosigned a note to help me get a set of drums, and rehearsals for my first tour as a professional drummer commenced.

Toronto was an exciting trip. We had a two-week engagement at the Edison Hotel at 335 Yonge Street, right in the heart of Toronto's booming music scene. Neon signs flickered all around, beckoning kids to come in, hear some great rock and roll and rhythm and blues, and have a drink or two. Just a few years earlier, Bill Haley of "Rock Around the Clock" fame had played the Edison. Next door to the Edison was Le Coq d'Or, a club that would later be known as the place that launched the career of The Band. While I was playing in Toronto, Le Coq d'Or was hosting Narvel Felts, a fantastic singer from Missouri. His saxophone player, Jerry Tuttle, would play in a band with me later on.

The Toronto audience was a fairly sophisticated one, and they knew what good music sounded like. Unfortunately, we weren't able to arouse our Canadian audiences. I felt sorry for Johnny, but we simply had a terrible show. Our band was bad, and even though I was still learning to play the drums, I wasn't the worst musician in the group. At the end of our engagement, the club owner at the Edison pulled Johnny aside and told him, "This is the worst show we've ever had in here. Maybe you should just play in the South." I found out later that the owner called our booking agent and told him that he should drop us because we would ruin his reputation if he continued to represent us.

On the drive back to Nashville, we stopped at Niagara Falls. As we were walking to the falls, we spotted one of rock and roll's greatest wonders, the "Killer," Jerry Lee Lewis, looking out at the powerful waterfall. Although he was a big star, we weren't afraid to approach him and introduce ourselves. After a brief conversation, he matter-of-factly said, "Well, boys, Jerry Lee has seen Niagara Falls. Let's go!"

Once we got back to Nashville, I was eager to establish good credit, so I took my earnings from our Canadian engagement down to Hewgley's Music Shop and paid off the note on my drums.

The next weekend, we were scheduled to play a show in Livonia, Georgia. After our terrible stint in Toronto, this was a chance for us to redeem ourselves and to test the theory that southern audiences might like us more than our Canadian neighbors did. Luckily, the audience seemed to enjoy Johnny's southern drawl and his slow, easy delivery, and I left the show feeling better about the situation I had gotten myself into. But that feeling didn't last long. The next day, Johnny called Kent to tell him that he had run out of bookings and was going to disband the group. So there I was, with no money, no work, and a set of drums that I couldn't really play.

Things didn't get much better for the next month or so. Kent and his wife were having problems, so we all moved out and tried to survive on the little bit of money that we had among us. Although we were in a tough situation, I couldn't bring myself to swallow my pride and ask my dad for help. But I did ask my mother, who came through with some much-needed financial support, just like she always had. With her help, I was able to hang on.

Because there wasn't any work for us at the time, we had a lot of free time on our hands. Much of our time was occupied with board games. But we also spent a lot of time writing songs. Kent was very interested in songwriting, and he allowed me to add a word or two here and there or to play along with him on the harmonica. One time, Kent was working on a song that he was writing with Marijohn Wilkin, who had already written such hits as "Long Black Veil" and "Waterloo." The song was called "I Just Don't Understand," and I worked up a harmonica part for it that would be my ticket to the session world that I dreamed of.

One of the songs we wrote came from an idea that a guy at the Old South Jamboree had given me. Gil "Chick" Metters has started a song called "Cherry Berry Wine," but when he hit a wall and couldn't finish it, he told me that I was welcome to take a stab at it. I sang what he had given me for Kent, who was enthusiastic about our ability to finish it. The song opened a lot of doors for me later on. Kent and I wrote two other songs that were recorded: "Funnel of Love," which was the B-side of Wanda Jackson's huge 1961 hit "Right or Wrong" (and that was recorded by Rosie Flores in 1999), and "A Little Bit of Heaven," which was recorded by Earl Sinks—who went by the stage name Earl Richards—in 1962. "Funnel of Love" has been in three movies and recently came out as Cyndi Lauper's new single.

One Saturday night, Kent, Snuffy, and I were down at Tootsie's Orchid Lounge, the famous watering hole located beside the Ryman Auditorium and a favorite spot for *Grand Ole Opry* stars to relax during the show. I was watching a jam session between the great steel guitar players Buddy Emmons and Jimmy Day. In addition to being a first-call session player, Emmons had been playing with Ernest Tubb's Texas Troubadours, adding a jazz touch to Tubb's iconic honky tonk sound, and Jimmy Day was playing with Ray Price. I had never heard steel playing like this before. Each of them tried their best to upstage the other, showing off their best licks and trying to outsmart the other guy. On one tune, Jimmy was playing a break that intrigued Buddy, and Buddy was sitting back to watch what he was doing. When it was Buddy's turn to play, Jimmy took advantage of Emmons's inattention and reached over to snatch the steel bar that Emmons used to play the instrument. Buddy, though, was unflappable. He calmly finished drinking the beer he was nursing, turned the empty bottle on its side, and used it instead. That just knocked my socks off.

While I was being mesmerized by two of the greatest steel guitarists ever to touch the instrument, Kent was trying to find us some work among the *Opry* regulars who hung out at Tootsie's. With the sounds of Emmons and Day ringing in my ears, Kent told Snuffy and me that he had landed us a gig with *Opry* star Jimmy C. Newman. Newman came from Mamou, Louisiana, and had been a member of the Opry since 1956. His musical style blended the sounds of the honky-tonk with those of the Cajun music that he grew up with, and that distinctive sound had helped to make him a mainstay on the country charts.

Newman had a performance scheduled at the NCO club in Fort Jackson, South Carolina, the next day, and he was in need of a band. Having learned that Kent thought I could play anything, I asked him, "What am I playing?"

"Piano," Kent replied. "You do play piano, don't you?" I'd already learned that I shouldn't say no in situations like these, at least if I wanted to work, so I told him that I could. But, I informed him, I didn't know any of his music.

Eager for work, Kent said, "He will teach us in the car." So we scrambled home to pick up our instruments and clothes, and we made it back to the *Opry* in time to leave Nashville at midnight for the long drive that lay ahead.

When we got in the car, Jimmy started teaching us some of his biggest hits. It turned out that I already knew a couple of his most famous songs, including "A Falling Star" and "Cry, Cry Darling." But Jimmy also wanted us to play some Cajun music as well. Although it was one of the things that distinguished him from other country acts of the day, I hadn't heard Cajun music before, and I spent half the night trying to get a sense of its structure and style. I was hanging on the best I could during the performance, but I'm not sure that we gave him the backing we needed. Either way, Jimmy was incredibly nice to us, and he treated us like a real gentleman and a professional. We remained friends until he passed away in June 2014.

As a hungry young musician, these road gigs offered much-needed money, but they were not always the most musically rewarding experiences. Sometimes these short-term gigs would yield great friendships, like my trip with Jimmy C. Newman did, but just as often, the circumstances surrounding the gig were tough. This was the case when I was hired to play with Red Sovine, who had made a niche for himself doing country songs with long recitations of sentimental stories, and Stonewall Jackson, who had a hit with Marijohn Wilkin's "Waterloo." The trip was arranged by Wayne Gray, a guitar player I had met during my time at the Old South Jamboree.

"I'm putting together a band for Red Sovine and Stonewall Jackson to play the summer fair circuit," he told me. "Can you play drums?"

"Not only can I play," I replied, "but I just happen to have some." Although I wanted to be picky and hold out for a guitar job, I figured that it wasn't the time to negotiate. Besides, the drum parts in country music seemed simple to me at the time. (As time passed, I realized that I was being naive and that country drumming was a special art, just like any other kind of music.)

We spent the summer on the road, playing fairs and festivals all through the Midwest. At the beginning of the summer, the band included Bill Johnson, a steel player who was a buddy of mine from the Old South, and Art Bishop, who played bass. Later that summer, Johnson quit and was replaced by Eddie Raeger. Our long trips in Art's un-air-conditioned Aero Willys gave us lots of time to talk and share musical insights, and it was here that Art taught me—a young rocker—a lot of the basic drum patterns used in country music.

Not only were these road trips long and arduous, they also were paved with one trap after another. It's pretty easy for a road musician to get lured into destructive habits, as I learned one day as we were on our way from Michigan to Iowa. Art decided to stop in Calumet City, Illinois, a suburb of Chicago. He warned me, "This is a very rough place. Don't talk to anyone, or even look at anyone." We went in a very rough-looking club where an equally rough band was trying to entertain the patrons with some poorly executed country music. I sat in a booth trying not to look at anyone, hoping that we would get out of there in a hurry. Before long, a guy dressed in a trench coat walked up to me and offered to sell me some pills. He opened his coat to show me the pockets that lined its inside. In them were medicine jars of pills in every size and color.

I'd had one bad experience with pills when I started on the road with Red and Stonewall. For my very first gig with them, we had a long overnight trip that started at the end of the *Opry* broadcast and ended with a matinee performance in Lima, Ohio. I was excited about my new opportunity, and between the adrenaline and the uncomfortable seats in the car, I struggled to get any rest. By about 10 a.m. the next morning, I was feeling awful and started to worry that I wouldn't be able to stay awake for the matinee. Seeing my pain, Art Bishop held out his hand and said, "Here, kid. Take this pill, and you will be fine." I refused, but after a while, I agreed, sure that it wouldn't work. The pill—I think it was called an "ole yellow"—hit me just as I was setting up the drums. I think I could've threaded a sewing machine with it running. We were set up right next to the rodeo ring, where cowboys were trying to ride bulls. In the middle of our set, one of the bulls jumped up on the stage, scattering everyone in the band except me. I just looked that bull in the eye and kept playing. Afterward, the guys in the band told me I was crazy and that I could have been killed by that bull. My experience with "uppers" was over for good.

With my bad experience in mind, I just told the man in Calumet City, "No, thanks," and prayed that he would go away. He took the hint and wandered off.

Although I filled an immediate need, it quickly became clear that my drumming needed a lot of work to meet Stonewall Jackson's needs. Like a lot of country singers at that time, he knew about hard work. The story around Nashville was that he came to Nashville from Moultrie, Georgia, in a dump truck. When I was on the road with him, he had just had a monster hit with "Waterloo," and he also sang the great ballad "Life to Go" and my favorite, "A Wound Time Can't Erase," written by Bill Johnson. When Stonewall would sing "Waterloo" at a county fair, he would look back at me, smile, and stomp the stage like the bass drum, trying to get me to push even harder than I already was. I know he could stomp the stage louder than I could ever play the bass drum. Others heard my struggles, too, as I learned one night after a fair gig in Champaign, Illinois. Carl Smith, a successful country singer in his own right, was talking with Stonewall, and I overhead him saying, "You know, 'Wall, this boy back here . . . I know he is probably great at something, but he sure can't play drums." Carl didn't know that those were my sentiments exactly!

Just as Jimmy C. Newman didn't hold my poor showing in his band against me, neither did Red Sovine. Red was a real prince whom I admired for many, many years. In 2008, I had the pleasure of inducting him into the West Virginia Music Hall of Fame the very same night that I was inducted as well.

The transition from college life to life on the road was a tough one, but I was beginning to make important contacts with musicians around Nashville and to show them that I was willing to take on just about any musical challenge. I might not have been the best musician to play the piano or the drums, but I was willing to work hard to get a good sound from the instruments. And I was a quick study, thanks in large part to the great solfeggio training I received from Mme. Longy. It wouldn't be long before word of my eagerness and musicianship helped me land in the very Nashville recording studios that I had been dreaming of since my first visit to Music City.

CHAPTER 5

MUSIC CITY OPPORTUNITIES

In 1960, Nashville had many opportunities for an aspiring musician to try to make a living. Although the city's music publishers and recording studios were putting hit after hit on the charts, it still had something of a small-town atmosphere, and it was relatively easy to get started, as my travels with Jimmy C. Newman, Stonewall Jackson, and Red Sovine would indicate. Nashville was also a town that was willing to take a risk on unproven talent, hoping that a hard-working and talented recording artist, songwriter, or session musician might turn out to be a great investment in the long run.

Cedarwood Music, under the leadership of its cofounder Jim Denny, was one of those companies that was interested in emerging talent. When I got to Nashville, Cedarwood was a real force in the country music business, having published dozens of songs that had gone to the top of the charts. Like most publishers on Music Row (and in the music industry more generally, for that matter), Denny hired a talented pool of songwriters whose main job was to turn out high-quality material that recording artists would be interested in cutting. The Cedarwood roster included such powerhouse songwriters as Mel Tillis, Marijohn Wilkin, and Wayne Walker.

Denny was always on the lookout for new talents, and my friend Kent Westberry was one of his rising stars. One day in the summer of 1960, Kent asked me to come to Cedarwood with him as he pitched some new songs and to play along on the harmonica. When he sang "I

Just Don't Understand," I filled all the gaps in the lyrics with my bluesy harmonica, just like I had done during our work sessions at home. Denny heard what I played and was impressed.

"That harmonica is a nice touch," he said. "We'll let him play it when we do the demo." Demos—or demonstration records—were one of the main tools that publishers had in convincing recording artists and record producers to cut their songs. It painted a picture of the song and tried to make the song even more appealing than it already was. But even more importantly for me, demonstration sessions were a great way for musicians to get their foot in the door of the session scene.

As I was starting to get excited about the possibility of doing a demo session, Kent introduced "Cherry Berry Wine," the song that Kent and I had finished together. "We've got a song here that we wrote together," Kent said, "and Charlie sings it much better than I do." I sang it just like I had at home, and Denny was clearly impressed and suggested that I sing it on the demo session as well.

Here was an opportunity to start working with the hotshot players I fell in love with during my first visit to Nashville. But before I could go into the studio, I needed to become a member of the Nashville musicians' union. Although I was already a member of the Miami local, it was so corrupt that I had a bad taste for the union in general. Denny called the union hall and set up an appointment with George Cooper, the president of the Nashville local. When I went down to meet him, it quickly became clear that Nashville was not Miami. Mr. Cooper was a stern-looking southern gentleman, and his gruff voice was particularly effective in explaining all the union's rules and enforcement policies. As he talked about policies and procedures, his eyes lit up. It was clear to me from that first meeting that he was a no-nonsense, commonsense leader who tried to be fair to all parties. (Little did I know at the time that I would be connected to his family one day by marrying his granddaughter.)

I started going to Cedarwood every day to cut demos of the dozens of new songs that were written there every week. Demo sessions were steady work and paid a decent wage that helped prevent me from taking a non-music job to pay the bills. One of the best things

about this work was that I got the opportunity to play in many different musical styles and to meet a cross-section of the people who made
Nashville's music industry work, including the many people who
came through to meet with Denny's partner, Lucky Moeller, who ran
one of Nashville's biggest booking agencies at the time. It wasn't long
before my versatility and commitment paid off and the doors to the
studio scene began to open for me.

One day, Denny received a call from Owen Bradley, the producer
who had invited me to watch my first Nashville sessions. He was looking for someone to play blues harmonica on a demo session with a
young Johnny Rivers. Rivers had written a song in the Jimmy Reed
style, and it cried out for harmonica. Immediately, Denny recommended me for the gig. When Denny told me that I was going to be
playing harmonica for one of Bradley's sessions, I was thrilled. As
much as I had been trying to make my way as a guitarist, the compe-
tition in that arena was steep. But the harmonica seemed like it could
be my ticket.

Denny informed me that the session leader was Grady Martin, the
guitarist I had met when I visited the Brenda Lee session. Rumor was
that Grady could be tough on new musicians. When I went into the
Bradley studio, I saw Johnny Rivers talking with Owen and Grady.
Grady had his back to us and looked like a mountain. Denny introduced me.

"Grady," he said, "here's the guy I told you about."

Grady didn't even turn around. He just looked over his shoulder
and gruffly said, "You play blues harmonica, kid?"

Timidly, I responded. "Yes, sir."

"Let me hear you play something," he demanded. I pulled out the
harp and stumbled through a couple of Little Walter licks.

"Well, I guess you'll do," he said.

Johnny Rivers was thrilled, and I was still in a state of shock. My
head reeling, Owen recognized me from my first visit. "Hey! I know
you!" he said.

"Yes, sir," I replied. "I auditioned for you in 1959."

I was surprised by his ability to recall the details of my visit. "You played the guitar and sang a Chuck Berry song, right?" he asked. I nodded. "I didn't know you played harmonica too. Guitar players are plentiful around here," he observed, "but that harmonica is special."

The band came in at 2 p.m., and we did the song. Afterwards, Denny told me that even Grady was raving about my playing. That was my first big test, and I passed with flying colors.

By September 1960, I was itching to get back into the studio, but I was still working the road, playing drums with Red Sovine and Stonewall Jackson. The road felt like an endless trail that led nowhere, and although the drums paid the bills, they didn't provide me with any musical fulfillment. We were out in Iowa to play a fair, and were lounging in the hotel before the show. A hotel porter knocked on the door of my room to tell me that I had received a long-distance phone call in the lobby. In those days before cell phones, people rarely made long-distance calls, and I was worried that something was wrong with my mother or my dad. I ran to the lobby, bracing myself for the news. To my surprise, it was Jim Denny.

"Charlie," he said, "I've played your demo of 'Cherry Berry Wine' for Archie Bleyer, and he wants to sign you to a recording contract. He will be in town next week to meet you." Bleyer was the owner of Cadence Records, one of the most successful independent labels in the country. He had released great hits with the Everly Brothers, Andy Williams, Johnny Tillotson, the Chordettes, Julius La Rosa, and many others, and he had also been the music director for *The Arthur Godfrey Show* on television. My mother was a huge Godfrey fan, and when I told her the news later, she was thrilled.

I was stunned at this news. "Really?" was all I could say in response.

"Yes," Denny replied. "And I want you to get off the road and be available for Archie. I will give you enough demo sessions to pay your bills."

I was overjoyed! A chance to record and—most importantly—no drums! I thanked Denny profusely and began to dream of life as an artist. I had almost given up the idea of being a recording artist, and now an opportunity was staring me in the face.

Shortly after I finished my last stint with Stonewall and Red, I went down to Denny's office to meet with Archie Bleyer. As I waited for him to arrive, I sat in an office chair and played the guitar, trying to calm my nerves by doing something that was familiar and soothing. He walked into the room, and Denny introduced me. As I stood to shake his hand, the guitar strap got caught on the chair, and I couldn't get up. What a way to make a great first impression! Luckily, Archie just laughed, clearly amused at the situation but not making fun of me. Immediately, I felt at ease.

He was very excited about "Cherry Berry Wine" and thought it could be a hit. "I would like to record it soon," he said. "I'll work out the details of the contract with Jim, and perhaps we can record it at the end of the month." Of course, the only thing I could say in response was an enthusiastic "Yes!"

At the end of October, I entered the studio to record my first single. It was like a dream come true to be in the studio with the very same musicians who had knocked my socks off during my visit little more than a year earlier. Harold Bradley, who had played lead guitar on the demo session, was there, even though he didn't normally play lead in sessions. Archie had liked what Harold played on the demo, and he wanted him to do the same thing on the single. Floyd Cramer was the pianist, Hank Garland was playing bass guitar, and Ray Edenton was holding down the rhythm guitar. On drums, Doug Kirkham kept a steady beat. We cut "Cherry Berry Wine," and then did a Marijohn Wilkin song called "My Little Woman" for the single's "B" side.

Apparently, there was a lot of excitement about the single because it was released right away. It was customary for the bigger publishing companies to promote the songs they published, so Denny had a promotion man named Curly Rhodes, who plugged my record on radio stations all through the South, including in cities like Birmingham, Atlanta, Charlotte, Columbia, Savannah, and Jacksonville. Cadence even got my picture published in *Seventeen* magazine, alongside starlet Ann-Margret, as an up-and-coming young artist. In early November, Archie told me that I would need to go on the road to promote the record after the beginning of the year. Denny informed me that there weren't any demo sessions scheduled for the remainder of the year, so I might want to visit my dad in Miami after the stop in Jacksonville. I decided that was a good idea, and I stayed in Miami through the Christmas holiday. But, even though I was there for a visit, I couldn't help but make music with some of my old buddies, too. Kent and Snuffy had returned to Miami to play a gig at the Bird Bowl Lounge and asked if I would play guitar with them for the rest of the year. It was a no-brainer to me, although it was a tough gig, six nights a week from 9:30 p.m. to 3 a.m. The fact that Jim Isbell was their drummer made it even more enjoyable.

January came quickly, and it was time for me to leave on my first tour as an artist. Archie arranged for me to fly directly from Miami to Chicago, my first long commercial airline flight. I hadn't taken the Chicago weather into account when I packed my bags in sunny Miami, and, when I arrived, I realized that it was far colder than I ever could have imagined. The light jacket I was wearing did little to stop the wind from cutting through me; I don't think I'd been that cold since the third grade.

Cadence's head promotion man, Bud Dollinger, met me at the gate. When he saw me, he was flabbergasted. "For God's sake, kid, is that the only coat you have?" he asked incredulously. "This isn't Florida!"

Sheepishly, I said, "This is it."

"We'll be shopping tomorrow," he matter-of-factly replied.

When we arrived at the hotel, Bud went straight to the telephone to call Archie. "Where did you find this kid?" he inquired, astonished. "He doesn't even have a coat!" The next day, we went to a department store and bought a very nice black overcoat, the nicest one I'd ever owned. He must have thought that I was a bumpkin, and I probably didn't do anything to convince him otherwise. I just didn't feel comfortable around him from the very beginning, and I had a very hard time trying to feel at ease.

The first leg of the tour took us through the heart of the industrial Midwest, with stops in Chicago, Detroit, Cleveland, and Pittsburgh.

Although his job was to promote my record and, hopefully, my career, it seemed that Bud was more interested in visiting with his old station manager friends. He'd talk with them about all sorts of things, and then, almost as an afterthought, he's say, "This is Charlie McCoy. He has a new single, 'Cherry Berry Wine.'" Some of the stations put it on the air immediately, and others told us that they would play it later. I may have felt like an afterthought, but it turns out that both Bud and Cadence had a great reputation among station managers, and because of my affiliation with them, I got the opportunity to be heard in some markets that would have been impossible for a new artist. Most new artists wouldn't even be able to get in the door of those stations, let alone on the air.

Pittsburgh brought my first opportunity to appear on television. They had a show that was modeled after the popular *American Bandstand* program that Dick Clark hosted in Philadelphia. It was called *The Clark Race Show*. These programs wouldn't allow the musicians to perform live. Instead, the musicians went through the motions, pretending to play their instruments and lip-synching with their recordings. If you watch some of the old *Bandstand*-style programs today, you'll notice that the music normally sounds just like the recording because it *is* the recording. But, in those days, it was still a rare treat to see a picture of your favorite musicians, let alone a close-up moving picture, and the kids just loved it. So I played *The Clark Race Show* with my beautiful Les Paul Custom sounding as silent as when I played for Dicky Doo. Also on the show that day was Smokey Robinson and the Miracles, who were there to promote their new Motown single, "Shop Around."

From Pittsburgh, we headed off for several dates along the East Coast. In Philadelphia, I appeared at a dance that was sponsored by a local radio station. There was a live band there, but I was still supposed to lip-synch to my record. After I did that, the band asked me if I wanted to sit in and play guitar on a couple of songs. Bud resisted at first because he had seen many artists who didn't have the musical abilities to join in and ended up making fools of themselves. But I was so tired of lip-synching that I would not be denied. The band wanted to play some blues, and when they did some B. B. King, it was right up my alley. I really let my Les Paul loose and had a great time. For the first time, I think I might have impressed Bud.

The next stop was Baltimore, where I was scheduled to appear on Milt Grant's television show. Bud informed me that one of my label mates, Johnny Tillotson, would be there as well. I'd met him years earlier at one of the Bob Green dances in Miami, around the time that his "Poetry in Motion" was climbing the charts. The girls went crazy when he did his lip sync, setting the bar very high for me. When I did my lip sync, I got the feeling that the girls were just biding their time until they could see Tillotson again. After the show, he came out to sign autographs and confirmed my suspicions. He had a nice crowd of people who were interested in him. As he was sitting on the edge of the stage, Bud told me to observe how he interacted with the audience.

"Watch this guy," he said. "He looks at every single person, speaks to them, and makes them feel special." I still had a lot to learn about handling an audience, but Tillotson gave me plenty to work with.

When we got to Hartford, Connecticut, we were snowed in for a couple of days. Downtime can be difficult when you're on the road, but there's typically a lot of it. Although the hours leading up to show time are pretty hectic, there are plenty of hours in hotel rooms with little more to entertain you than the local television stations, your instruments, and your creativity. Luckily, on this occasion, we had been joined by the newest Cadence artist, Lenny Welch, whose "Since I Fell for You" was on its way to becoming a monster hit. Lenny loved B. B. King as much as I did, so he and I stayed out of trouble by playing and singing the blues together.

After all the travel to promote the record, "Cherry Berry Wine" made it to the prestigious *Billboard* pop chart. It reached number 99, where it stayed for one week before falling off the chart. Although it wasn't a big hit, I was able to return to Nashville with my head held high and a song that had made it to the charts.

Archie liked the way that I played and sang the blues, so we tried to record a couple of Chicago blues classics, "Rooster Blues" and "I Just Want to Make Love to You." Unfortunately, the record was a giant flop. Later, he also had me record an instrumental single that featured my harmonica, so he flew me to New York to record "Mississippi Blues" and "Theme from *Hippodrome*" with future music industry mogul Tony Mottola on lead guitar and a live string section. I remember one of the session musicians laughing when he saw my ten-hold harmonica on the music stand. I supposed it must have looked like a toy to him, but after he heard the playback, I suppose he conceded that it could make real music. Unfortunately, these sides were never released.

My time with Cadence was short-lived, lasting from the fall of 1960 to Archie's retirement in 1962. The label had released many million-selling hits over the years, and they struck "super gold" in October 1962 with a comedy album by Vaughn Meader. The album was called *The First Family*, and it was a spoof on President Kennedy and his family. It sold more than six million copies in two months, and Archie saw this windfall as an opportunity to shut the company down. He sold the catalog to Andy Williams and enjoyed a much-deserved retirement.

After my time on the road and my first—albeit limited—success as a recording artist, I was beginning to think that I might be even more successful with hard work and the right circumstances. But, at the same time, I had the opportunity to continue developing as a session musician thanks to Jim Denny, who called me to play on several demo sessions for Cedarwood. Those demos could open still more doors for me in the session world, which also looked very promising. In the short term, I decided to focus on the session work that Denny was offering, but I always kept an eye on opportunities to be a recording artist.

In hindsight, my decision was a wise one because the door to the top-flight session work was about to open. In May 1961, Denny came to me with news that Chet Atkins wanted me to go to RCA's studio to record with a new artist named Ann-Margret. She was going to cut Marijohn and Kent's song "I Just Don't Understand," and he wanted me to play the exact same thing that I had played on the demo. I couldn't believe it. Chet Atkins had asked for me! This is what I had been dreaming about!

When I got to the studio, I was overwhelmed. First, Ann-Margret was a beautiful blond bombshell, just eighteen years old, and my twenty-year-old self was entranced. And then I looked around the room, saw the band I was going to be working with, and almost had to pinch myself. These were the same musicians I had seen at work during that magical first trip. Floyd Cramer was on the piano, and Bob Moore was playing upright bass. Buddy Harman was holding down the drums, and three guitarists—Hank Garland on lead, Ray Edenton on rhythm, and Harold Bradley on bass—were prepared to play whatever they were called to do. Thankfully, Harold had been the leader on Denny's demo sessions, so at least there was one familiar face in the room.

A remarkable guitarist in his own right, Chet was a very soft-spoken man. He seemed to enjoy giving young musicians a chance to make it in the business, often hiring people who showed great potential and using them for sessions until they were in great demand. Then he would let them spread their wings and give a new crop of musicians an opportunity to prove themselves.

Denny went with me to the studio so he could introduce me to Chet. Like Owen Bradley, he remembered me and my audition.

"You played a black Les Paul Custom, right?" he asked. Chet was quite the gearhead, and he was constantly trying to develop new and improved designs for guitar bodies, necks, and electronics.

"Yes," I replied, surprised that he had remembered me.

"You should have played that harmonica for me," he admonished. "We might have done something."

At the end of the session, Bob Moore asked me if I was busy on Friday. My appointment book looked like a polar bear in a snowstorm. I had nothing booked for eternity at that point.

"I'm free," I told him.

"Great," he said. "I would like you to play on a session with Roy Orbison."

I couldn't believe it! I'd been a big fan of Orbison's records ever since I'd heard his big voice on the radio. When Friday came around, I headed down to RCA, where Bob introduced me to Roy and to Fred

Foster, the owner of Monument Records, Roy's label. Immediately, I was surprised that Orbison didn't talk with the same authority that he sang; he was very soft-spoken. And just as surprising was the fact that Foster asked me if I was still with Cadence Records. I didn't even know that he was aware of my Cadence deal.

I looked around the room and saw some familiar faces in the band. Buddy Harman was behind the drums, Floyd Cramer was playing piano, Boots Randolph was on saxophone, and my new "old friend" Harold Bradley was holding down the rhythm guitar. There was also one noteworthy new face: Scotty Moore, the same guy who had played lead guitar on Elvis's records, on lead. I was in some pretty tall cotton.

Roy started playing and singing "Candy Man" while accompanying himself on guitar. He said he needed someone to come up with an introduction. I had an idea right away, but being the new kid on the block, I didn't think I should speak up. Time passed, and still no one had any ideas.

Worried that I might be breaking an unwritten rule of session work, I walked over to Harold, who I knew wouldn't steer me wrong, and very quietly said, "Harold, do you think it would work if I played this lick?" I played the first half of the line. "And the whole band then played this?" I played the second half.

Harold blew my cover, shouting, "Hey, guys! Charlie has a great idea." Then he turned to me. "Show it to 'em, Charlie."

Timidly, I played what I had played for Harold. Roy said, "That's great! Let's do it just like that, and you take the solo on harmonica." I was definitely feeling pretty good about myself when I heard those words. Nashville's session greats actually accepted my idea, and they let me play a solo to boot! After the session, Fred Foster came over to congratulate me.

"Great job today," he said. "If your deal with Cadence doesn't work, come out and see me."

Two songs from that session went on to be hits for Orbison, "Candy Man" and "Blue Bayou." I played on only one more song with Roy: "Pretty Woman." Boots Randolph was there with all his saxophones, and Roy wasn't hearing harmonica on the song. Fred asked me to find something else, but, with three guitars, bass, and Boots's tenor saxophone on the signature lick, there wasn't a lot left for me to play. Boots suggested that I use his baritone saxophone, which normally plays in the bass register, to accent the lick's bass notes. "Pretty Woman" turned out to be one of the greatest rock-and-roll hits of the 1960s.

My first year in Nashville was a busy one as I tried to build a name for myself as a session musician, recording artist, and sometime songwriter. By the start of 1962, I was poised to take advantage of some of my experiences and was hustling to find more opportunities to play and sing.

CHAPTER 6

—

THE STUDIO SCENE

Nashville is a "bandwagon" town. When word gets around that a new musician has something special to offer, everyone seems to use them. After "Candy Man" hit the airwaves, my telephone started ringing off the hook. In 1961, I played on more than forty sessions, and by 1962, my session work doubled to more than eighty sessions. By the end of 1962, I had the opportunity to play just about any session that I wanted. I was working almost every single day, sometimes even playing on two or three sessions on a given day. My dream of being a first-call session musician was being fulfilled.

It was pretty easy for a young musician to become a bit cocky about being in with the A-Team studio players. I started to do things that were a little idiosyncratic, like wearing a silly little rain hat to the studio or carrying my harps around in a cigar box. But at the same time that I was starting to feel like something special, the novelty of my blues harp was starting to wear off. Producers began asking, "Could you play not quite so funky?" or "Could you play closer to the melody?"

In his characteristically gruff way, Grady Martin helped me understand how I could find my place in a session arrangement. We were doing a session at Owen Bradley's studio. During the first take of one of the songs, I started feeling my oats, playing nearly every lick I knew. I looked over at Grady and saw him shooting me a dirty look. When they played the tape back, I walked over to Grady to ask him if something was wrong.

"You're playing too much," he said. "Listen to the words. If you can't hear and understand every word, you're playing too much." This was the best advice that anyone ever gave me about studio playing. For the rest of my career, I let this be my guide: Less is more. Take a listen to some of Grady's playing, and you'll hear a perfect illustration of this concept.

Over the course of the first couple of years of studio work, I started to develop my own approach to the harmonica, thanks in large part to the suggestions of producers and my session musician colleagues. I spent a lot of time learning how the other instruments on a session sound and teaching myself the licks that the other musicians were playing on them. I also started leaving out some of the heavy blues tone in my sound, using it only sparingly in those moments that really called for it. And I also played a lot more attention to the melody and the spaces between the lines of lyrics. Through that careful attention to nuance and detail, my harmonica playing was transformed from a catchy novelty that could wear out its welcome into a country music mainstay.

Nashville had been associated with a country music for several decades by the time I got there, thanks in large part to the *Grand Ole Opry*, which broadcasted from radio station WSM on Saturday nights. But it wasn't a major recording center until the middle of the 1950s, when the Bradleys opened the Quonset Hut studio and RCA Victor built a permanent facility. When I got to Nashville, the recording scene centered around these two studios, as well as a few others that lined Music Row. These studios were booked solid, with three-hour sessions running at least three times each day, if not more frequently. Thanks to the leadership of the Nashville union local president George Cooper, sessions ran on a very strict schedule, starting at 10 a.m., 2 p.m., 6 p.m., and 10 p.m. It was normal for the session musicians to pack up their gear at the end of a session to head across the street to another studio to do another session. It was a real boom time for someone who was hoping to get involved with session work because there was plenty of it.

The core group of Nashville session musicians was known as the

Nashville A-Team, and it was this group of musicians I had met when I came to the city the first time. In the early 1960s, the first-call guitarists were Hank Garland, Grady Martin, Ray Edenton, Harold Bradley (who often played an electric "tic-tac" bass guitar), and Velma Smith. The pianists were Floyd Cramer, who later left session work when his song "Last Date" hit the charts, and Hargus "Pig" Robbins. On upright bass was Bob Moore, Junior Huskey, or Lightnin' Chance, and sometimes Joe Zinkan, who had been recording in Nashville since the Delmore Brothers were making records there in the 1930s. The top drummer was Buddy Harman, who was able to hold down a steady shuffle, a big booming rock beat, or a tasteful jazz backup when the situation called for it. And there were two main vocal groups that provided the backgrounds. The Jordanaires (Gordon Stoker, Neal Matthews, Hoyt Hawkins, and Hugh Jarrett, who was later replaced by Ray Walker) were the all-male group who had backed Elvis on records and television, and the Anita Kerr Singers (Anita Kerr, Dottie Dillard, Gil Wright, and Louis Nunley) were called for mixed chorus sessions. Sometimes an additional singer, such as the great high-soprano singer Millie Kirkham, would join us as well.

Because the same people were playing on one session after another, we got to know one another's musical tendencies and started to develop a fairly quick and easy way of working with one another. That was absolutely necessary because the producers were expecting us to cut four songs in each three-hour session, and time was money. In a normal session, we would get there a few minutes early to set up our instruments and to warm up a bit, sharing conversation about something in the news or joking around with each other. Of course, we'd also meet the singer and try to make whoever it was feel at ease so that the day's work would go smoothly and everyone would be happy with the results of the session. Then, when the clock reached the top of the hour, it was time for work to begin.

Many times, we didn't have the opportunity to hear the songs that we were going to record until the session itself. Most of the time, the producer or artist and repertoire (A&R) person would play a demo recording supplied by the publisher, and we would immediately start thinking of ways that we could improve upon it. Sometimes we would change the tempo or the rhythmic feel to create a specific mood, and, unless there was a string or horn arrangement that we needed to work with, we would also build the introductions, transitions, and codas as we listened. Then we would try out a few of these ideas, but always with efficiency in mind. We couldn't go on with this experimentation forever because we really had only about forty-five minutes for each song. Eventually, we would settle on an arrangement that every-body—especially the singer and the producer—liked, and we would do the first take. From that point, we would listen to the playback of that take through a set of large speakers mounted in the studio and begin to tweak what we had done the first time through. Sometimes that meant changing the key to fit the singer's voice a little bit better or replacing the intro with another lick that someone suggested. After a couple more takes, everyone would be satisfied with the results, and we would move on to the next song.

Although we worked quickly, we weren't simply playing to a for-mula. Instead, we had to develop some fairly interesting ways to play the instruments and to create sounds that no one had ever heard before. On Bobby Bare's recording of "Detroit City," for instance, they decided that they wanted the sound of a guitar tuning up to be built into the record. All the guitar players were occupied playing other parts. I'd been hired to play harmonica on that session, but didn't have anything to do during that introduction. Since I had a free hand, I tuned the bass string of the guitar while Jerry Reed played it. Another time, I was playing a session with Ray Stevens for the R&B singer Rodge Martin. Bob Johnston, the producer, wanted a bass line that sounded like the one in Ben E. King's classic "Stand by Me," but he wanted it to have a different tone quality. Bob suggested that Ray, who was a great keyboardist and trumpet player, play the bass line on the Hammond B-3 organ's bass pedals, but Ray didn't play the organ bass in the typical style. Eager to keep the producer happy, though, Ray pushed the organ bench out of the way, got on his knees, and played the bass notes with his hands.

One of the things that made it possible for us to work so quickly was a system of shorthand notation that was developed by Neal Matthews of the Jordanaires. Later known as the "Nashville Number System," it uses Arabic numerals to indicate the chord changes of a particular song. Rather than thinking of chords with letter names like C, D, E, and so on, the Nashville Number System gave each of those chords a number. With letters, every time a singer changes key, you have to think of new note names. But with the Nashville Numbers, the relationship between the chords remains the same. It may not seem like a big difference, but it shaved minutes off each session and made things run smoothly.

I first became aware of the Nashville Number System during my first visit to Nashville, when I noticed that Neal Matthews had written numbers down on a sheet of paper. I had learned to associate Roman numerals with each chord in my high school music theory class, so I quickly realized that these Arabic numerals represented the chord changes of the songs they had just recorded. Neal and the Jordanaires were really the first ones to use the Nashville Number System. When I started working with the A-Team, no one else had adopted it yet. But it made perfect sense to me. I used the ear training skills that I had learned with Mme. Longy to transcribe the changes of the songs for a session in Nashville Numbers after hearing a demo recording or a live run-through at the beginning of the session.

One day, guitarist Wayne Moss and I were on a session, and he asked me if I understood what Matthews was doing, and I explained the system to him. After a short explanation, Wayne tried to write down the changes of the song we were learning. He showed me the paper and asked me to check its accuracy. With just a few mistakes, he had caught on in a hurry. From that session on, Wayne would transcribe the changes of every song we were learning and have me check his work. After a while, other musicians started to take notice. Harold Bradley overheard us talking about the numbers one day and asked us what we were doing.

"I'm explaining Neal's music shorthand to Wayne," I said.

"Can you explain it to me?" he asked.

I was more than happy to show Harold this system, and, before long, he was in on the numbers game too. Other musicians were starting to notice what we were up to and started trying to write the numbers as well. Pretty soon, most of the session musicians in Nashville were writing numbers, and it remains a vital tool in Music City still today. In fact, it's used all over the world, as I've seen in my travels to Europe and Japan. There have been three books published on the subject, one by Neal Matthews and two by guitarist Chaz Williams. I really like Chaz's first book because he asked some of Nashville's session players to write charts on five country standards to show the different ways that musicians can use the system for their own needs.

The success of the Nashville system can also be traced to the producers who signed recording artists, hired session musicians, and helped to get good songs in the hands of their artists. Chet Atkins at RCA Victor had been a session musician for many years before moving up the ranks and becoming a full-time producer, so he knew the kinds of challenges that recording posed. Chet's philosophy seemed to be to hire some of the best musicians he could find—especially the younger ones who needed an opportunity to prove themselves—and give them the room to create. Prior to being a session musician, he had played with a number of big country acts and was very interested in jazz as well, and I think he valued that creative freedom. That's how the iconic "Floyd Cramer style" of piano playing came to be so closely associated with country music. He heard the demo recording of "Please Help Me I'm Falling," which he was considering for singer Hank Locklin, and noticed how he would slide into a note by hitting the note immediately below it. He hired Cramer to play the session with Locklin, and the Floyd Cramer style became one of the standard sounds that any country pianist has to master. Chet also had a knack for pushing people to play things that were out of their comfort zone, which is how I came to play vibraphone on recordings. Chet produced dozens of great hits, including Skeeter Davis's "End of the World," Bobby Bare's "Detroit City," Floyd Cramer's "Last Date," and the Browns' "The Three Bells."

Owen Bradley, on the other hand, was meticulous in his efforts to build the best arrangement possible for each song. A pianist in a country club dance band, he understood how an arrangement could make or break a good song, and he set the bar very high in all his work. He was a master of taking a song apart, reconstructing it, and making it better than before. His abilities as an arranger are evident on some of his biggest hits, including Patsy Cline's "Crazy," Brenda Lee's "I'm Sorry," and Loretta Lynn's "Coal Miner's Daughter," not to mention Jack Greene's "There Goes My Everything," Cal Smith's "Country Bumpkin," and Bobby Helms's "Jingle Bell Rock."

Many songwriters owe Owen a debt of gratitude, not only for recording their songs, but for making them much better. Once I was talking with Owen about which production he was the proudest of. Expecting to hear him say on of his classic recordings with Patsy Cline, Brenda Lee, or Loretta Lynn and Conway Twitty, I was surprised when he said without hesitation, Wilma Burgess's "Baby." The melody and responses that he developed between Wilma, Hal Rugg on the steel guitar, and my harp part made the song really special. I would like to take credit for inventing that harp part, but it was all Owen.

I arrived on the Nashville session scene at an absolutely amazing time for music. Throughout the 1960s, the city's recording studios produced such great country hits as Patsy Cline's "Crazy," Jim Reeves's "Welcome to My World," Jimmy Dean's "Big Bad John," and Marty Robbins's "El Paso," among hundreds of others, and the A-Team musicians shaped the sounds of those records. Nashville was also one of the places where Elvis Presley recorded, as did the Everly Brothers, Connie Francis, and Patti Page, all of whom had hits on the pop charts. As a kid in my early twenties, I had the opportunity to play with some of the leading country and pop recording artists of the day, including many of the stars of the *Grand Ole Opry*, the barnstormers who played fairs and festivals around the country, and musicians working in the pop field. Every day brought an opportunity to collaborate with musicians who were well established in the industry, others who were climbing the ladder to stardom, and still more whose recording careers were ultimately fairly brief. Regardless of who was recording at the time, though, the folks on the A-Team did their best to make the artists feel like they were the most important people in the room at the time. After all, they trusted us to support their art by giving each track our best effort, and that was a very special privilege that we all took seriously.

Starting in the middle of the 1960s, I played on an average of more than four hundred sessions each year, a streak I kept up for fifteen consecutive years. That's more than one a day, and many of them were scheduled two or three in a single day. Needless to say, it's a challenge to recall the details of each session that I've played on, especially after several decades. Looking back at my datebooks from this period in my life, it's clear that my life was a whirlwind, but I was having a great time and making a great living.

The dean at the University of Miami had been wrong in thinking that I needed to prioritize my orchestral bass playing because part of my success as a studio musician rested on my willingness to play many different instruments, sometimes during the same session. Although my harmonica playing was the main reason I was hired for sessions, I was also called on to play guitar, bass, trumpet, and, on Bobby Bare's iconic recording of "Detroit City," the guitar's tuning pegs. Thanks to Chet Atkins, I started playing the vibraphone after he asked me to play a few notes on a tune that didn't need harmonica; I ended up buying a set of mallets and going into the studio early so I could practice every chance I got. During that time, I was never hurting for work, and each new instrument and each new session brought an opportunity for creative reward.

By the middle of the 1960s, Nashville was becoming a popular recording destination for recording artists from all around the world. The city began to gain a reputation for the many talented musicians who worked there and the ease with which everyone worked together to make great records. Pop artists like Perry Como, Connie Francis, Henry Mancini, Cliff Richard, Patti Page, and others came to Nashville for a change of pace and an opportunity to work with a fresh group of professionals. Unfortunately, as word about Nashville began to spread through the industry, it became almost impossible for the A-Team musicians to do all the work. They would have needed to be in two places at once to meet the increasing demand for Nashville session time.

With more session work available, musicians started coming to Nashville specifically with the goal of becoming a session musician. Road musicians who were working with *Opry* stars saw an opportunity to settle down and get out of the tough grind of road work. Folks like Pete Wade, Buddy Spicher, Weldon Myrick, Lloyd Green, Pete Drake, Henry Strzelecki, and Willie Ackerman were part of this crew. Other musicians who had been in Nashville for a while, including Wayne Moss, Kenny Buttrey, and Hal Rugg, also took advantage of this need to enter the studio for the first time. From Muscle Shoals, Alabama, Rick Hall, who had been producing great R&B records for artists like Wilson Pickett and Aretha Franklin, brought his all-white rhythm section composed of pianist David Briggs, bassist Norbert Putnam, and drummer Jerry Carrigan to Music City. Folks came from Louisiana, like guitarists Jerry Kennedy, Billy Sanford, and Fred Carter Jr. They came from Georgia, like instrumentalist Ray Stevens and guitarists Jerry Reed, Chip Young, and Joe South. Horn players and arrangers came to the city as well, and many members of the Nashville Symphony Orchestra started doing sessions as more and more artists called for them. There were musicians everywhere!

Chet Atkins, Owen Bradley, and Don Law were the big-three producers when I came to town, working for RCA Victor, Decca, and Columbia, respectively. With the growth of country music's popularity and the increased recording activity around Nashville, a number of producers were able to score hits and to develop their own approaches to record production. To get a record on the charts, a producer had to find great artists, hire session musicians who would fit well with their sound, and come up with a way to market them to an audience. If you listen to the recordings that came out of Nashville during the 1960s and 1970s, you'll be able to hear each producer's mark on the recordings they oversaw. As a session musician who worked for all of them, I had to learn what they were looking for and try my best to make a meaningful contribution.

Fred Foster at Monument Records built the most important independent label in Nashville during the 1960s and 1970s. He was passionate about instrumental recordings, and Boots Randolph, steel guitarist Jerry Byrd, and I were the beneficiaries of his excitement. Under his direction, Monument was a success right from the start, landing a country and pop hit with Billy Grammer's 1959 recording of "Gotta Travel On." His work with Roy Orbison, Dolly Parton, Jeannie Seely, Henson Cargill, the Gatlin Brothers, and Billy Swan secured his legacy.

Shelby Singleton and Jerry Kennedy came to Nashville at the same time, landing in Music City in 1961. Shelby worked for Mercury Records, which was trying to build a country catalog, and he jumped into his task with both feet. In his first full year (1962), he oversaw more than two hundred sessions. He was a hit maker, even recording three number-one songs in a single day in 1961: Ray Stevens's "Ahab the Arab," Leroy Van Dyke's "Walk on By," and Joe Dowell's "Wooden Heart." Shelby also oversaw some great R&B recording in Nashville with Brook Benton, Peggy Scott, and Jo Jo Benson. He later went on to establish his own label, Plantation Records, where he helped Jeannie C. Riley break into the country and pop charts. In the studio, Shelby was always full of great sayings. He evaluated every take on a numerical scale; it was either a 7, a 7 1/4, or a 7 1/2. When we finished, he'd say, "There's your record, fine as frog's hair!"

When Shelby launched Plantation in 1966, Jerry Kennedy was the obvious choice to replace him as Mercury Records' staff producer. He was a real musicians' producer who hired people he trusted and let them play. Between releases for Mercury and its subsidiary label, Smash, Jerry scored hits with Roger Miller ("King of the Road"), the Statler Brothers ("Remember When"), Jerry Lee Lewis ("What Made Milwaukee Famous"), and Tom T. Hall ("Old Dogs, Children, and Watermelon Wine").

When I arrived in Nashville to audition in 1959, Don Law was the staff producer for Columbia Records. His artists included Johnny

Cash, Marty Robbins, Carl Smith, Carl and Pearl Butler, and many others. Columbia Records was a major player here. When Don retired, his assistant, Frank Jones, took over. Frank didn't miss a beat as Columbia carried on their excellent work. By the late 1960s, Billy Sherrill and Bob Johnston were also producing for Columbia, but using two very different approaches.

Billy Sherrill, who produced for Columbia and its subsidiary Epic Records, was a real "song man." Unlike Owen and Chet, whose artists usually brought their songs to the session, Billy was personally involved in picking all the songs that his artists recorded. Billy was also a talented songwriter, and on many days, he would be finishing a new song in the morning for a session he had booked at two in the afternoon. Among his memorable hits are Tammy Wynette's "Stand by Your Man," Charlie Rich's "Behind Closed Doors," David Houston's "Almost Persuaded," Joe Stampley's "Soul Song," Tanya Tucker's "Delta Dawn," and Johnny Paycheck's "Take This Job and Shove It."

Bob Johnston is probably best known for producing such acts as Bob Dylan, Leonard Cohen, Johnny Cash, and Flatt & Scruggs. He tended to make records by letting the musicians have some space to create their own sound, and he was much more hands-off in his approach than Billy Sherrill was. Among the many sessions that I worked for Bob, my favorite was his very first one: a Patti Page session that produced "Hush, Hush, Sweet Charlotte." Patti was at the end of her contract with the label, and Bob Mersey, Columbia's A&R director in the New York office, gave Johnston the opportunity to produce the session after he heard some demos that he'd produced. The company had nothing to lose on this untested producer because they were letting Page go, but Bob surprised them all. Using contacts he had in Los Angeles, he got the rights to "Hush, Hush, Sweet Charlotte," which was slated to be the theme for an upcoming movie. Johnston hired me to be the session leader and to bring in his usual rhythm section and strings. Patti, who is one of my favorite singers, was her usual gracious self and was very patient as she watched this first-time producer try to do something with this song. In the end, the session resulted in a hit record, and everyone was pleased with the results.

Noel Ball, a local radio disc jockey, also produced many sessions, and he always hired me to be the leader. As a disc jockey, he had discovered Chase Webster, who had scored a hit with "Moody River" in 1961, and then took over Arthur Alexander's productions from Rick Hall in Muscle Shoals. Noel was friends with Randy Wood, who ran Dot Records in Los Angeles and was the same guy who owned Randy's Record Shop, the source for the blues recordings I bought when I was a kid learning to play blues harp. The radio station that Noel worked for was located in the basement of the Maxwell House Hotel in downtown Nashville. One night while I was driving home from a session, I tuned in to Noel's show. As he started a record, I heard him say, "I think something is burning." When the song ended, I could hear the needle just running in the groove. The next morning, I found out that the Maxwell House had burned to the ground. Luckily, Noel escaped harm. My favorite Noel Ball production was Arthur Alexander's "Anna," which features a haunting piano riff played by Pig Robbins.

There were many other producers who supervised sessions in Nashville throughout the 1960s, and I worked for most of them. Bob Ferguson, Chet Atkins's second-in-command, secured his legacy by producing Connie Smith, whose first single, "Once a Day," reached number one on the charts. Ken Nelson at Capitol Records commuted to Nashville from Los Angeles, producing Sonny James, Faron Young, Ferlin Husky, and the Louvin Brothers and, in Los Angeles, recording the great Bakersfield Sound artists Buck Owens, Wynn Stewart, and Merle Haggard. Bob Montgomery, working at United Artists, also enjoyed great success on the country and pop charts, most notably in his 1968 production of Bobby Goldsboro's "Honey."

As the kinds of music that we recorded in Nashville became more sophisticated, many of our sessions required arrangers to write parts for the strings and horns. Unlike rhythm section musicians, string and horn players typically use written notation, so the arranger created backgrounds for them to play. In some cases, as with Cam Mullins's outstanding arrangements for Ray Price or Bill Hall's string arrangements for Roy Orbison, arrangers were as important to an artist's overall sound as was his or her own unique way of singing. Others—like Anita Kerr—recorded on sessions in addition to creating memorable arrangements. In some cases, a producer would hire an arranger to do most of their string sessions. Bill McElhiney is a great example of that as he was Owen Bradley's arranger of choice. You can hear his haunting strings on Brenda Lee's "I'm Sorry."

In addition to writing string and horn parts, the arrangers brought ideas that they thought would make a song a hit. Don Tweedy, for instance, did many arrangements for Bobby Goldsboro, and he would call me to play harp, vibes, and melodica on the same song just to get more variety on the cut. Another time, Cliff Parman, who was one of the earliest string arrangers in town, brought an arrangement for a song about Indians that had a section for the drums to change over to an "Indian beat." When we came to that transition in the session, I looked up to see Cliff doing a war dance, holding his fingers behind his head like they were feathers. It was hard to hold it all together to get through the take! Bill Justis, who, as an artist in Memphis, had a huge hit with "Raunchy," liked to fill his charts with goofy sayings that we had to read as we played the chart down. Talk about inside jokes!

Bill, Boots Randolph, Ray Stevens, and I often came together to provide a funky horn section. During the mid-1960s, he was doing a series of instrumental albums for Mercury, and one of the songs that he wanted to cut was a saxophone instrumental that had previously been on pop radio. He hired me to play the solo because, as he said, I was "the only sax player in the union who can play that bad"!

I've had the great pleasure to work with a number of great arrangers as I've recorded my solo albums. Bergen White, who was Bill Justis's protégé, wrote beautiful string arrangements for "The Christmas Song" and "Theme from *A Summer Place*." Buryl Red, who first came to town to record music for elementary school textbooks, is an amazing vocal arranger who has had great success with a male choir called the Centurymen. He contributed some stunning arrangements to my first Christmas album. Bill Pursell, a graduate of the Eastman School of Music, should be listed in the dictionary entry for "genius." An amazing pianist, he had a monster hit on the song "Our Winter Love" in 1963. His arrangements for me include "Shenandoah," "I Honestly Love You," "Evergreen," and many songs on my first Christmas album.

No story about recording in Nashville would be complete without mentioning the great background singers who contributed to so many classic recordings. When I came to Nashville in 1960, almost all the backing vocals were provided by two groups: the Jordanaires and the Anita Kerr Singers. The Jordanaires, who rose to fame as Elvis's backing group, were an all-male group consisting of Gordon Stoker, Neal Matthews, Hoyt Hawkins, and Hugh Jarrett; Ray Walker later replaced Jarrett. If you wanted a group of mixed voices, then the Anita Kerr Singers were the ones you wanted to call. Anita was a gifted arranger and musician who played vibes on many RCA records. Consisting of Anita, Dottie Dillard, Gil Wright, and Louis Nunley, the Anita Kerr Singers can be heard on such great recordings as Brenda Lee's "I'm Sorry" and Bobby Helms's "Jingle Bell Rock." When Anita retired from the group, they carried on as the Nashville Sounds. There were also some freelance singers like Millie Kirkham, Dolores Dinning, and Helen Chance, who sometimes joined the existing groups or, if an all-female group was needed, formed a backing group for sessions.

As the number of sessions began to grow in the mid-1960s, there was a deep need for additional backing vocalists. The Nashville Edition—Ricki Page (later replaced by Wendy Suits), Dolores Dinning Edgin, Joe Babcock, and Hurshel Wiginton—helped fill that void. The group can be heard on Freddie Hart's "Easy Lovin'," as well as many of Billy Sherrill's productions, including Charlie Rich's great "Behind Closed Doors." Eventually, they became the staff vocal group on *Hee Haw*, where I would work many hours with them.

In the mid-1970s, the Lea Jane Singers—Lea Jane Berinati, Janie Fricke (and, later, Sharon Vaughn and Judy Rodman), Duane West, and Tom Brannon—worked a lot of sessions. I first met Lea Jane when she worked as a secretary at Columbia Records. She was friends with engineer Neil Wilburn, who let her observe Bob Dylan's sessions there.

One day, I saw her listening to a playback and taking notes. I looked over at her paper and saw that she had transcribed the melody and chords and was taking the lyrics down in shorthand. I didn't know that she was musical, but it turns out that she has perfect pitch, and she can even write an arrangement while she is singing. Lea Jane is an exceptional talent, and her group contributed to a lot of great recordings over the years.

An often-overlooked part of the Nashville Sound came from the engineers who recorded, mixed, and mastered the recordings that we made. In many cases, they also designed the tracking rooms and the circuitry that was responsible for turning our music into electrical signals that could be captured on tape. Creative people in their own right, no one would have been able to hear what we were playing without their hard work. I've worked with far too many engineers through the years to mention them all, but I have worked with several who stand out as my favorites. The Quonset Hut was staffed by Selby Coffeen, Mort Thomasson, Lou Bradley, Neil Wilburn, Charlie Bradley, and Ed Hudson. At RCA, Bill Vandervort, Chuck Seitz, Jim Malloy, Al Pachuki, Les Ladd, and Tommy Strong held down the control room. At Woodland Studios, which Gillian Welch and Dave Rawlings currently own, David McKinley, Brent King, and Ernie Winfrey made us sound great. My session buddy and bandmate Wayne Moss is one of my all-time favorites, and his Cinderella Sound is one of my favorite places to record. Jack Clement hired Charlie Tallent to design a state-of-the-art facility at the Cowboy Arms Hotel and Recording Spa. When the Bradleys sold the Quonset Hut to Columbia, they built a new studio, known as Bradley's Barn, in Mount Juliet, and Joe Mills and Bobby Bradley were important engineers there. Out at Monument, Glenn Rieuf, Chad Hailey, and Chip Young stood out, as did Quadrafonic's Gene Eichelberger. Mercury hired Tom Sparkman to engineer many of their recordings. And there were several independent engineers around Nashville who were brought in to work with specific clients, including Eric Paul (who is one of my all-time favorite engineers), Ron "Snake" Reynolds, Billy Sherrill (the engineer, not the producer), Bil VornDick, and Lee Hazen.

Studio life in the 1960s was a constant whirlwind of excitement and creativity, and I feel very fortunate to have had the opportunity to work with such an excellent community. At the end of the day, we were all dedicated to doing our best to make the artist feel safe to be creative, to help the labels that hired us score hits on the charts, and to create music that was interesting and well played. As artists came and went, my studio colleagues and I were a constant, and I have an enormous amount of respect for everyone I worked with during those years. It was a thrilling time to be making music, and the folks I collaborated with made it all the more rewarding.

—

CHAPTER 7

THE ARTISTS

The Nashville studio scene was populated by dozens of exceptional session musicians, arrangers, producers, and engineers, as well as the many secretaries who helped keep the business moving forward. But we all would have sat around with nothing to do if it weren't for the artists who came to Nashville to record with us. I've had the opportunity to record with hundreds of singers over the years, and, although some of them came and went, others became lifelong friends. After nearly six decades and thousands of recording sessions, many sessions blur together, but a few stand out in my memory.

Many of the A-Team session musicians recorded solo projects during the 1960s, especially when instrumental records began making waves on the radio. Chet Atkins had one of the best known of these albums with his 1966 release, *Chet Atkins Picks on the Beatles*. I played on those sessions, which featured many of the Beatles' earliest hits, including "I Feel Fine," "Can't Buy Me Love," and "Yesterday." But if you turn the sleeve over, you'll see a picture of a small boy with a harmonica, not a picture of me. When my dad saw this, he was furious! He didn't want people to think that a kid was playing harp on Chet's albums, especially when it was his kid who was doing the work. I mentioned it to Chet, who told me to apologize to my dad on his behalf. On his next album, Chet included a quotation: "Charlie McCoy is the harmonica player on Chet's albums." When he did the *Superpickers* album in 1974, Chet included a photo of all of us on the album's cover, a compliment that helped make me well known within Chet's circle of fans.

Boots Randolph, the saxophonist, was a master musician who played background parts on so many classic rock and pop recordings, including Brenda Lee's "Rockin' Around the Christmas Tree," Elvis Presley's "Return to Sender," Roy Orbison's "Pretty Woman," and too many more to mention. In 1963, he'd had a hit with "Yakety Sax," a song that has been associated with comedic silliness thanks to the British comedian Benny Hill. He was also a great jazz musician and a world-class musician all the way through his eightieth birthday. He invited me to play harmonica (both bass and standard) on his cover of the *Sanford and Son* theme song, which was one of the most fun things that we did together. I also played twice at a golf tournament that he hosted near his hometown of Cadiz, Kentucky. Sadly, we lost Boots in 2007. He had agreed to do a guest solo on my *Over the Rainbow* album, but he passed before I recorded it.

Pianist Floyd Cramer, too, enjoyed a lot of success as a solo artist. I met Floyd back in 1959 during my first visit to Nashville, and he played on the very first recording session I ever did. After his single "Last Date" took off in 1960, he began to pursue a solo career, eventually leaving session work altogether. He was such a great session musician, and his contributions to Elvis Presley's "Heartbreak Hotel," Patsy Cline's "Crazy," and so many more hit records were significant.

Elvis Presley was an important figure in Nashville's development as a recording center during the late 1950s and 1960s. After his initial success on Sun Records, Sam Phillips sold Elvis's contract to RCA Victor, and, over the course of his career, he recorded over two hundred songs at RCA's Nashville studio. My first opportunity to record with Elvis came in 1965. The tremendous volume of recording that we were doing in Nashville at that time prevented Elvis's regular session musicians from playing the gig, so Scotty Moore—Elvis's lead guitarist—called Grady Martin, Pig Robbins, Henry Strzelecki, Kenny Buttrey, and me to play on the soundtrack for his new movie, *Harum Scarum*. Having been a big Elvis fan for many years, I was very excited to receive the call.

When Elvis walked into the studio, there was an aura around him that I have rarely felt with any other artist. His presence commanded my attention. I quickly learned, though, that Elvis didn't walk around like a big star, but was, in fact, the most polite star I've ever worked with. He made it a point to speak with each musician, shaking his hand and saying, "It's good to see you. I'm happy to have you here today."

At the end of the *Harum Scarum* session, I figured that it would be the only Elvis session I would ever do. I had been called to play rhythm guitar, and I didn't have much of a chance to show them my strengths. Fortunately, Scotty convinced the powers that be that I was a valuable guy to have around, so I ended up with the opportunity to work on six more film soundtracks and five additional albums with him. Elvis didn't care for a lot of the movie music, but he remained professional, always treating each song as if it were special.

Elvis liked to record late at night, in part because he wanted to bypass the crowds that gathered outside the studio waiting for a glimpse of the star or an autograph and in part because he was a night person. When we booked an Elvis session, we were asked to keep it a secret, but someone must have let the word out because there were many times that people were hanging out in the parking lot. Elvis's close friends, known as the "Memphis Mafia," came to all the sessions, remaining almost invisible while we were playing. Whenever there was a playback, though, they appeared out of nowhere, standing, grooving, snapping their fingers, and saying, "That's great, Elvis!"

The Memphis Mafia guys added an interesting dynamic to the sessions. During our late-night sessions, the studio normally brought food in around midnight. One time, they brought hamburgers, fries, and all the trimmings. There was a large milkshake cup filled with dill pickle spears. Jerry Carrigan, the drummer on the session, reached for one of them when, out of nowhere, a hand grabbed his wrist and a voice said, "Those are Elvis's pickles." On another occasion, we took a break, and I headed to the men's room. As I started in, one of the Memphis Mafia guys said, "You can't go in there right now." I stood there waiting. After a minute or so, Elvis came out, and the guy said, "Okay, you can go now."

Another night, a bunch of us got into a discussion about how to disarm a man with a gun. Elvis, known for his interest in martial arts, volunteered to show us how it was done, so he asked Red West, one of the Mafia guys, to come at him with a gun. Red pulled out his pistol and emptied all of its bullets. Chip Young, worried about the safety of some acoustic guitars that were propped up against a sound baffle, was getting ready to move his guitar when Elvis knocked the gun out of Red's hand, causing it to fly across the room, where it landed—barrel first—in the back of Chip's guitar. Elvis apologized profusely and told him to pick out any guitar that he wanted to make up for the damages. Chip, though, knew that he had something special, replying, "No, I now have the only guitar in the world with a hole made by Elvis!"

Johnny Cash, like Elvis, got his start at Sun Records in Memphis, and by the middle of the 1960s, he was a major star for Columbia Records. My father, who didn't care much for rock and roll and country music, introduced me to Cash's music one evening in the mid-1950s. He came home from work and told me that we were going out to a restaurant for supper. When we were shown our table, he said to me, "I want you to hear something." He went over to the jukebox, put a quarter in—in those days, jukeboxes would give you six plays for a quarter—and played "I Walk the Line" six times.

Cash had an aura around him, too, and everyone in the room watched what he was doing. My first session with him was also in 1965. Don Law's office called me and asked, "Can you play like Dylan?" Of course, I answered yes. Cash, who was a huge Bob Dylan fan, wanted to record one of his songs, "It Ain't Me Babe," and he wanted the sound to be raw. To accomplish that, I played the harp upside down. I also played on his recording of "Orange Blossom Special," Chubby Wise's famous fiddle tune. I had never played it before, but I loved to hear fiddlers do it. Johnny asked me to play the first half of the solo and gave Boots Randolph the second half. To play the chords like a fiddler would, I had to use harps in two different keys. Johnny was impressed with what I'd done, and, after the session, he asked me to show him how I played it. At the end of the lesson, I gave him the two harps that I'd used on the record.

I recorded many more sessions with Cash over the years. In 1981, he starred in a film about a guy who couldn't read called *The Pride of Jesse Hallam*. During the sessions for the film's soundtrack, I realized that this guy was a genius who was in complete control of his artistic vision. He knew exactly what he wanted to hear, and he also knew how to tell us so that we could create the sound he was listening for.

My connections to Johnny Cash and his family run deep. I recorded with his wife, June Carter, before she was ever married to Johnny. Before the session, I went over to her house in suburban Madison to rehearse the song with her. Her daughter, Carlene, was about two years old at the time, and when June introduced her to me, Carlene announced, "There's a 'nake [snake] in the pond." Carlene—all grown up—toured Denmark with me in 2006. And in an even stranger connection, I found myself in the office of Dr. John Witherspoon, an excellent ear, nose, and throat doctor, after having some trouble with my ears on airplane descents during my European travels. A harmonica fan, Dr. Witherspoon—whose daughter, Reese, won an Oscar for her portrayal of June Carter Cash in the 2005 film *Walk the Line*—fixed me right up.

When most people think of the Nashville Sound these days, they think of three singers: Patsy Cline, Jim Reeves, and Eddy Arnold. Unfortunately, I never had the chance to work a session with either Cline or Reeves, both of whom died tragically in the prime of their careers. I did play on some of their recordings, though, because the labels hired me to add backing—what we called "sweetening"—to some tracks that they had in the vaults. I especially loved Reeves's singing, and I would have loved to be in the room while he was singing live. On the other hand, I had the chance to work with Eddy Arnold many times. The ultimate southern gentleman, he was always friendly and professional, and, even some thirty years after doing my last session with him, he always treated me like an old friend when I saw him.

In the 1960s, Nashville was a city full of amazing country singers, and, as a session musician, I had the chance to record with many of them. Connie Smith, who later toured Japan and Denmark with me, is one of the most amazing country singers to ever grace a Nashville studio, and I was fortunate to play on many records with her during her time at RCA and Columbia. Charley Pride, who was the first African American artist to have big success on country format radio, was a phenomenal artist who was passionate about country music, even recording a tribute album to Hank Williams. Brenda Lee, who was singing on that first session that I witnessed back in 1959, was another fantastic singer who, at Owen Bradley's suggestion, normally hired me to play vibes right behind Brenda. And Skeeter Davis, whose "End of the World" was a major hit, was one of the nicest artists I ever had the pleasure of working with. Her strong faith in God allowed her to live and work with cancer for many years, and, during our visit to Japan, she touched many lives.

Sonny James, known as "The Southern Gentleman," was a gentleman in every sense of the word, and I was lucky to play on a few of his records. He called everyone "Dear Heart." A creature of habit, he always recorded in the morning. He brought two thermos bottles, one with coffee and one with tea. He brought two guitars, one for the rehearsals and one for the recording. He would have Ed Grizzard, the maintenance man at the Bradley studio, sprinkle the rug where he would stand with water. He patted his foot so hard that it could raise a little dust if it were not sprinkled. Sonny was the first artist to take a Jimmy Reed song ("Bright Lights, Big City") and have a country hit with it.

Nashville was also home to many recording artists who performed in some of the more traditional styles of country music. Many of these acts played on the Grand Ole Opry and had come up through the radio barn dance programs, which were quite common in the 1940s and 1950s. Bluegrass, honky tonk, and old-time music were quite common in Music City, and I was fortunate to play on many sessions in those styles as well.

Kitty Wells, known as the "Queen of Country Music," and her husband Johnny Wright were both regulars in my datebook. Kitty, whose real name was Muriel Deason, was the first female country artist to sell a million copies of a single record with her, thanks to her 1952 hit "It Wasn't God Who Made Honky Tonk Angels," and Johnny was, with Jack Anglin, a member of the duo Johnny & Jack. I played on sessions for both of them, but our connections went far beyond the sessions themselves. John Sturdivant, who played with me in a band called the Escorts (see chapter 8), married Kitty's daughter, and Johnny's daughter Sue and their granddaughter played softball against my daughter. It was also on a Johnny Wright session that I met Russ Hicks, who would go on to be a musical partner for many years. And their son, Bobby, made one of my favorite country records of all time, "Here I Go Again."

The influence of Kitty Wells was strong in the work of Loretta Lynn, who came to Nashville from eastern Kentucky via the Pacific Northwest. I was privileged to work many sessions with her over the years, and I always enjoyed her interesting way of describing things. One day, we were recording at Bradley's Barn, and Owen had put me in an isolation booth. Loretta said, "I can't hear the French harp."

"The harmonica is in a booth. You can hear it with the earphones," Owen replied.

"You can call it a harmonica if you want to," she said, "but it ain't nothing but a French harp. That's like when you get four fiddles together and call 'em strings. It ain't nothin' but four fiddles." Loretta also never said "earphones." Instead, she called them "hear phones." When you think about it, she's right.

Another time, I was booked to work with Loretta at RCA's Studio A. I was coaching a girls' softball team called the Demons, and I had to run to practice as soon as the session was finished. The logo on our team's hat was a devil's head. As I walked into the control room to say hello, Loretta looked at me and said, "Here we are, talkin' about things that makes us scairt, and the first thing you do is walk in here with a dad-blamed devil on your hat."

After Owen sold the Quonset Hut studio to Columbia, he built a new studio out in the country called Bradley's Barn. It burned in

1980, destroying all the equipment. But the biggest loss was a book of unique things Loretta had said that Owen had been keeping.

To many people, Lester Flatt and Earl Scruggs were the face of bluegrass music for many years thanks to their television programs and their appearances on *The Beverly Hillbillies*. I became a real fan of theirs during my early years in Nashville, so I was happy when they called me to play on an album with them and Doc Watson in 1967. Grady Martin and I were the only "outsiders" in the session; it was a straight-ahead bluegrass session with some stellar picking. They set up in a circle around the main microphone, and they stepped closer to the mic when they had a solo break or a backup fill. They were doing it just like they had in the early days, using their spacing around the microphone to balance their sound. I'd guess that's where some of the extra bars in bluegrass music come from, too, because it takes a bit of time to get from one place to another. I became great friends with Uncle Josh Graves, their dobro player, who was always wanting to go back in a corner somewhere to play the blues.

The Osborne Brothers—banjoist Sonny and mandolinist Bobby— were a favorite group of mine from the time I heard their version of the old ballad "Fair and Tender Ladies." One time, Owen Bradley and Sonny were in a debate about a banjo part. After a while, Sonny stood up and said to Owen, "Look, I've played it this way all my life, and I've made a fortune." With that, the conversation was over. Not many people could have the last word with Owen Bradley.

Governor Jimmie Davis, the author of the famous song "You Are My Sunshine," is probably the oldest artist I've ever recorded with. I worked with him several times, the last time when he was ninety-eight years old. When we were on a break during that session, I told him that we had just come back from Japan and had closed the show with "You Are My Sunshine." Everyone in the place was singing along. With a great deal of enthusiasm, Jimmie asked, "Can you get me booked over there?" He lived to be 101 years old.

Although Nashville is best known as the home of country music, many pop artists also came to Music City during the 1960s, and I worked with many of them. An effortless singer, Perry Como, who was great friends with Chet Atkins, came to Nashville to record his 1965 hit "Dream on, Little Dreamer," which features my harp playing in the introduction and returned for his 1969 hit "Seattle." In 1963, Bobby Vinton came to Nashville to record his huge pop hit "Blue Velvet," my first session with him. You can hear me playing the vibes and orchestra bells on that record. Tony Martin, who sang in the style of Vic Damone and Al Martino and was married to the actress Cyd Charisse, came to Nashville to record cover versions of big country hits. The producer told us to play just like the records we were covering, some of which I had originally played on. When I started to play exactly what I had played on the hit country version, Tony Martin came over to me and said, "Hey, buddy, could you not play that thing so corny?"

I never had the chance to work with Frank Sinatra, but I worked with his daughter, Nancy, twice, first on an album that she recorded in Nashville and later on the soundtrack of the Elvis movie *Spinout*. The country album, which we did in 1968, was produced by Lee Hazelwood, and Jim Malloy, an engineer from Hollywood whom RCA had transferred to Nashville, hired the musicians. Jim had called me to play vibes and harp, but for the first eleven songs, there was no harp. We started rehearsing "Jackson," the great Billy Edd Wheeler composition, and I said to Jim, "Last chance for harp." Jim went to Lee and said the same thing. Lee, who had a rough edge and a weird sense of humor, said, "Okay, let him play the [expletive] harp if it will shut him up." I did, and it was the only hit from the album.

On two different occasions, Bob Johnston brought Paul Simon and Art Garfunkel to Nashville to record, first for their 1965 record "I Am a Rock" and again in 1968 for their big hit, "The Boxer." "The Boxer" features some of Fred Carter Jr.'s outstanding guitar work, as well as my contributions on the bass harmonica. Paul Simon was in complete control of these sessions, telling me exactly what he wanted to hear on the bass harmonica. All I had to do was perform the part that he invented. Occasionally, Garfunkel would suggest something, and Paul would dismiss him, saying, "No, Artie. That won't work." In

1970, Simon flew me to New York to play bass harmonica on a song called "Papa Hobo." We spent five hours working on sixteen bars of music. We would work out the part and start recording it, and then he'd decide that he didn't like the microphone we were using and would have me cut it again. On the next take, he'd decide that he didn't like the notes we'd chosen. We went back and forth, changing microphones and notes, for hours. But, although it may have been a taxing session, I think it's clear that Paul Simon was right. History has proven his genius, and I am happy to have been on those classic recordings.

Paul Simon wasn't the only person to bring me to New York for session work. In 1962, Shelby Singleton took Pig Robbins, Bob Moore, Buddy Harman, Jerry Kennedy, Harold Bradley, Ray Edenton, Bill Justis, Boots Randolph, Ray Stevens, and me to New York to do sessions with Damita Jo, Brooks Benton, and Nana Mouskouri. For the Benton session, Jerry Kennedy and I went to the studio and found ourselves to be the only Caucasians in the place. The arranger seemed to have a chip on his shoulder that a white musician had been hired for the session, but everyone else was very nice to me. Later on, Brooks came to Nashville, where he recorded his huge hit, "Hotel Happiness."

On that same trip, I had an opportunity to do a session with Quincy Jones and his big band. The group had twelve brass players: four trumpets, four trombones, and four French horns. The main song on the session was "A Taste of Honey," which was then a hit for Herb Alpert and the Tijuana Brass. Since I wasn't playing on that song, I was allowed to sit in the middle of the studio and listen to those high-caliber musicians play an amazing Quincy Jones arrangement. The song I played on, "Shagnasty," was a blues number featuring a blind saxophonist named Roland Kirk, who could play two saxes at the same time. When I returned to Nashville, I told all the jazz buffs I knew about the session, and they were envious. Rahsaan Roland Kirk was very well respected for his contributions to avantgarde contemporary jazz. That's one of the things about session work; you never know who you might have a chance to work with!

By the late 1960s, Nashville became an important place for the younger generation of folk and rock musicians to record as well. A lot of this music wasn't heard on the mainstream AM stations that were playing the pop and country hits of the day. Instead, they were on campus radio stations and FM stations, which were just starting to emerge in some markets. These "underground" stations made room for musicians like Joan Baez, Buffy St. Marie, and others. Their leader was a Minnesota-born songwriter who was making big waves in New York: Bob Dylan. And it was thanks to Dylan that many folk-rock acts and singer-songwriters came to Nashville, offering still more opportunities for studio work in the second half of the 1960s and the first few years of the 1970s.

Dylan's introduction to Nashville came through the producer Bob Johnston. Johnston had proven his worth to Columbia Records after he produced Patti Page's hit record "Hush, Hush, Sweet Charlotte," and the label decided to offer him the opportunity to produce Dylan as a reward. As part of the gig, he moved to New York, where he could work more closely with Dylan and other Columbia artists there. When he left, he told me that he would get me tickets to a Broadway show if I ever came up to New York, and, when I visited the World's Fair in 1965, I called him to take him up on his offer.

"No problem with the tickets," he told me. "Are you free this afternoon?"

"Yes," I said.

"Come to Columbia Studio," he replied. "I want you to meet Bob Dylan."

I headed over to the studio, where Johnston greeted me and introduced me to Dylan. He surprised me by saying that he had a copy of my "Harpoon Man" record, which I had made with the Escorts. Then he told me that he was going to cut a song called "Desolation Row."

"Why don't you grab that guitar and play along?" he asked. There wasn't much to lose, so I agreed, picked up the guitar, and set up next to a microphone. In two takes, Dylan, a bassist, and I made a critically acclaimed recording that appeared on his *Highway 61 Revisited* album. I'm often asked about my guitar work on "Desolation Row," and I must give credit where credit is due: I was playing a very poor imitation of Grady Martin classical guitar sound. Grady inspired every guitarist who ever heard him, and, like everyone else, I did my best to play like him. The notes could be copied, but Grady's impeccable taste was all his own.

Because the impromptu session with me went so well, Johnston was able to convince Dylan to come to Nashville by telling him that all the sessions in Nashville were as easy as the one we'd just done. He came down in 1965 to work on his *Blonde on Blonde* album. Johnston hired me to bring in the regular rhythm section that we had used to do demos for Bob back when he was pitching songs for Hill and Range: Wayne Moss on guitar, pianist Pig Robbins, bassist Henry Strzelecki, drummer Kenny Buttrey, and me. In addition to this group, Dylan brought Robbie Robertson and Al Kooper with him. We were booked for a 2 p.m. session, but he didn't arrive until around six that evening. He told us, "I haven't finished writing the first song. Just relax, and we'll do it when I have it finished." That song—"Sad Eyed Lady of the Lowlands"—was finished at four the next morning. A fourteen-minute ballad, it was a tough assignment to fight sleep while trying not to make a mistake.

On another *Blonde on Blonde* session, Johnston told me that Dylan wanted to do a song in the style of a Salvation Army band and asked me to find a trumpet and trombone player.

"Does it have to be good, or will 'funky Salvation Army' work?" I asked.

Bob replied, "The funkier, the better."

"I can play trumpet," I said, "and I'll call a trombone player. What time should I have him here?"

"Midnight," Bob answered.

My old buddy Wayne Butler, who played with me in the Escorts, was a fantastic trombone player, so I called him and told him to be at the studio at midnight. Wayne came in around 11:45, and we got started almost right at midnight. By 12:17, the record was done, and Wayne put his horn in its case and went home. The song was called "Rainy Day Women #12 & 35." Everything was live, including the yelling that you can hear in the background. In his book, Al Kooper said that he saw me play the trumpet and the bass at the same time during this session, but it didn't happen. I knew how to do it thanks to my work with the Escorts, but I didn't play both on that record. I did, however, show Al how I did it, so perhaps his memory is a little bit cloudy in that respect.

Blonde on Blonde took thirty-nine hours to record.[2] That was an eternity by Nashville standards, where we could cut an entire album in two or three sessions. For his next Nashville album, *John Wesley Harding*, we were done in nine and a half hours.[3] The band on that record was mostly Kenny Buttrey and me. On his third album, *Nashville Skyline*, Pete Drake came in to play steel guitar, and newcomers Charlie Daniels and Norman Blake played guitar. His last album, *Self Portrait*, was an overdub session with Buttrey and me; we were working to some of Dylan's demos.

In all those sessions, one thing never changed: Dylan said very little. As the session leader, I frequently asked him if he thought a certain idea would work. His answer was always the same, as if it were a tape recording: "I don't know. What do you think?" Finally, I stopped asking. I figured that, if he didn't like something, he would tell us.

Dylan's four Nashville albums were very successful and critically acclaimed, and, as a consequence, he put a stamp of approval on Nashville that encouraged artists working in all kinds of music to come here to record. After Dylan, a parade of artists arrived, including Joan Baez, Buffy St. Marie, Leonard Cohen, Gino Vannelli, the Byrds, Paul McCartney, Ringo Starr, Linda Ronstadt, Leon Russell, Manhattan Transfer, and Peter, Paul, and Mary, among many, many others. In my opinion, Dylan opened the door wider for Nashville musicians than any other artist before him. After recording some of his biggest albums here, we all wish that he would come back again.

One of those artists, the Canadian songwriter Leonard Cohen, is the source of my all-time best session story. Bob Johnston brought Cohen to Nashville so he could put some of his poems to music. Accompanying him was a banker from Toronto named Zimmerman.

Everyone called him "Zim." He was shorter than me and always wore a three-piece suit, and he had a passion for playing the Jew's harp, carrying around a bandana with a half dozen harps of different sizes. We were booked for five nights' worth of sessions, each of which was scheduled from 6 p.m. to 1 a.m. Bob asked me to hire the regular guys: Pig Robbins, Henry Strzelecki, Kenny Buttrey, and Wayne Moss. The first night, we recorded one track before heading out for the dinner break.

"Come on, guys," Bob said, "I want to buy you all a drink." It wasn't customary for us to drink during a session, but Bob assured us that it would be fine. We headed to a place called Ireland's, which made a wicked drink they called a "Leprechaun." I stuck with beer, but the other guys had Leprechauns. After two drinks, Bob figured that we'd better head back.

When we returned to the studio, Cohen said that he wanted all of us to sing on the song that we had recorded prior to the break. When we started, the Leprechauns got in the way. Pig started laughing, and then everyone else would follow. No matter how hard we tried, we couldn't get through the song without breaking up. After about twenty minutes, Cohen came out of the control room, and he was absolutely furious.

"I want these people gone!" he shouted. He wasn't kidding.

We all felt awful, and, as we were packing up, Johnston came out and said, "Listen, guys. This is my fault. You will get paid for all the sessions." No one said a word.

Just a bit later, Bob came up to me and said, "He wants you to come back tomorrow night."

"What will I play?" I asked, a bit surprised.

"Bass," he answered.

The next night, I came to the studio with a bass case in one hand and my harp case in the other. I noticed the door was ajar, so I pushed it open with my foot and charged right in. All the lights were out, and it was completely dark in there. Someone had placed a big divider right in front of the door to prevent anyone from seeing into the studio. As I busted in, I tripped over the edge of the divider and fell.

Lying there, I let my eyes adjust to the darkness. As I picked myself up, I looked around and saw one small candle burning in front of Leonard's microphone. He was singing, completely oblivious of my graceful entrance. I went to my stool, took the bass out of its case, tuned it, set it down, and walked into the control room. There was Johnston, engineer Neil Wilburn, back-up engineer Ed Hudson, and Zim.

"Learn this song," Johnston said. "When Leonard is ready, we're going to roll tape."

We listened to Leonard practice, and I learned the song. After about twenty minutes, Zim leapt out of his chair and shouted, "Oh my God! I feel like playing!" He grabbed his Jew's harps and headed for the studio. The rest of us just looked at each other, stunned.

"Well, I guess they're ready," Johnston said.

I took my place, and we started to play this very mournful song, which Leonard was singing with a very sad voice. I was glad that it was dark in the room because it was all I could do to keep a straight face. The whole time, we could hear this Jew's harp going "boing, boing, boing."

When we rolled tape, Leonard made a mistake about thirty seconds in. We restarted, and he made another mistake. After about nine or ten times, Leonard said, in a very deep voice, "Well, Zim, I guess it's time." He went over to his guitar case and pulled out a whip that was about five or six feet long. He handed it over to Zim and turned his back. Zim hit him on the back seven or eight times—not extremely hard, but not real easy either. Zim then handed the whip back to Leonard and turned his back to let Leonard hit him seven or eight times. As I watched this unfold, I was determined that I was not going to be the next person to feel the lashing of the whip. My grip on the bass went from playing position to baseball bat position as Leonard turned the whip on himself, shouting, "Out devils!" Then, almost as an afterthought, he looked me right in the eye and said, "How about you?"

"I don't know about you," I said, my hands tightening their grip on the bass neck, "but I played the hell out of my part."

"Well, okay," he said, after what seemed like an eternity. Out of the corner of my eye, I saw the three guys in the control room duck their heads behind the console to conceal their laughter. It was, hands down, the strangest thing that I ever witnessed in the recording studio.

When all is said and done, I've had the chance to record with many of the greatest recording artists of the past sixty years. But none made my grandmother, Mrs. Esther Kelley, happier than Maude-Amie Humbard. Maude-Amie was the wife of Rex Humbard, a televangelist from Ohio, and she was a featured singer on their broadcasts. Bob MacKenzie, a new producer with Heart Warming Records, had been hired to produce a session with Maude-Amie. This was his very first project, and he pulled all the musicians together before the session to talk about how he wanted to change the production of gospel music. He wanted to feature more instruments on the records, and he wanted us to get away from arranging the last line of the song for the record's introduction.

The session started, and Bob was working out an introduction with the piano player. "Now, I just want to create a mood rather than playing a specific melody," he said.

Maude-Amie ran out of the control room, saying, "No, no, no! I just want that harmonica to play the last line of the song for the intro." Bob tried to talk her out of it, but she was determined. Later, Bob was passing the fills around to all the instruments, and Maude-Amie jumped in again.

"No, no, no! I want that harmonica to play the intro and solo and fill the verses and choruses," she said. Bob talked her out of that idea, convincing her that it would be too much harmonica. The session continued, and we made a good album for her.

Shortly after her sessions with us, Maude-Amie talked about her recent trip to Nashville on the Humbards' broadcast. "My trip to Nashville was a wonderful experience," she told her television audience. "There was this young man there who played the harmonica like it came from heaven."

My grandmother, who played piano for two churches and was a devout Christian, was a loyal viewer of the Humbards' program, and she was elated to hear Maude-Amie Humbard talking about her grandson. She hadn't really understood why I wanted to move to Nashville or what I was doing there, and she was disappointed that I hadn't chosen to pursue a career in religious music. But at that moment, she thought that I had finally arrived!

I feel very fortunate to have enjoyed the opportunity to make musical history with so many of these outstanding recording artists. Although I often didn't receive credit on the album sleeves or in record reviews, that was part of the business. I was happy to have a chance to make music my life and to earn my living from it. Session work provided a steady income and consistent creative challenges, and I am grateful for the opportunities that have been presented to me.

CHAPTER 8

—

THE RECORDING ARTIST

Although my session work was pulling me toward country music more and more, I continued exploring my rock-and-roll interests with some Nashville-area musicians. Originally called Bobby Williams and the Night Lifters, I got involved with them toward the end of 1961, when Snuffy Smith called me to substitute for him as the group's bassist. I hadn't played much bass by that point in my life, but I thought it could be fun. Snuffy, who had a gig with an *Opry* act the next night, told me to meet the guitarist—a fellow from South Charleston, West Virginia, named Wayne Moss—to learn the tunes. He was a fantastic guitarist who was as skilled as many of the session guys I'd been working with.

My first gig with the Night Lifters was at the army base at Fort Campbell, Kentucky, northwest of Nashville, and it was a lot of fun to play with a great rock-and-roll outfit. I played a few more gigs with them after Snuffy joined a road band and couldn't commit to the Night Lifters anymore. I was worried that these performances would conflict with my session work, but since the gigs were only on the weekends, I gladly accepted an opportunity to play rock-and-roll music. The band consisted of pianist Bill Aikins, saxophonist Jimmy Miller, Wayne Moss, me, and Kenny Buttrey, the best drummer I had heard since Jim Isbell. Bobby Williams held down the lead vocals, and the group also had a female vocalist named Pat Campbell. After a while, Bobby also let me sing a few songs now and then.

Over the short time that I played with the Night Lifters, I noticed that there was quite a bit of tension between Bobby and the band. It came to a head after a gig at Fort Campbell when the entire band quit. We had all ridden up together, as was our custom, so it was a long, silent ride back to Nashville. When we got back to our cars, Bobby left immediately, and the band stood around talking. They wanted to continue working together, and they were looking for someone to serve as the group's front man. Bill Aikins asked me if I'd like to become a permanent member of the band and fill that role. I was definitely interested in the opportunity to front a great group, but I also couldn't prioritize a rock-and-roll band over the steady work that I was getting in the studio. After some convincing, I agreed to try it for a while. They changed the name of the group to Charlie McCoy and the Escorts, and my tryout session lasted seven years. Even when I wasn't excited to play a four-hour rock-and-roll gig at the end of a week of fifteen or more sessions, it was a blast to play the hit songs of the day in front of a live audience.

After Cadence Records went out of business in 1962, I had put the idea of being a successful recording artist out of my mind and was working hard to continue building a reputation as a first-call Nashville session musician. But Fred Foster at Monument Records had other ideas. He had seen how my first Cadence single had broken into the *Billboard* charts, and he thought that he might be able to create an environment in which I could create interesting music and reach a broader audience. At a session one day, he pulled me aside to talk to me about my artistic aspirations.

"I heard that Cadence shut down," he said. "I would like to have a chat with you. Why don't you come out to my office?" I knew that Fred Foster had one of the greatest ears for talent in the record business, right up there with Sam Phillips and Archie Bleyer. He was responsible for giving Kris Kristofferson a shot, along with Billy Grammer (who provided the first Monument hit with "Gotta Travel On"), Boots Randolph (whose Monument single "Yakety Sax" was an international hit), and Dolly Parton. Years later, he even spotted the talent in a young Vince Gill, some fifteen years before his first single, telling me that Vince was going to be a superstar. I was honored that he would think that I might have what it would take to be a successful artist on Monument. The next chance I got, I headed out to Fred's office in Hendersonville, about fifteen miles from downtown Nashville, where he told me that he wanted me to make some records for him.

One of Fred's greatest attributes was his willingness to let artists record what they wanted to. After all, in most cases, he had discovered them when they were doing the thing that interested them most, and he wasn't going to try to push them in artistic directions that were uncomfortable. When I asked him what kind of music I should record for him, he gave me carte blanche. With the small success that I'd had with "Cherry Berry Wine," he thought that I might try singing again. With a man with his track record telling me that I could record anything I wanted, my desire to be a recording artist was rekindled.

For my first Monument single, I decided to take the Escorts into the studio to record three sides. We cut "My Babe," a popular Chicago blues number written by the great songwriter Willie Dixon; "Do You Want to Dance," which had been a hit for Bobby Freeman in 1958; and the Carole King-Gerry Goffin song "Will You Still Love Me Tomorrow?" Fred released "My Babe" and "Will You Still Love Me Tomorrow?" as a single, but it got absolutely no airplay. It was just the first of many disappointments. The Escorts played around with all the pop sounds of the day, especially the "Motown sound," and we took the band into the studio time after time to cut singles that we thought were interesting. But, after eight years, we had experienced almost no success aside from a novelty song called "Harpoon Man," which later inspired Kris Kristofferson to write the line "I took my harpoon out of my dirty red bandana" in his hit song "Me and Bobby McGee." Every time I wanted to quit trying to make it as a recording artist, though, Fred would give me more encouragement, telling me, "Just keep on trying. You'll find it!"

Although our singles weren't successful, I was having a lot of fun playing with the Escorts. For a while, we had a horn section comprising Bill Aikins on trumpet, Jimmy Miller on tenor saxophone, and Johnny Sturdivant on baritone saxophone. When Jimmy Miller left the group, we brought in Quitman Dennis and began to play more rhythm and blues than rock and roll. In 1963, we cut down to five pieces to get more work, but we were spoiled by the sound of the big horn section. I recalled seeing a guy in a club one time playing bass with one hand and trumpet with the other, so I started experimenting with it in hopes of filling that void. I discovered that I could do it if I kept the bass parts simple, so I worked that into our show when the songs called for horns. Voila! We had a six-piece band!

By the middle of the 1960s, the Escorts were traveling all throughout the southern United States, even as I was booked solid with studio work. One time, we were playing back-to-back gigs at a tobacco festival in Statesboro, Georgia, and the army base at Fort Campbell, Kentucky. We had to drive all night to make it, so we each took turns at the wheel and slept when we could get the chance. As Quitman Dennis was taking his turn, I fell asleep in the front seat, only to be rudely awakened around four in the morning by a voice saying, "We've been stopped by the police, and they're going to put Quitman in the Macon, Georgia, jail!" We followed the patrol car downtown to the police station, and I went in to talk with the officer in charge. He was a short, heavyset man with a crew cut, a white short-sleeve shirt, and a bow tie.

I asked him what the charges were. "Speedin' and pullin' a trailer with no license," he said in a very thick southern drawl.

"In Tennessee, you don't need a license for a utility trailer," I replied.

The man jumped up, leaned across the desk, and shook his finger in my face, shouting in his best redneck brogue, "You ain't in Tennessee now, boy!"

I tried to reason with him. "We have to be in Kentucky tonight. What can we do?" I asked.

"You can talk to the judge," he said, "but it's Sunday, and he always goes fishin' on Sundays."

I asked if I could post bail, and he said no. I pleaded with him, "We've got to do something."

He laughed and said, "If there is any upstanding citizen in Macon that would come down here and speak up for you, then I'll take your fine and let you go."

Luckily, I had an ace up my sleeve. "There's a guy who is a news anchor on a local TV station named Howard Absalom," I said. "I know him."

The desk sergeant laughed and said, "Howard Absalom is out of town this week."

Then a guy who was passing through the station said, "No he's not, I saw him on the news last night."

Howard Absalom was the father of John, one of my best friends in Fayetteville. I had met Howard Absalom maybe two times in my life. I wasn't sure if I could bring myself to call this man at 4:30 in the morning and ask him to come downtown to bail out a bunch of musicians, but I was desperate. I thought that my dad would do the same thing for John if he were in trouble, so I called reluctantly, expecting to wake him up. To my surprise, he answered. I apologized for waking him and explained the situation. He told me that he and his wife were packing for a vacation, and it would be absolutely no trouble to come by the police station to get us out of this mess. Before long, we were on our way to Fort Campbell with the voice of that drawling desk sergeant ringing in my head.

Another time, the Escorts were booked to play a fair in Champaign, Illinois, where we were scheduled to play a set of our own music and to back up a pop artist named Freddy Cannon. When we rehearsed with Cannon, he told us, "Listen, guys. I do this song called 'Buzz, Buzz, a Diddle It.' When it gets to the middle part, I want you guys to go crazy. Do anything you want to do."

When Freddy came on, it was dark. The stage was on the infield of a racetrack, and the audience was sitting on the track and in the grandstands. With the glare of the stage lights, it was impossible to see beyond the edge of the stage. We started the set and were grooving along, and before we knew it, it was time for "Buzz, Buzz, a Diddle

It." We got to the middle part of the tune, and Freddy looked back at me and said, "Okay, go crazy!" I couldn't do much because my guitar cable had me tethered to an amplifier, and Wayne Moss and Kenny Buttrey were similarly tied down. But the horn section—Quitman Dennis, Bill Aikins, and Johnny Sturdivant—jumped off the stage and started running through the audience with the spotlights chasing them around the infield. Freddy was left in the dark. After what seemed like an eternity, Freddy came over to me and asked me to bring the guys back on stage.

"You told them to go crazy," I replied. "There's no way I can get them back on stage now."

Freddy was mad! He tried to start singing, but the spotlights would not leave the three horn players, who continued to run around in the audience. I think Freddy learned an important lesson that day: think long and hard before you ask musicians to "go crazy."

Although there were times that I was too exhausted at the end of a long week of session work to go out with the Escorts, I had a great time playing with such great musicians and keeping my finger on the pulse of contemporary popular music. Over the years, some of the city's best musicians played with the Escorts. In addition to the original lineup, Mac Gayden, who later wrote "Everlasting Love," played guitar; and Jerry Tuttle, Wayne Butler, Bergen White, Benny McDonald, and Eddie Tinch contributed to the horn section. Unfortunately, the band never scored a hit in its seven years of existence, despite Fred Foster's continued willingness to support our creative work. Every time I talked with Fred about my frustrations, he would reply calmly, "Just keep on trying. You'll find it." But by 1968, I had to leave the Escorts because I was too busy with my session work and my young family, even though I really wanted to keep going with them.

One of the best things about living and playing music in Nashville is that there are so many exceptional musicians who are interested in trying new and exciting things. The studio musicians I worked with were accustomed to playing in a wide variety of styles and to developing new ideas quickly, but the nature of session work didn't really allow us to spend a whole lot of time developing projects over the long term. The Escorts had provided an opportunity for us to do some original material, to develop a sound that we liked, and to build a regional audience for our music. But, by 1969, session work and family life were taking up all my time, and I wasn't really interested in being a regular member of a band.

Some of the other Escorts had different plans. That year, Wayne Moss, Kenny Buttrey, and Mac Gayden, along with pianist David Briggs and bassist Norbert Putnam, decided to put together an instrumental project that could show off some of their talents as performers and arrangers. After playing together in the studio for a bit, they thought that they needed to expand their instrumentation to create a fresh, new sound, so they called Bobby Thompson, Buddy Spicher, Weldon Myrick, and me to help.

Several of us had played together in the Escorts, and we knew that rhythm and blues was a common language for us. But R&B just didn't fit with our group. Then we tried to play country together, but that wasn't really all that new. We were just about to give it up and pull the plug on the project when Bobby and Buddy came in with an instrumental arrangement of the Beatles' hit "Hey Jude." As we ran it down, each of us found space to play in our own style. And it was then that our sound was born. Rather than trying to make us fit into a single style—much as a typical recording session might—the arrangements that we started to develop gave us the room to contribute in our own particular ways. As a consequence, the sound that emerged was the sum of each of our talents. We decided to call the group Area Code 615 to reflect our connections to Nashville.

Kenny had been working with a New York-based producer named Elliott Mazer, and he mentioned the project to him during a session one day. Mazer wanted to hear it, and when he did, he was excited about what we were creating. He offered to try to land us a major record deal, and we agreed to let him try to find a company that wanted what we had to offer. In a short time, he had interest in Polydor, and we signed with them. With a record deal in hand, we made Elliott a recording engineer so he could be part of the project.

Our first album included a mix of original material, arrangements of pop hits like the Beatles' "Lady Madonna" and Mason Williams's "Classical Gas," and country tunes like "Crazy Arms" and "Ruby." We were able to get some national attention thanks to Johnny Cash's television program, which allowed us to pantomime our recording of the old fiddle tune "Katy Hill." (Because we weren't actually playing, David and Norbert switched instruments just for the fun of it!) One of the tunes, "Stone Fox Chase" even garnered some international attention. Featuring just Kenny and me, it was used as the theme song for the popular BBC television program *The Old Grey Whistle Test*. In 2003, rap artist Bubba Sparxxx used part of it on his single "Johnny Mathis."

With the help of a San Francisco lawyer named Brian Rohan, Elliott was able to get us a booking at the Fillmore West, which was famous as the birthplace of such rock groups as Moby Grape, the Grateful Dead, and Jefferson Airplane. In January 1970, we traveled to San Francisco to play for four nights on a bill that included Country Joe McDonald and the Fish as the opening act and a headlining act called the Sons of Champlin. It was a weird scene for some of us studio guys who had only seen the skull orchards in the South and the NCO clubs on military bases. The room was huge, and the high ceiling collected a large cloud of marijuana smoke that left my head floating by the end of each night's show. The audience wasn't too sure about us either because our clothes and hairstyles were not the same as what the San Francisco hippies were wearing. Our look represented the very thing that they were protesting against. I could hear snide remarks from the audience, saying, "Welcome to the Establishment." Our first set was good, but we didn't have enough good material for a second set. Luckily, Buddy Spicher bailed us out with his version of "Orange Blossom Special," and the audience went wild. As always, "O.B.S." paid dividends!

For me, the highlight of our visit to the Fillmore was having Linda Ronstadt sit in with us. Linda loved country music, and she sang "Silver Threads and Golden Needles" and "I Can't Help It, If I'm Still in Love with You." Her recordings of these songs would play a big part in my recording career some years later.

At the end of the fourth night, we weren't feeling too good about our debut in the "Marijuana Rock" scene. On the way back to the hotel we started singing to the tune of a song from *The Wizard of Oz*, "Ding, Dong, the Code is dead." We recorded only one more album, *A Trip in the Country*. Polydor, which had made a sizable investment in the group, wanted us to start touring, but with each of us staying busy in the studio, at the *Opry*, and with our families, it was just out of the question. We had created the group on a whim, never thinking that anything would come of it. When we refused their request, Polydor dropped us. Although our albums didn't sell very well, they did go on to influence many musicians over the years.

After the Code's demise, Wayne, Kenny, and Mac decided to keep pursuing the band idea. They liked the rock scene a lot more than the rest of us did. Adding keyboardist John Harris (aka Dr. John) to the group, they rechristened themselves as Barefoot Jerry, taking the name of an old guy they knew who ran an old country store in the Great Smoky Mountains. Wayne asked me to be a part of the group, but I was hesitant for the same reasons that I didn't want to continue with Area Code 615. I agreed to help them record their first album. We recorded a tune called "The Hospitality Song," which was to be the first song on their initial album. With that song as a demo, they landed a deal with Capitol and were given the green light to record their first album at Wayne's Cinderella Studio, which is located out in the suburbs away from Music Row.

During the tracking of Barefoot Jerry's first album, we ran into some problems that made it rather difficult for me to continue working with them. In my mind, I was there to help them record an album, and, since I was doing more than four hundred sessions each year, I was very busy down on Music Row. As a consequence, I wanted to work quickly and efficiently, just as each of us knew how to do. Mac, who was totally committed to this project and wasn't trying to balance other work, had different ideas about the pacing of the project and wanted to stretch out the production process. Wayne had me play bass in the control room and take responsibility for starting and stopping the tape machine. The second day I worked with them, I could only stay until 4:30 because I had a 6 p.m. session downtown. We were doing a very easy three-chord song, and it was taking much too long for musicians of our caliber. Concerned about my commitment downtown, I made some remark to everyone that I thought we were working below our capabilities. But, since Mac wanted to take his time with it and was committed for the long run, it wasn't important to him to cut tunes quickly. I decided then and there that I was not interested in continuing with the Barefoot Jerry project. I was too busy downtown to be in a band that wanted to live in the recording studio.

The band went on to make six albums and to enjoy some regional radio success. Their song "You Can't Get Off with Your Shoes On" was played quite a bit, capturing some of the "southern rock" craze that was taking off in the early 1970s. Barefoot Jerry fit right in with that vibe. They were immortalized in the huge Charlie Daniels hit "The South's Gonna Do It Again": "All the good people down in Tennessee are digging Barefoot Jerry and the C.D.B."

There were many personnel changes in the group over the years. Some of Barefoot Jerry's members were guitarists Wayne Moss, Mac Gayden, Dave Doran, Barry Chance, Vip Vipperman, Fred Newell, Bobby Thompson, and Jim Colvard; keyboardists "Dr. John" Harris, Buddy Skipper, Warren Hartman, and Steve Davis; banjoist Buddy Blackmon; steel guitarist Russ Hicks; drummers Kenny Buttrey, Kenny Malone, and Si Edwards; and vocalist Terry Dearmore. John Moss did their mixing and occasionally played percussion. I rejoined the group for their sixth album, *Barefootin'*.

Although my recordings with the Escorts hadn't been very successful, Fred Foster continued to support my desire to become a successful solo recording artist. In 1967, I recorded my first album, *The World of Charlie McCoy*, which included such rhythm and blues tunes as "Jump Back Baby," "Up Tight," "Turn on Your Lovelight," and "Harpoon Man." The highlight of that album was a version of the Beach Boys' hit "Good Vibrations." The Beach Boys had created these lush stacked vocals that sounded absolutely amazing, so we tried to emulate that sound with my harmonica. We ended up layer-ing eight tracks of harmonica to get that sound!

The World of Charlie McCoy was a lot of fun, but it didn't do much in sales or airplay. But, in 1968, we cut *The Real McCoy* (the first of two albums with that title). It was my first all-instrumental album, and we did a lot to show off my harmonica playing. We decided to take advantage of the fact that an album has two sides to present one side of pop songs and another side of country ones. The country side consisted of such tunes as "Orange Blossom Special" (which I had recorded with Johnny Cash back in 1965), "Harper Valley, PTA," and "Today, I Started Loving You Again" (which I recorded in only twenty minutes). Country radio picked up the album and gave it some airplay.

In 1970, my relationship with Monument Records came to an end. That year, Fred signed a distribution deal with Columbia Records, and they decided to cut my albums from their active list. A hands-on label owner, Fred called me up to break the news. He believed that I should continue recording instrumental albums, but, unfortunately, Columbia wasn't interested in them. And then he showed me what a supportive person he really was. He offered to release me from my contract so I could keep recording instrumen-tals. I knew that he was right, especially after the airplay that "Harper Valley PTA" had received. But I didn't want to leave Monument because I really enjoyed working for Fred.

I thought about Fred's offer for a while and began to consider all the possibilities that lay ahead of me. I needed a label that would sup-port my vision and not try to put me into a creative corner. At the same time, I wasn't in much of a hurry to sign a new contract because I was swamped with session work. One day, I was on a session for Capitol Records, and I struck up a conversation with their head man in Nash-ville, George Richey. We talked about my situation, and he said that he would love to sign me with Capitol to make some instrumentals. With regret, I said good-bye to Monument and signed a contract with Capi-tol. I recorded a few songs—including "How Can I Unlove You," "Loving Her Was Easier," and "Easy Lovin'"—for Capitol's Ken Nelson to review in Los Angeles. George said he would take it to Nelson personally.

In late summer 1971, I received a phone call from Tex Davis, the country record promotion man at Monument, asking me to come out to the Monument office so we could go to lunch. I didn't know Tex very well because he joined the label right before I left. He was a morning disc jockey in the Norfolk area when he met Fred Foster. Before that, he had been involved with Gene Vincent and the Blue Caps and cowrote the huge rockabilly hit "Be Bop a Lula." With his experience and contacts in radio, he was a natural for the country promotion job with Monument. Over lunch, he told me an unbelievable story.

"There is a radio station in Pensacola with a disc jockey named Charlie Dillard," he said. "He started playing your cut of 'Today, I Started Loving You Again' as he went into the news. His telephones lit up with people wanting to know who the artist was and where they could buy it. He was very curious and started playing it every day. Every day, the same results. He called Monument, and Fred directed him to me. He said, 'Tex, you've got a hit record here if you will just put it out.'"

Tex explained to him that the album wasn't even available anymore and that I was no longer with the label. Apparently, he told Tex, "If I were you, I'd put out the single and get Charlie back on the label."

Tex called the head of promotions at Columbia and told him the story. He wasn't impressed and wrote it off as a fluke. He said that, if Monument no longer had a contract with me, they should just forget about the whole thing.

Tex was undeterred. He went to Fred, who told Tex to continue investigating the situation and to keep him informed of his findings. Now Tex had a "gut feeling," which can be very informative for people in the talent business. Over lunch, Tex asked me about my situation with Capitol. I explained that we had done a session and that George Richey was personally taking it to Los Angeles. Disappointedly, Tex said, "If anything changes, let me know."

Another week passed, and the telephone rang with Ken Nelson, head of Capitol Records, on the line. "Charlie," he said, "I've just heard this session that you and George did. I don't like it, and I don't want it. George never should have recorded an instrumental without clearing it with me first. I never would have agreed."

"I'm sorry you don't like it," I replied. "What can we do now with the masters?" I hoped to make something out of my work in the studio.

"Call accounting, find out how much we have in it, send us a check, and it's yours," he said. And just like that, my time with Capitol Records was over.

I called Tex to explain what had happened. "That's great," he said, "but this is not a done deal. The Columbia people aren't exactly chomping at the bit to put out an instrumental. Come out and talk to Fred about this, and let's see what we can do."

Fred knew that Columbia would need to get on board before we could do anything with the album. "Columbia will never consider this unless you are signed to Monument," he said. "I tell you what: you give me your word that you won't sign anywhere else until we get this resolved, and if they decide to put it out, you'll sign back with us." That's vintage Fred Foster. His word is better than a contract. I was happy to wait.

In the meantime, Charlie Dillard kept calling from Pensacola, and Tex made it his personal crusade to get this record released. He finally browbeat the Columbia people into giving the record a try in 1971.

When the record was finally released, I saw firsthand why Fred had hired Tex. He had a bulldog's tenacity. He had to fight to get radio stations to add the record one station at a time, and it was a long, slow process. Many times, I would hear him yelling at the music directors of major radio stations, and I thought that he'd blown our chances of getting airplay.

One time, he was on the phone with the music director of WJJD in Chicago. Tex called him every week to inform him of the album's upward climb in the charts, but the music director would not be persuaded. "I wouldn't play an instrumental if Jesus Christ put it out," he exclaimed.

Tex screamed some expletives and slammed the phone down. He was red in the face and really mad. Then he smiled and said, "Don't worry. We'll get WJJD." And he was right. The record ended up on WJJD's top twenty. With that kind of promotion behind it, the album made steady progress up the charts each week. In the end, it made it to number 15 on the Billboard country singles charts.

After all the work that Tex had to do to convince Columbia to release my record, its chart success convinced them that we needed to release an album quickly to capitalize on the single's success. My first Columbia album, also called *The Real McCoy*, took the first side of the 1968 album and the session from Capitol and added four new songs. The album also had a fantastic cover image that was designed by Bill Barnes, who was interested in breaking free from the standard close-up head shot that was featured on the covers of most Columbia albums of the time. Using his zany creativity, he photographed a harmonica sitting in a hot dog bun on an American flag plate. I loved it!

The album took off and started climbing the charts. Tex and I traveled to record stores on the weekends to do in-store promotions. In all, we appeared at forty-seven different stores, which one Columbia promotion guy told me was a record for a single artist. And I managed to do all of that while keeping a busy session schedule, playing on more than four hundred sessions a year. To make it work, we had to fly out so we could make the most of a Saturday, and then we normally took an early flight back to Nashville on Sunday. When the alarm went off at 5 a.m., Tex was always wide awake, probably because he had gotten up that early to sign onto a morning radio show for so many years. I never knew how anyone could be so chipper at that hour.

The new *The Real McCoy* was a big hit, selling more than 400,000 units. In 1972, I received a Grammy Award and a Country Music Association Award for the album. Not bad for an instrumental album! Our next single, "I'm So Lonesome I Could Cry," peaked in the top thirty, and my second album with Columbia, *Charlie McCoy*, reached number 2 on the *Billboard* album chart. I love the version of "The First Time Ever I Saw Your Face" that we cut for that album, and Curly Chalker's steel playing on "Danny Boy" is absolutely beautiful. By my third album, *Good Time Charlie*, I was beginning to hit my stride as a solo artist, and the album reached the number 1 spot in all the music charts. Between the first five albums, we sold more than a million units.

One of the reasons that *Charlie McCoy* and *Good Time Charlie* did so well was that we stuck with Tex's promotion plan. As with *The Real McCoy*, we were on the road most weekends, signing autographs at record stores and other events. I learned a lot about the record business through these travels.

On one trip, we visited a Columbia Records convention, where Tex and I had a discussion with the promotions man who represented New England. He had heard about our in-store appearances and asked if we would come to Boston. Country records weren't selling very well in New England, so artists had neglected the region. I was game for anything, so I told Tex that I would be willing to go there if he would take us to a Red Sox baseball game and to a great seafood dinner. He agreed.

Our appearance in Boston was in a large department store. The record department set up a huge display with my album covers hung everywhere, and they provided a small booth for me to sign autographs in. But no one came. Newspaper ads and some limited radio coverage hadn't drawn people to the event. I sat there for around thirty minutes when a lady approached the stand. Thinking she was there for an autograph, I readied my pen. But instead of asking for my signature, she said, "Can you tell me where to find the ladies' room?" Ten minutes later, another woman approached me asking, "Can you direct me to housewares?" To some artists, this could have been embarrassing, but to me, it got to be funny. Finally, a guy came along and bought six copies of my *Charlie McCoy* album. We all felt better, and began to think that he was the beginning of a rush that would come later. The sad truth, though, was that he was the only one. In two hours, I managed to sell six albums and give two women directions. As we were leaving, the manager of the record department said, "You sold three times as many as the last artist who was here." The last artist had been Jody Miller. We may not have sold hundreds of records, but the baseball and seafood were great!

Another time, Tex and I booked a record promotion trip to Missouri, flying from Nashville to St. Louis, where the Columbia promotions man would take us on a tour of several small, rural department stores. Our day was scheduled to start in Rolla and continue to two nearby towns. It was a summer day with temperatures in the 90s and soaring humidity.

As we pulled into the parking lot of the first store, I noticed a flatbed truck with a band that was setting up. "Look," I said to Tex. "There's a band."

The record buyer sheepishly said, "We thought you might play a couple of songs to help with the in-store appearance. These guys are the best band around, and they know all your music." My instincts told me to say no, but I gave in and said, "Okay, but just a couple."

The Columbia guy parked the car across the parking lot from the stage. I reached into the trunk to pull out my harps, as the buyer rushed across the lot and up on stage to introduce me. He must have run to the stage to make sure that I wouldn't change my mind.

Looking like an insurance salesman with a briefcase full of harmonicas, I strode across the parking lot. The flatbed was very high, and the small stepladder they had used to climb onstage didn't give me much of a chance to make a graceful entrance. People in the audience were looking at me and trying to figure out what was going on. Since my first album cover didn't have a picture of me on it, many of the folks in the audience had no idea what I looked like.

I walked to the mic and said, "Folks, I'm going to have a little chat with the band and then I'll play some songs for you." The flatbed was very narrow, and there was barely enough room in front of the drums to squat down to open my harp case. By now, the band had gathered around me.

I looked up and said, "How are y'all doing?" None of them said a word. I thought, "I am in *so* much trouble here."

"Can we do 'Jackson'?" I asked.

After what seemed like an eternity, the band leader—identifiable because he was wearing a different colored shirt than the other band members—looked at me and said, "No." He didn't say, "We don't know it" or "We've forgotten it." He just said, "No."

"How about 'Rocky Top'?" I asked.

Once again, forever passed before the bassist said, "We used to do 'Rocky Top,' but I forgot the words."

"No, you don't understand," I said. "You don't have to sing it! I'm going to play it."

"Oh!" he sighed. Then I realized that it wasn't just that these guys didn't know my music. They didn't even know who I was!

We struggled through "Rocky Top," and the audience seemed to really like it. Between the nerves and the heat, I was soaking wet, and sweat was filling my eyes. I turned to the band and asked, "Can we do 'Today, I Started Loving You Again?'"

The leader nodded yes.

"You guys just start a vamp," I said. "I'm going to talk over it, and then I'll play the song." As I turned to the audience, there was no music.

I looked back and said, "You guys go ahead and start!" Once again, I turned to the audience, but there was no music.

I turned around and counted, "One, two, three, four!" Again, nothing.

The bandleader asked, "You want an intro or something?"

"Yes, please," I replied, frustrated. "An intro." The audience loved it because it was the only one of my songs that most of the people there had ever heard before. Although I was ready to get off the stage, the audience liked it, so I thought I'd try one more. I turned to the band and shouted, "'Orange Blossom Special'!"

The drummer yelled back, "Please don't play it too fast."

By then, I'd had enough, so I hollered back, "Y'all keep up!"

We made it through the first half of the tune, and I looked back at the drummer, who was as red as a stoplight and had his mouth closed and his jaws puffed out. I thought, "This guy is going to croak if I don't end this song right away." I played the second verse very short, and when I went to the second chorus, a drumstick flew past my ear. I wrapped it up, thanked the band, and got off the stage. I was soaking wet, just the way I wanted to meet my fans in the record department.

As we were walking into the record store, I noticed that the band was hurrying to break down their gear. "They must have another gig," I said to Tex.

The record buyer said, "They're going to your next store."

Sensing my frustration, Tex stepped in and said, "No, absolutely not! He's not playing again."

Experiences like that one led me to form my own band. At first, I decided to hire a steel guitarist to join me in these performances because the steel was such an important sound to my early recordings. Weldon Myrick, who had played on my first album, was a regular in the *Opry* staff band and couldn't play on the weekends. Luckily, I met Russ Hicks, a native of Beckley, West Virginia, during a session with Johnny Wright at Bradley's Barn. We were born only twelve miles apart, yet we didn't know each other until that session. When I asked Russ if he'd like to join me on the weekends, he said he'd be happy to. For a short time, Russ and I played with Boots Randolph and Floyd Cramer, who usually toured with Chet Atkins. Chet was taking time off, so they called me to fill in.

As the recordings continued to gain momentum, I started getting calls to work in some clubs where I would need an entire backing band. I turned to some of the core members of Barefoot Jerry to do these shows with me. In addition to Russ, Si Edwards played drums, Buddy Blackmon was my bassist, Barry Chance played lead guitar, and Sherry King played keyboards for a short time before moving to Indiana. After a while, Barry left the group for another gig where he could play more often, and Buddy suggested a guitarist friend from Athens, Georgia, named Vip Vipperman. He joined us in Houston one night and stayed on as Barry's replacement. Later, Buddy—whose main instrument was the banjo—had a chance to work in a band with his idol, the bluegrass legend Earl Scruggs. He left, and Russ's brother David came to play bass.

In the mid-1970s, Fred Foster signed a young singer from Tuscaloosa, Alabama, named Laney Smallwood. Her second record, "That I Love You, You Love Me Too Love Song," was a hit reaching all the country charts, and Fred wanted Laney to get some experience singing on live concerts. Since she was so young, he wanted to make sure she could travel with someone he trusted, so he called me to see if I would let her work some of our shows. I had played on her album session and was happy to have her join us. I was very impressed with her when, on the first show, she told the band, "I am *not* one of the boys!" From that moment on, she had the band's respect.

When she and Russ met, it was instant attraction. It made me think of an interview that I had heard with Little Richard. He said that, when he started to tour in the 1950s, mothers would warn their daughters about these stars. Little Richard told the interviewer, "The mothers didn't know that there was nothing to worry about with me, but my band was serious." Fred had nothing to worry about with me, but Russ was serious. Before long, Russ and Laney were married. When their first daughter was born, Laney said to me, "This may be hard to understand, but at this moment, my career means nothing to me. If you want to find another singer who is serious about a career, I'll understand." With her priority on family, she gave up the chance at stardom. She said, "I still would like to sing." It was a no-brainer for me. Things would not be right without her.

The success of my recordings also drew attention back home in West Virginia. In 1972, Johnny Witt, the mayor of Fayetteville, called to tell me that folks back home were proud of me and that they would like to honor me at the annual Fourth of July celebration. I suggested that we stage a charity concert. It was a huge success, and, after the concert, Witt and Walter Caldwell, the head of the American Legion post, suggested that we make it an annual event. I agreed, and we decided to donate the funds to the town park. Over the course of the next eighteen years, I brought some of Nashville's hottest acts to Fayetteville, including Barefoot Jerry, Mel Street, the Statler Brothers, Barbara Mandrell, Tammy Wynette, Don Williams, Crystal Gayle, and Mel Tillis, among many others, to play in my hometown. Several of the artists gave part or all of their artist fees back to the town, including Barbara Mandrell and the Statlers. The town recognized the Statlers' generosity by naming the baseball field after them, and they named the park, which is just a short walk from one of the houses where I lived as a kid, after me. Another fun part of the experience was trading hometown visits with the Statlers, who lived across the mountains in Staunton, Virginia, and Tom T. Hall, who hailed from Olive Hill, Kentucky.

Living and working in Music City made it possible for me to record with the best of the best. When I recorded my albums, I decided to take advantage of my position as a session musician to hire the best musicians I knew. Unlike most producers, who would stick with the same musicians, singers, and engineers from one album to the next, I decided to change musicians on every session. I am sure that I have used more musicians than just about anyone in Nashville. On my first thirty-nine albums and instructional videos and books, I have used 426 musicians, singers, and engineers.

In 1972, Fred suggested that I should do a Christmas album in the near future. I thought about it for a year, and then I went into the studio in December 1973 to cut an album for the next Christmas season. For that album, I hired three of the best arrangers I knew: Bill Pursell, Bergen White, and Buryl Red. Buryl had access to a great children's choir and an excellent adult choir. He arranged my "one-man band" for a tune called "Christmas Cheer." Bill's strings were brilliant, and he had the idea to use two classical harpists on the album. Bergen's strings were beautiful on "The Christmas Song," as well. And I got the chance to sing again on two tunes: "Christmas Time's a-Comin'" and "Angels We Have Heard on High."

For my 1975 album *Harpin' the Blues*, I had the chance to work with two New Orleans legends, clarinetist Pete Fountain and trumpeter

Al Hirt. I recorded the track for "Basin Street Blues" in Nashville and flew down to New Orleans with the tapes for an overdub session. The morning of the session, the taxi drove me right down Basin Street. I thought that was a good omen. Pete and Al had worked club dates until the wee hours the night before, and I had booked a morning session. I almost felt guilty about it, but then I heard them play. They were brilliant. They needed only one take! I would have stayed longer, but there was no need.

In 1977, I cut a version of the traditional ballad "Fair and Tender Ladies" that had me singing several vocal parts at the same time. I wanted to do an entire album by myself, so I took the tape to Fred for his approval. He said, "I think this is a hit. Let's release it as a single!" The record made it to number 33 on the *Billboard* chart some fourteen years since I was last on the charts with a vocal. Thanks to the single's success, we did an album of Appalachian music, called *Appalachian Fever*, in 1979. The cover features me looking out over a beautiful river back home in West Virginia. The band was an all-start cast, too, including the Charlie McCoy road band with Buddy Blackmon on banjo, Buddy Spicher on fiddle, and Uncle Josh Graves on dobro.

In all, Monument released fourteen albums of my music, and I am proud of every one of them. Fred Foster was patient with me and had a better vision of "the real McCoy" than I did at times. Unfortunately, the label started to have some financial problems in 1979. Even after the great success, Columbia and Monument parted ways, and Fred tried out a distribution deal with Mercury that didn't work. He told all the artists on the label that he was going to file for Chapter 11 bankruptcy, and he offered us all releases from our contracts. I believed in Fred and felt certain that he would be able to rebound, and I stayed with him because, even though being an artist was secondary to my studio work, I was quite fond of making solo records and playing live. Unfortunately, in 1983, he sold the catalog to Sony, and MTM Records, which was owned by Mary Tyler Moore, bought the office building he had on Music Row. He also sold Combine Music, his publishing company. It broke my heart for Fred, who was one of the pioneers in our music business and was forced to give up the company that he had built from scratch. And his right-hand man, Tex Davis, was without anything to promote, despite being one of the greatest record promoters ever to work in Nashville. Thankfully, Fred was inducted into the Country Music Hall of Fame in 2016, and his support for interesting and creative musicians has been recognized for the special thing that it was.

—

CHAPTER 9

HEE HAW AND OTHER TELEVISION APPEARANCES

In the summer of 1969, CBS began airing *Hee Haw*, a country-themed variety show in the style of the highly popular show *Rowan and Martin's Laugh-In*. Starring Roy Clark and Buck Owens, the show was set in Kornfield County and featured a whole host of great country recording artists as special guests. It was immensely popular, and, although CBS canceled it after only two years, it was picked up as a syndicated program, where it ran for more than two decades.

I didn't have much experience on television aside from a few appearances on some local country music programs, but thanks to my reputation as a session musician, I got a call in 1970 to play on *Hee Haw* with the legendary rhythm and blues musician Ray Charles. He had been enjoying a lot of attention from the country field ever since his 1962 album *Modern Sounds in Country and Western Music*. I had a great time playing with him because, as a long-time rhythm and blues fan, I'd been interested in his music for quite a while.

A year or so after that performance, I received a call from George Richey, the music director for *Hee Haw*. He told me that Sam Lovullo, the show's producer, wanted to hire me as a regular member of the staff band. I was certainly interested in the opportunity to try something new, but I was concerned that television work could conflict with my session work, and I didn't want to lose those opportunities for a show that could be canceled any time.

"The band doesn't play that much," he said. "Why don't you try it once?" I decided to give it a shot for one season, knowing that I could never commit to it full time.

Like *Laugh-In, Hee Haw* wasn't performed as a continuous live show, but was instead recorded in segments that they would later edit and assemble into a full program. It was a high-energy show with lots of quick cuts from one segment to another. To produce the show, the *Hee Haw* gang would spend the entire month of June making the thirteen episodes that would air from September until Christmas, and then they returned in October to make the thirteen shows that aired between January and April. The rest of the year, the show would rerun the episodes.

Like recording sessions, *Hee Haw* was a model of production efficiency. They would put up the set for "The Barber Shop," "Junior's Used Car Lot," or "The Culhanes," fix the lights, and then shoot all thirteen spots of that segment. They also kept a mini-cornfield set up all the time to tape skits with the musical guests. It wasn't uncommon for us to record five musical guests with all their comedy skits in one day! As it turned out, the band worked only eight or nine days out of the thirty days that it took to produce thirteen episodes.

The person who managed all the record keeping related to this rigorous production schedule was Sandy Liles, who kept track of which artists and cast members performed in each skit and what songs everyone performed. Sandy probably knows more about what has been taped for *Hee Haw* than anyone else alive. It stood to reason that, when the show stopped in the 1990s, Gaylord Entertainment kept Sandy on staff to serve as the show's archivist for future reruns, compact disc releases, and VHS and DVD reissues.

Hee Haw was taped at a local Nashville television station that barely had enough room for the cast, let alone the many guests who came to the show. There weren't many parking spaces at the studio, so the Nashville police had a field day writing parking tickets when we were taping Hee Haw. And, to make matters worse, the audio equipment at the station was insufficient, and Larry Sullivan, the show's audio engineer, had to work miracles to get such a good sound for the show.

The first month of production was a lot of fun, and there weren't many conflicts with session calls, so I agreed to finish the season before reevaluating the situation. I enjoyed the work, and, in some cases, I had recorded with the musicians several times before. I ended up working as a band member for several years under Richey's music directorship.

In 1978, Sam Lovullo called me into his office. "I think our band needs a leader," he said, "and you are the most logical guy for the job."

"Sam, I'm not sure if I'm going to come back after this taping session," I replied.

"Well, I hope you do," he said. "But, in the meantime, will you lead the band?" I was honored to be asked, especially after I learned that the band had recommended me for the job.

I went into the studio for a taping session, and when I was finished, Sam called me into his office again. "George Richey is going to marry Tammy Wynette. He's going to be her manager and business agent, so he'll be leaving the show. I want you to be the music director."

I was shocked. I hadn't even decided whether I was going to stay with the show, and now I was being presented with a big opportunity. It was becoming clear to me that Sam wanted me to become the band leader so that I could become familiar with all the workings of the show and take over the music director's position if it ever became vacant. And now it was.

My first instinct was to say no. I was certain that this would take up even more time, and I really didn't want to miss calls for session work. But, at the same time, I enjoyed working with the band and with the cast members, who were becoming more and more like a family. And it was great to spend time with some of the true legends of the country music business. Grandpa Jones, Roy Acuff, and Minnie Pearl had roots in Nashville's early days, and Roni Stoneman's family had been recording since the middle of the 1920s. Gordie Tapp, Archie Campbell, Lulu Roman, and George Lindsay had also become great friends. After some thought, I told Sam that I would try it for one season. I ended up serving as *Hee Haw*'s music director for fourteen years.

The band we had when I became music director was stocked with exceptional pickers and singers, including several who came from the session scene. Jerry Whitehurst played piano, Henry Strzelecki was our bassist, and Willie Ackerman sat behind the drums. Bobby Thompson played banjo and acoustic guitar, Leon Rhodes and Dale Sellers were our lead guitarists, Curly Chalker played steel, and Tommy Williams was the fiddler. And we had the exceptionally talented Nashville Edition—Wendy Suits, Dolores Edgin, Joe Babcock, and Hurshel Wiginton—covering the backing vocals.

An additional bonus to being *Hee Haw*'s music director was the opportunity to work with Buck Owens's fantastic band, the Buckaroos. Buck was a no-nonsense guy, and his band always came in well rehearsed, ready to play, and early to set. Buck liked to do his business and get out of the way so that the next act could begin taping. When Don Rich, his lead guitarist and fiddler, died in a motorcycle crash in 1974, Buck never replaced him and just let Terry Christofferson, who played great steel and lead guitar, cover the duties. A couple of times, when Buck taped his solos, he asked me to sit in on lead guitar. I borrowed Terry's red, white, and blue Telecaster and, if just for a bit, got to play with the Buckaroos.

As the music director, I was responsible for a lot of work beyond just making sure that the band was ready to back up the guests on the show. I tried to help Larry Sullivan with the audio by telling him about the arrangements and showing him who had solos so that he could adjust the levels as necessary. There was also quite a bit of union paperwork because the music director serves as a kind of union steward. Thankfully, Sam's right-hand gal Marsha Minor provided help with a lot of that.

The first thing that I tried to do as the music director was to convince Sam to commit to a firm production schedule. In my estimation, a firm schedule would be helpful in two ways. For the musicians, it would allow us to know exactly when we weren't available for session work. After all, *Hee Haw* was a good gig, but it wasn't as steady as session work, and we needed to be able to maintain our accounts. For the crew, a regular production schedule could alleviate the congestion in the tiny television studio because people wouldn't have to stand around waiting for their turn to get in front of the camera. Sam loved the idea, and we quickly adapted to the new process.

A couple of years into my tenure as music director, the show's production moved to Opryland. There, we had state-of-the-art facilities for video and audio production and all the space we could ask for. We had gone from working in an underequipped television studio that wasn't designed for music production to production facilities that, as far as audio was concerned, rivaled the studios on Music Row. At Opryland, I worked with audio engineer John Long, who was a brilliant audio mixer. He was unappreciated by the higher-ups at Opryland Productions, but I'll put the audio from those direct-to-videotape recordings up against any other show that has ever been recorded in a similar fashion.

As the Nashville record business became more and more corporate and Hollywood-like, it became common for artists to come to *Hee Haw* with road managers who sometimes served as their sound men. One day, we came back from a lunch break to find a guy in the audio control room turning knobs.

"Can I help you?" I asked.

"I'm the road manager and sound man for the artist who is going to tape next," he said, "and I'm here to mix his part of the show."

Opryland had pretty strict rules about who could use the equipment. "We sure would like to have your help," I calmly explained, "but nobody but an Opryland engineer can mix here."

He was not happy to hear this news. "I always mix for my artist," he insisted.

Maintaining my professional attitude, I explained, "I appreciate that, but you won't be mixing here, company policy." He stormed out of the booth to find the artist, who told him that everything would be just fine if he just came in to provide some pointers. He returned, but was definitely not a happy camper.

That guy got his revenge on me a few months later. I was booked to open a show for two other acts in Birmingham, one of which was the act with the angry sound man. On my live show, I played keyboard while Laney Smallwood Hicks sang. My buddy Barry Chance was playing with the middle act, so I called and asked him if I could play their keyboard. He agreed. When we arrived at the auditorium, I walked onstage, spotted a keyboard, and walked over to it. I asked the house sound man if the keyboard was turned on yet. No sooner did my question leave my mouth than I heard a voice shouting from backstage. It was the angry sound man! It turns out that the keyboard was for his act, and he decided to make sure to mark his turf. When all was said and done, I played Barry's keyboard, and the show went on without any problems.

Another time, a well-known artist came to the show with a new sound man. We had taken a lunch break before we were scheduled to start recording with this artist. When I got back to the studio, there was the sound man, walking to every microphone and shouting, "Whoooooaaa! Whoooooaaa!" Then he told our monitor mixer, "That is a little extreme at 10K," meaning that it was a little loud in the frequencies above ten thousand cycles. He tested the monitors for forty-five minutes, constantly tweaking things. The director called me into the control room to see if I could get him to settle on a monitor mix.

"Can you do something about this sound man?" he asked. "He is going to run us into heavy overtime. We really need to get going."

I went over to the sound man and said, "We've got to get started. Let's get the band on the stage." I've always preferred just getting on with the show.

"Oh, sure. I just wanted to make sure the monitors were right for the band," he said.

The band came out, and the bass player walked up to his microphone and said, "Test, test. One, two . . . Who set this monitor? It's all wrong."

Sheepishly, the sound man said, "Oh, my setting was just a place to start."

The longer I was at *Hee Haw*, the more I realized how important the show was to Nashville and the country music industry. But, although we managed to be the television home of country music after many other syndicated programs went off the air, we also brought guest artists who specialized in other musical styles. Vic Damone, Roy Rogers and Dale Evans, Los Angeles Dodgers manager Tommy LaSorda, Pittsburgh Steelers quarterback Terry Bradshaw, and Gov. Lamar Alexander of Tennessee all appeared on the program. In the mid-1980s, the legendary entertainer Sammy Davis Jr. was scheduled to appear. Curly Chalker, *Hee Haw*'s original steel guitarist, was very excited when he learned the news because it would give him a chance to play some of the jazz and big band style chords that he couldn't normally play on a straight-ahead country chart. Sammy wanted to sing "Look Down That Lonesome Road," a great blues standard with lots of room for extended harmonies, as a duet with Roy Clark, who played excellent jazz lead guitar. The arrangement we worked up was a soft swing that featured Curly with an acoustic bass and drum backup. Curly was on fire that day, and Sammy was definitely into what Curly was playing. I remember telling John Long, "Man, Curly is visiting heaven right now. He's accompanying a great artist who is really grooving and digging his playing." That's the most any of us could ever ask for.

One of the show's most popular segments was "The *Hee Haw* Banjo Band," which featured Grandpa Jones, Roni Stoneman, Bobby Thompson, and Roy Clark. Later, we had a fiddle band that featured Roy, Ramona Jones, Tommy Williams, and a guest artist like John Hartford, who could play the fiddle. These segments were a lot of fun, and they showcased Roy Clark's remarkable versatility. We asked Sam if we could have a harmonica band, too, and he quickly agreed. The group featured Roy, Grandpa Jones, Gordie Tapp, and me. We were occasionally joined by special guests, such as Stan "The Man" Musial, the Baseball Hall of Famer for the St. Louis Cardinals who had been my boyhood idol. We also invited Wayne Raney and Lonnie Glosson, who had radio shows on WCKY in Cincinnati and XERF in Del Rio, Texas, to join us. They played country records and sold harmonicas and instruction courses through mail order. In my mind, they were two of the real pioneers of country harmonica playing, and it was a magical experience to have them on stage with me.

A lot of people who watched *Hee Haw* will undoubtedly remember the *Hee Haw* girls with their cut-off shorts, Daisy Mae tops, and southern belle personas. But there was much more to them than their stage characters. Most of them were aspiring actresses who were trying to get a break in movies or television. They were consummate professionals, and we never had to wait for them to get their parts right. It was always the other cast members or the guest artists who needed multiple takes. They also cared a lot about the show and were team players. Among the girls who were on the show when I was there were Misty Rowe, Gunilla Hutton, Marianne Gordon, Irlene Mandrell, Victoria Hallman, Lisa Todd, Barbi Benton, Diana Goodman, Kathy Baker, MacKenzie Colt, Linda Thompson, Donna Stokes, Becky and Lindy Norris, and Dawn McKinley. Alice Ripley, who joined the show in our last season, went on to Broadway and won a Tony Award in 2009.

In 1978, the producers tried to capitalize on the show's success by creating a spinoff called *The Hee Haw Honeys*. It was a situation comedy that starred Kenny Price, Lulu Roman, Gailard Sartain, Misty Rowe, and Kathy Lee Johnson, a talented singer who would later marry NFL football star Frank Gifford and host the popular *Live with Regis and Kathy Lee* television program. We used the *Hee Haw* band and the Nashville Edition for the musical backing and recorded the show at the same Nashville television studio where we started taping *Hee Haw*. The show ran for only one season.

My dad always loved to come to *Hee Haw* because of all the stars and the girls. He was one of those guys that the ladies liked to make over. The cast members always asked about him, and when he came to visit, everyone—including Sam—treated him like royalty. Those visits to the set were great memories for him.

In 1980, Sam had an idea to get some of the best instrumentalists in country music to come together for a segment called the "Million Dollar Band." As he planned it, the group would feature Roy Clark playing and introducing the all-star band, Floyd Cramer on piano, Chet Atkins on guitar, Boots Randolph on saxophone, Danny Davis on trumpet, Johnny Gimble on fiddle, Jethro Burns on mandolin, and me on the harmonica. Sam got confirmation from all the parties, and he started making plans for how he could work us into the show. He knew this would be a big hit with the fans of *Hee Haw*.

But it almost came apart before the Million Dollar Band ever hit the airwaves. One afternoon, I was in the office that Fred Foster allowed me to use at Monument when I received a phone call from Chet.

"You know that 'Million Dollar Band' segment that Sam wants to do?" he asked. "Well, I don't think I want to do it."

I knew that Sam would be devastated if this segment fell through. "Are you in your office?"

"Yes," he replied.

"Don't move! I'm coming right over." I sprinted down the alley to the RCA studios, where Chet had an office. For Sam's sake, I swallowed my pride and begged Chet to reconsider. After some time, Chet agreed to try it. It turned out to be one of the most popular segments ever on *Hee Haw*. At the time of this writing, the only surviving members of the Million Dollar Band are Roy Clark and myself.

From time to time, we would have a guest performer on *Hee Haw* who was unknown and had little professional experience. Usually, they were brought on to try to get the show into a certain television market. One time, we had a female singer from Los Angeles. She was rehearsing with the band on the set, which had risers with many levels, and I was in the control room.

"Charlie," the director asked, "do you think that this song is too low for her?"

"Yes," I said. "I'll see if she can raise the key."

I walked out onto the set and asked her, "Do you think you could do this song up a step?" anticipating that she would understand that I wanted her to raise the pitch of the song one key higher.

"No problem," she replied and moved up to the next step on the riser.

One summer, some of the members of the *Hee Haw* cast played some live shows in the style of the old package shows that toured the southern United States when I was a kid. The show featured the comedians in the group, including Gordie Tapp, George Lindsey, and Grandpa Jones, as well as Gunilla Hutton, Misty Rowe, and some of the other *Hee Haw* girls. Providing music and dance for the show were the Moonshine Cloggers, the Nashville Edition, and, of course, the *Hee Haw* band. When the regular *Hee Haw* band couldn't get away, I brought my regular road band: Russ Hicks, David Hicks, Vip Vipperman, Si Edwards, and Laney Hicks. We played about eight or ten shows, and the highlight for me was always George Lindsey's monologue. He is such a great stand-up comedian that, even though I knew what was coming, he still made me laugh every time. Gordie Tapp, too, was a great comic and a truly professional entertainer who served as the glue that held the show together.

Over the course of the years I was on the show, the band personnel changed very little until the middle of the 1980s. When we learned that Bobby Thompson, the best banjo player I had ever heard, had been diagnosed with multiple sclerosis, I was devastated. His shoes were so big that I decided to fill them with two great players, Buddy Blackmon and Russ Hicks. Russ could play almost every instrument on the stage, so he made a great utility man for the *Hee Haw* band. When Curly left the group, Russ took over the steel guitar duties full-time. Henry Strzelecki had to leave the band due to ear problems; David Hicks filled the bass duties. And Dale Sellers left the show to play with Wayne Newton in Las Vegas.

After a couple of seasons at Opryland, the show was bought by Ed Gaylord, who went on to buy the *Grand Ole Opry*, Opryland, TNN, WSM Radio, and the Opryland Hotel. Almost overnight, *Hee Haw* went from being a sort of family production to part of a very large corporation. For our twenty-fourth season, the people who sell ads decided on a radical format change. They fired a lot of the *Hee Haw* Honeys, the whole band, and the Nashville Edition. I was in Europe when I found out. When I returned, I scheduled a meeting with Sam and the Gaylord people. I fought in vain to save the jobs of these people who had been so loyal. They explained to me that they wanted a "younger" band. They would leave the music ability up to me but they had to approve on the "looks" of each band member. I appealed to Sam but his hands were tied. The only job I was able to save was Russ Hicks's.

The new *Hee Haw* band was great and packed with some of Nashville's greatest young talents. Tony Migliore played piano along with Kip Paxton on bass and Shannon Ford on drums. Vic Jordan was on banjo and acoustic guitar, Vip Vipperman on lead guitar, Downs

Thompson on fiddle, and Russ Hicks covered the steel guitar. Lea Jane Berinati led the new vocal group. Unfortunately, the twenty-fourth season proved to be the last. It's hard to know how much the new format had to do with the show's demise. Perhaps the Gaylords wanted out of the investment, and they knew that the new format would be the end of us.

All in all, *Hee Haw* produced twenty-four seasons, and I was there for the bulk of the show's run. In the time I was with the show, I made eight solo appearances and one with Laney Smallwood Hicks. I played with dozens of talented musicians and had the chance to meet some people I had immense respect for. I also had the chance to learn from Sam Lovullo, who was the center of gravity for everything that happened at *Hee Haw*. Every morning, he greeted every cast member, every crew member, the stagehands, custodial crew, and anyone else who was involved in the show. He made everyone feel important. The *Hee Haw* experience was one of the best I've had in the music business, and I will always treasure the friends and memories that I made there.

Over the years, I was involved in several other television projects, but most of them didn't have the longevity of *Hee Haw*. One of the first was *The Nashville Palace*, which ran as a summer replacement show in 1980 and 1981. We recorded it at the Roy Acuff Theater at Opryland, and each of the seven shows we taped had a different host. The first show was hosted by Roy Clark. After we finished taping, Roy came back to the dressing room to thank us and to share a cold drink. Someone came to the door to let him know that the executives from NBC were waiting for him, but he made them wait while he enjoyed a beer with the band.

A special part of *The Nashville Palace* was a segment called "Boots," which was set in a club like Gilley's in Houston. To give us a better idea of how we should plan the music and the choreography for the segment, Jean Whittaker, the show's choreographer, and I flew to Los Angeles to see the premiere of the film *Urban Cowboy*, which helped to make country dancing popular across the United States for a few years in the 1980s. In later years, I would play several telethons in support of Mickey Gilley's arthritis foundation. They were hard work, with lots of downtime over the eight hours of live television but never enough to leave the premises. Through that work, we became friends, and he came to Fayetteville to play my hometown festival.

Starting in the late 1980s, I began working on the *Country Showdown*, a nationwide talent contest that is broadcasted to stations across the United States and that has featured such artists as Garth Brooks, Martina McBride, and the Sweethearts of the Rodeo. At one of our shows, we witnessed the singing debut of eleven-year-old Miley Cyrus, whose father, Billy Ray, was hosting the event. Over the course of my more than two decades with the show, sponsorship changed hands between Wrangler, True Value, Dodge, GMC, Jimmy Dean, and Colgate. I was responsible for the band, which has consisted primarily of keyboardists Tony Migliore and Bobby Ogdin, bassist David Hicks, drummer Jerry Kroon, acoustic guitarist and banjoist Buddy Blackmon, electric guitarist Vip Vipperman, steel guitarist Russ Hicks, and fiddler Hoot Hester. In 2009, the *Showdown* did a tribute to my career with a medley of songs that I had played on. Host LeAnn Rimes and the contestants took part in a medley that included "Candy Man," "Delta Dawn," "He Stopped Loving Her Today," "Baby," "I Was Country When Country Wasn't Cool," and "Orange Blossom Special." The show is still going strong at the time of this writing.

In 1983, The Nashville Network, known as TNN, launched on basic cable and helped to promote country music entertainment in ways that local television stations no longer did. Cable television was more common in small towns and rural areas than it was in cities, and country music seemed to be a natural fit for it. The first primetime show on TNN was *Nashville Now*, featuring long-time Nashville radio personality Ralph Emery. Jerry Whitehurst, who had once hired me to play on the syndicated show *Pop Goes the Country* and *That Good Ole Nashville Music*, led a great band with Billy Linneman on bass, Clay Caire on drums, Fred Newell and John Clausi on guitar, Hoot Hester on fiddle, and Larry Sasser on pedal steel guitar. I performed as a guest on the show six or seven times. Ralph was always a great host and really helped me promote my records.

In 1994, I was invited to play on a TNN show with a very interesting concept. Each episode of *Yesteryear* focused on a single year and showcased the big hits of the day. Because they didn't just focus on country hits, we had a band with horns, a full rhythm section, and, of course, background vocals. Bill Walker, the great Nashville arranger, was the music director, and he provided a lot of written arrangements for us to play. I thought it was a great concept, but it lasted only one season.

TNN also had a great show hosted by Lorianne Crook and Charlie Chase called *Music City Tonight*. Buddy Skipper, the show's music director, had hired a band that featured George Tidwell on trumpet and Denis Solee on saxophone, but The Nashville Network's advertising gurus decided that the show needed to be "more country." Tidwell and Solee were let go, and Buddy filled the spot with me playing harp and vibes. The first week I played the show, two of the guests were rock-and-roll legends Bo Diddley and Chubby Checker, real country artists if there ever was.

Buddy had assembled a killer band. He and Rodger Morris played keyboards, Larry Paxton was on bass, and Bob Mater was the drummer. Gary Burnette and Bill Hullett played guitars, and Tommy White was the steel player. The vocal group—Jana King leading Stephanie Hall, Mark Ivy, and Guy Penrod—was also great. But the centerpiece of the band was Wanda Vick, a world-class musician who could play any acoustic instrument, including fiddle, banjo, mandolin, dobro, and acoustic guitar. She's not too shabby on electric guitar and steel guitar either.

Buddy Skipper is the most organized music person with whom I have ever worked. Each day when I came to the studio, I barely had to think because Buddy had already done everything that needed to be done. I worked there for eight months, leaving when the show was canceled at the end of a two-year run.

More recently, the RFD cable network has allowed me to get back on television from time to time. Since 2009, Ralph Emery has hosted an interview show with lots of video clips and a live call-in segment that allows fans to talk directly to the artists. When I appeared there, it seemed to be the fastest hour I've ever spent on a television program.

Also in 2009, I appeared on *Larry's Country Diner*, hosted by Larry Black. Larry is a veteran of country radio and has hosted many "country reunion"-type shows for different cable networks. *Larry's Country Diner* is set in an old country diner with Larry serving as its owner, former WSM *Grand Ole Opry* personality Keith Bilbrey as his announcer and sidekick, and Jimmy Capps playing the role of sheriff and bandleader. It's a very spontaneous show with very little format and lots of off-the-cuff ad-libs. During my visit to the diner, I played "The Water Is Wide" with Jimmy on guitar and got a great reaction.

My television work has a lot in common with my session work. I always had to work quickly and efficiently because time was money in those production situations. It was imperative that I be able to mimic the sounds of hit records in the ways that I was sometimes called upon to call back the sounds from a demo recording. And I had the chance to work with some of the top professionals in a variety of fields, musical and theatrical. I'm glad that I took the chance and gave *Hee Haw* a shot because it opened a lot of doors for me and resulted in many great memories.

Emulating my boyhood hero, Stan "The Man" Musial.

Talented Johanna Dowling accompanies members of the advanced chorus at formal appearances or impromptu sessions.

Achievement By Chorus Brings Honor To School

IT REALLY WASN'T surprising that our chorus received superior ratings at the FVA Music Festival. As usual they were complimented for tune, tempo, meaningful and convincing presentation, etc.

Robed in purple and white, they've entertained at many school functions, plus giving annual recitals for Daughters of the Nile, South Miami Kiwanis, and singing at many other meetings and choral events.

One reason for their success is a long history of being together and working with the same director. Many of the present chorus members began their choral activities with Mrs. Margaret de Sola when she was teaching at Ponce de Leon Junior High in 1953.

The next year Mrs. de Sola and many of her pupils came to West Miami. Choral director there for two years, she "graduated" with ninth graders and became head of the music department at Southwest. An able musician herself, her talents are reflected in the achievements of her department.

There's special sadness and a special pride for departing senior chorus members especially those with a six year record.

Student director Charlie McCoy has a great hand for music.

161

Dig those white socks !

Directing the high school chorus.

High school music theory homework.

Top: The Agendas, my first band.
Bottom: The Escorts, my band in Nashville.

A Cadence Records artist, with my black Gibson Les Paul.

Members of the Nashville A-Team. From left to right: Ray Edenton, Bob Moore, Hargus "Pig" Robbins, Harold Bradley, and me.

With Elvis.

The Charlie McCoy Band.

Top: The *Hee Haw* Harmonica Band.
Bottom: With The United.

Top: With Druhá Tráva.
Bottom: With Mel Tillis, the guy who brought me to Nashville.

At the West Virginia Music Hall of Fame induction ceremony.

Harold Bradley inducting me into the Country Music Hall of Fame.

The Country Music Hall of Fame Class of 2009: me, Barbara Mandrell, and Roy Clark.

Still playing after all these years.

CHAPTER 10

—

AN ARTIST OVERSEAS

By 1974, I had been in Nashville for nearly fifteen years, during which time I had made records with hundreds of artists, built a reputation as a musical jack-of-all-trades, fronted a regional touring band, and, in my spare time, begun to establish myself as a solo artist. Because of my endless session schedule, touring was never a major priority. For the most part, I had limited my travels to locations within a day's drive from Nashville so that I could be back in time for sessions each Monday morning. But in the fall of 1974, international opportunities came calling, marking the beginning of more than four decades of great musical encounters with European musicians and audiences. These connections would allow me to continue making great music with talented musicians even as the market for country musicians in the United States focused on larger shows with elaborate staging and pushed some of the older musicians like myself to the wayside.

One day, I came home from work, and as soon as I walked in the door, my wife Susan said, "There's some man with an accent on the phone."

It was a long-distance call from Paris, and, although I didn't speak French, I decided to take a chance. Luckily, he spoke English.

"Hello, Charlie," the man at the other end of the line said. "My name is Jean. These are lyrics from a song we wrote called 'A Country Boy in Paris.'" And then he proceeded to recite them to me. Another line said, "Eddy came out with a loaf of bread, tipped his French beret and said, 'I'd like you to meet some Nashville friends of mine.'"

As we talked, Jean Fernandez informed me that he was producing Eddy Mitchell, one of the two biggest stars in France. Mitchell had started making hit records in the 1960s, but, by the time Jean called me, his career was in a slump. Jean was charged with getting Eddy back into the spotlight, and, after he'd heard our *Area Code 615* album, he was certain that our sound could work for Eddy. Jean and I decided to book three days of sessions with most of the Code at Wayne Moss's Cinderella Studio, where we had recorded the Code's albums. The combination clicked right away, and audiences were clamoring for Eddy again.

Rather than hiring French musicians for his live debut of the new sound, Jean and Eddy decided to bring our group of Nashville musicians to France to present a series of concerts at Paris's Olympia Theatre, one of the city's main venues. Our group included David Briggs, Wayne Moss, Kenny Buttrey, Russ Hicks, Dale Sellers, Jim Colvard, the Holladay Sisters (Mary and Ginger Holladay and Lea Jane Berinati), and the Jordanaires. My buddy Tex Davis from Monument also tagged along.

For most of us, this was our first trip to Europe, and we were so excited about it that nobody got much sleep on the overnight transatlantic flight. After flying all night, we arrived at Charles de Gaulle airport feeling mighty tired. A well-rested and smiling Jean Fernandez met us at the airport and informed us that we were going to rehearse.

"Tonight?" I asked.

"No! Now!" he replied. And off we went to a very long and exhausting rehearsal that I don't think anyone remembered. Quite a welcome to France!

The shows were a great success, and Eddy proved to be quite the showman. The audiences treated him like a real superstar, like American audiences treated Elvis. We were also treated like celebrities, which is not something that studio musicians are accustomed to. People there knew about records that we had played on that many of us had forgotten about, and many of them were exceptionally knowledgeable about our careers. It dawned on me that perhaps European audiences cared more about sidemen than Americans did.

The concerts were a lot of fun. We were able to show off a bit more than we might have in the United States, where sidemen were often expected to be heard but not noticed. But, during our first concert, Jimmy Colvard decided to try something different. He had the first solo and, armed with a thirty-foot guitar cable, walked all the way to the front of the stage to play it rather than standing in his spot. I looked over at Dale Sellers, who seemed surprised that Jimmy had done that. By the next night's concert, Dale found an extra-long cord so he could step to the front of the stage for his solos, too.

After the last concert, the owner of Eddy Mitchell's record label, Eddy Barclay, invited us to an after-party at his three-story apartment in the middle of Paris. There were quite a few people at the party, and many of them ended up in a designated "opium room" located on the bottom floor. It was a good thing that the room was located on the bottom floor because just walking by the door could have altered your state of mind.

Jean Fernandez's decision to bring Eddy to Nashville worked out well, leading him to record another seven albums in the city. They were all big hits in France. In 1977, Russ Hicks, Mary Holladay, and I joined Eddy for a one-week engagement at Paris's Palais des Sports, followed by a tour of Belgium and France. We visited Mons, Charleroi, Liege, and Brussels, and then, after a couple of days off, we went to Bordeaux, Toulouse, Lyon, Strasbourg, and Caen. Eddy had a super band, complete with another steel guitarist, harmonica player, and a brass section. The harmonica player, Jean-Jacques Milteau, is the most famous harp player in France, and he and I have become very good friends over the years. But, at first, I found it to be a bit unnerving to play with another harmonica player, especially because Jean-Jacques played through an amplifier while I went through the PA system and had to listen to the monitors to hear what I was doing. With so much volume on the stage, it was sometimes difficult to hear how I was fitting in with the rest of the group.

Eddy's manager, Claude Wilde, thought that Russ and I were country bumpkins, so he decided to introduce us to real French culture. He called a restaurant in Lyon that normally took a month to get a reservation because the chef is so well respected and, surprisingly, got us a reservation. It was one of the most elegant restaurants I have ever seen, and the food was very special. The main entrée was woodcock.

Everything was going great, and we were both behaving very well in our opulent environs. But, when the waiter came with the cheese plate, I let my bumpkin show, much to Claude's embarrassment.

"Do you have any *mimolette*?" I asked, remembering a great cheese that Eddy had served at his house.

Stepping back in disgust, the waiter replied, "Monsieur, *mimolette* is NOT French!" Although the name sounds French, Claude later informed me, *mimolette* is a Dutch cheese. Claude looked like he wanted to crawl under the table and hide from his uncultured companions. But, at the same time, it proved his point!

I had the privilege of joining Eddy Mitchell one more time in the early 1990s, when he appeared on a French program similar to the American show *This Is Your Life*, which celebrated an artist's career and brought mystery guests from their past for surprise visits. I was one of the surprise guests, playing "Rollin' in My Sweet Baby's Arms," a song that he had rearranged with the title "Je ne sais faire que l'amour." The moment I started playing, Eddy knew it was me and was thrilled that I'd made the journey to honor him on his special night. Of course, it was my honor because my association with Eddy gave me credibility with French audiences that has served me well over the decades.

After Eddy Mitchell brought the Nashville Sound to France, the folks at Columbia Records France decided that they needed to get into the act. They had an accordionist named Yvette Horner on the label, and they wanted to make a country record with her. We booked Owen Bradley's Quonset Hut with some of Nashville's finest musicians to accompany her. She arrived at the studio with a large entourage that included her producer, several label representatives, a film crew, and a radio announcer from RTL, a radio station in Luxembourg. During one of the sessions, the RTL guy did a live broadcast, bringing Nashville directly to the station's listeners.

Yvette was a remarkable musician who played the button accordion rather than the piano accordion that most American accordionists play. I read an article about her in *Paris Match* that talked about the décor of her home, which featured accordion-shaped curtains in the blue, white, and red colors of the French flag. Rumor also had it that she used to jam with the former president of France, Valéry Giscard d'Estaing, who was also an accordion player. She was a reading musician, so her arranger wrote out every note that she was supposed to play. She sight-read everything, even playing "Orange Blossom Special" with her right hand crawling across the buttons like a spider on speed. I have deep respect for her musicianship, and, just as I had with Eddy Mitchell, I appeared on the French version of *This Is Your Life* to honor her.

In 1979, I made my first trip to England, along with Lloyd Green and Johnny Gimble, to play at London's Wembley Festival. The festival was organized by a British man named Mervyn Conn, who was notorious for "gherming" the big stars, ignoring the lesser-known acts, and "poor-mouthing" everyone to get them to work cheap under the guise of promoting country music in the United Kingdom. (One of Tammy Wynette's backup singers joked that she wanted to create a t-shirt with little baby chickens that said "Mervyn's Martyrs: Cheap, Cheap, Cheap.") The Wembley Festivals went on for several years and always packed the fourteen-thousand-seat Wembley Arena with fans who were eager to see such artists as Johnny Cash, Tammy Wynette, Conway Twitty, and Crystal Gayle. I returned in 1980 and 1981 with Buddy Emmons and Pig Robbins.

Mervyn took the show to other parts of Europe, as well, with the hope of promoting country music throughout Europe. We traveled to Zurich, Rotterdam, Helsinki, Göteborg, and Frankfurt. As country musicians who were used to walking around in casual clothes, we stuck out quite a bit in some of these cities. In Helsinki, for instance, a group of us decided to visit a disco next to our hotel, but the bouncer wouldn't let us in because, as he shouted at us, he didn't like blue jeans.

Mervyn wanted to bring the show to Paris, but, because country music wasn't terribly popular there, he knew that the only way it would be successful was to hire a French star to headline the show. He asked me to contact Eddy Mitchell, who agreed to perform (probably for a lot of money!). There is no doubt that Eddy was the reason that the show wasn't a tremendous failure financially. But when Mervyn came to Eddy's dressing room to introduce himself, he launched into a big speech about how happy he was to be the one who could introduce country music to Paris, virtually ignoring the fact that Eddy had been at it for several years. When Mervyn left, Eddy, who spoke very little English at that time, smiled and said, "I have met God."

By the time I returned from the Wembley Festival in 1981, I had played in Europe five times, fitting my overseas journeys into a very busy schedule of session work, *Hee Haw* tapings, and concerts in the United States. I'd traveled to Europe primarily as a sideman, stepping out occasionally to show off as an artist. But, in 1987, the opportunity to present myself as an international recording artist appeared.

That year, I recorded a session with a Danish singer named Jodle Birge, which were led by a Danish guitarist named Nils Tuxen. Nils was an outstanding musician, arranger, and bandleader, and, to top it all off, he was also one of the nicest guys you would ever want to meet. Accompanying Nils and Jodle were Jodle's manager Calle Nielsen, the record label owner Mogens Villadsen, and a Swedish comedian named Yan Swahn. After the session, Nils approached me to let me know that Mogens was interested in recording a solo album with me for his label in Denmark. Since my deal at Monument had ended and I didn't have a label at the time, I thought I should give it a shot.

Mogens had big plans for the project. When we discussed the budget for the album, he told me that he wanted to do a double album with twenty or more sides. I asked him what he wanted me to record, and he gave me *carte blanche* to do whatever I wanted. That was quite a financial risk for him to take, especially considering that I was relatively unknown in Denmark.

I decided to remake some of my biggest hits and do some other songs, as well. Laney Smallwood Hicks joined me to sing four songs, including a great R&B record called "You've Got It All Over Him," which had originally been recorded by a group called the Jets. When I asked Mogens if he'd ever heard it, he said that he hadn't, so I thought that there might be an opportunity to break a record with Laney, too.

We recorded the album in July 1987. Mogens decided to split the material into two albums, one of which was mostly straight country music and another that collected several of rock, pop, and R&B tunes. He called the first album *Harmonica Jones*, which was also the title of one of the songs on the album. The morning before one of the sessions, I was eating breakfast when the idea for "Harmonica Jones," which was a play on words about someone who is addicted to the harmonica, came to me. Mogens thought it was a person's name and chose to name the first album after him. The second album, *Another Side of Charlie McCoy*, featured several of Laney's cuts, as well as new versions of Area Code 615's arrangements of "Southern Comfort" and "Katy Hill" and experimental versions of "Byrdland" and "Little Maggie" (which we did as a reggae tune). Unfortunately, Mogens never considered releasing "You've Got It All Over Him" because R&B was virtually unknown in Denmark.

Mogens invited me to tour Denmark that September to help promote the album. I arrived in Aalborg on a Saturday and was tired from the flight. Mogens and his crew let me have the rest of the weekend to myself to recover from the travels before I started the tour, so I went to my room and tried to sleep off the jetlag. Unfortunately, I overslept on Sunday morning and nearly missed breakfast, reaching the hotel restaurant as the staff was putting everything away. The guy in charge was willing to let me eat, but he barely spoke English, I didn't speak Danish, and the menu was entirely in Danish. I just pointed at a single word—*hønsalat*—and hoped for the best. When my chicken salad arrived, I was relieved. Later, when I was starting to get hungry for lunch, I learned that all the restaurants in Aalborg were closed until supper time at 7 p.m. On Monday, I traveled around

Denmark with a fellow named Thorkil Jensen, who took me to a family restaurant-bar called a *kro*. Denmark was having their national elections that day, and the bar was a polling place. That would never happen in the United States!

Country music was not terribly popular in Denmark, but the people who were interested in it were deeply passionate about it. Some radio stations play country music on weekly programs that last only an hour or two, and fans tune in for a rare opportunity to hear their favorite familiar artists and the latest musicians to break into their market. It was at one of these stations in Viborg that I met Kirsten Petersen, Denmark's most knowledgeable and enthusiastic supporter of country music. We did a two-hour interview on her show during my first visit. Since then, Kirsten has become a very good friend.

In March 1988, Calle asked if I would play with Jodle at Wembley, after which I could come to Denmark and play two concerts there. Although I wasn't terribly crazy about working for Mervyn Conn again, I convinced myself that it was worth it if I could support Jodle and Mogens.

The Wembley concert gave me the opportunity to meet up with Nils Tuxen again. He was playing with Jodle's backup band, a group called The United Steels of Europe. Featuring four steel guitarists, the United Steels had recorded a compact disc called *Devine Lines* and were putting out a sound that was absolutely tremendous. Nils was the leader, playing lead and steel. Jan Hartman was the bassist, and he was joined by drummer Hans Molenaar. André Sommer played keyboards and steel, and Koos Biel also played steel. They were all from Holland. French steel guitarist Jean-Yves Lozac'h and American fiddler Downs Thompson rounded out this incredible band.

Our two gigs in Denmark really went well. We played the first Aalborg Country Festival. The city fathers had me plant a tree in the park. It was right beside a tree that had been planted by Nana Mouskouri, whom I had recorded with in New York in 1962. Nils said there would be a lot more dates in the future if I wanted to play. Also, Jean-Yves Lozac'h offered to help me find work in France if I wanted.

When summer came, I joined Jodle and the United Steels in a

tour they were calling "The Jodle Birge Wembley Country Tour." We played all over Denmark and found enthusiastic audiences at every stop. Jodle was a very big star in Denmark, despite being decidedly "un-hip." The average country people really loved him, and he worked hard to reach out to them through a touring schedule that looked absolutely exhausting. Sometimes, we played shows in two towns in a single day.

Complicating matters was the general difficulty that came with travel in Denmark. Denmark is one mainland peninsula surrounded by several islands linked together by ferries that transport loads of cars, buses, eighteen-wheelers, and even trains from one place to another. One day, after playing an afternoon concert in Køge on the island of Sjælland, we were supposed to play a concert in Bogense, which is located on the next island over, Fyn. We played several encores at Køge, and we were unable to get to the ferry in time. We had to catch the next one, which had us arriving dangerously close to show time. Assessing the situation, Jodle stood up in the middle of the bus and said, "We are going to be late. I would like everyone to help with the equipment to try to start on time." We arrived at the small carnival in Bogense, where the rain was coming down on the crowd of people, hot-dog stands, and other attractions that lined the narrow road between where the equipment truck could park and the stage. Yet, amid all the chaos, Jodle—the great Danish country music star—carried his own equipment to the stage through the throng of adoring fans. I was duly impressed. You certainly wouldn't see many American artists who would do that.

I thoroughly enjoyed playing with the United Steels, and as studio work in Nashville started to slow down a bit, the prospect of touring was becoming more and more interesting to me. I returned to Europe to work with Jodle and the United Steels in 1989, this time bringing the Jordanaires with me. We played at Wembley and the second Aalborg Country Music Festival before I headed out on tour with the band. The tour took us to Aalborg, Munich, Bern, Strasbourg, Birmingham, London, and Hamburg, where Nils is currently living and working as a studio musician.

By 1990, the United Steels had undergone some significant personnel change. Nils had landed a gig with a German band, and their touring schedule made it impossible for him to stay with the group. Koos decided to quit playing for a while, and Jan Hartman needed to spend more time at home managing his music store. Hans suggested that we try two of his friends, guitarist Sjœrd Plak and bassist Tijmen Zinkhaan. Down two steel guitarists, they changed their name from The United Steels of Europe to simply The United. Through the years, these guys have not only become my favorite backing band—playing with me for the vast majority of my overseas appearances—but have become some of my best friends. We have taken vacations together, and we all know each other's families.

Denmark is connected by a bridge to Sweden, so we occasionally made trips over there, as well. Once, Calle booked me with a Swedish dance band called Birth Idoffs. Swedish dance bands are an immensely popular part of their culture, and they often have very good musicians and singers who sometimes become very wealthy as a consequence of their popularity. Calle booked me and Downs Thompson in a small town called Tingsryd for a dance that was supposed to start at 9 p.m. We drove to the big barn where we were supposed to play and hunkered downstairs in the warm dressing room to avoid freezing where the stage was located. At 8:50, I walked upstairs only to find that there wasn't a soul in the place. I was worried that we had made this trip to the country for nothing. At 9 p.m. sharp, the band started playing. At 9:10, I went back upstairs, certain that they were playing for the empty room that I had seen just a few minutes earlier. To my surprise, the place was packed, and several hundred people were dancing. At 9:30, the band introduced Downs and me, and I hit the stage. The first song went over well, and, as is my habit, I tried talking to the audience before I started the second number. Unfortunately, the crowd wasn't interested in listening to me talk. They just wanted music for dancing. Between sets, they all ran out to their cars to get a drink of their favorite alcoholic beverages because the venue didn't sell alcohol.

The next afternoon, we played a "dance band showcase" where

talent buyers, festival organizers and park owners could come and hear a lot of dance bands in one place. There were seven bands set up in a large semicircle around a floor that resembled a skating rink. At the end of the performance, Birth Idoffs drove Downs and me to Helsingborg, Sweden (the closest town to Denmark) to catch a ferry to Helsingør, where we could take the train to Randers.

I really liked the Birth Idoffs guys. Their music was very good, but sterile. To my ear, most Swedish dance bands have two major problems: (1) they play the same solos and fills every time they play a song, so there's little room for musicians to be creative on stage, and (2) they always have a keyboardist who plays a string or organ sound as a kind of musical wallpaper from the start of the song to its finish. As we got off the bus and started to say our good-byes, the guitarist asked me what I thought of Swedish dance music, and I told him that, while they were very good, it would be nice to see them cut loose and get a bit wild.

"The next time you see me," he said, "I am going to be very wild." There hasn't been a next time. I think the Swedish dance band experiment was a bust.

The association with Calle Nielsen and Jodle Birge turned out to be one of the most reliable ones that I have had in the music business. In nineteen years of touring Denmark, I never needed a contract with Calle, who served as my Danish agent. He was a tough negotiator, but whatever we agreed on, I could take to the bank. Calle and I became very good friends, as well, and it was a real treat to watch his family grow over the years. His wife, Bodle, was an excellent chef, and his daughter Christina was being groomed to work in the music business. His four sons—Nigge, Patrick, Mike, and Chris—were all very skilled athletes. They made history as the first four brothers ever to play in a first-division Danish basketball league game at the same time. I was also fortunate to watch Chris score his first soccer goal. Calle was very happy when I started to become interested in soccer, and we attended quite a few games together during my Danish tours. He had once dreamed of being a professional soccer player before an injury forced him to try another path. He still played soccer with his friends every weekend until he passed away during a game in December 2007. He was only in his mid-fifties.

Calle believed in me and in country music, despite the fact that interest in country music was often rather cold in Denmark. I'm sure that there were tours that lost money, but he kept the faith and invited me back for another visit. He was responsible for five of my solo albums: *Harmonica Jones*; *Another Side of Charlie McCoy*; *Wine, Candlelight, and Charlie*; *Choo, Choo, Ch'Boogie*; and *Charlie's Christmas Angels*. Calle was also my link to the many Danish artists with whom I've recorded and toured. I'm deeply grateful for his enthusiasm and support of my work over the years.

Jodle Birge, too, was a great friend, artist, and gentleman who made ninety-nine albums over the course of his long career. The snooty Danish press ignored Jodle and his music, but the average man on the street knew the lyrics to every one of his hits. During one of my visits, a group of reporters gathered to ask me why I was there to play with Jodle, who they thought was nothing more than a bumpkin. I was trying to be very careful in my responses because I knew that they were trying to get me to say something controversial that they could use against Jodle. I was doing just fine until one reporter finally managed to get under my skin.

"You could play with anyone you wanted," he said. "Why are you playing with Jodle Birge?"

"You just answered your own question," I replied in frustration. "I can play with anyone I want, and I *want* to play with Jodle Birge!" The audience felt similarly because, despite the pouring rain, not a soul left that sold-out concert. They knew that Jodle was not only a great musician, but a genuinely kind and generous man.

One time, I was staying at a hotel in Randers, the town where Calle had his office. Jodle was scheduled to play in Løkken, a town on the northwest coast, and he lived about thirty miles north of Randers. Knowing that I was there, Jodle drove sixty miles out of his way just to visit with me for ten minutes. That was typical behavior for Jodle. He never passed up an opportunity to speak with his friends, sign an autograph, and make the people around him feel very special.

He was also a musically adventurous artist who wasn't content just recording straight-ahead country music. One time, Jodle recorded some Hawaiian songs in Danish at a studio in Denmark, and he contacted me about meeting them—along with a contingent of Danish journalists—in Hawaii to add some guitar and harmonica to the tracks. Calle hoped that these recordings would have an authentic Hawaiian touch, and he thought that the change of venue would be helpful. I told Calle that the best Hawaiian steel guitar player in the world, Jerry Byrd, lived in Honolulu, and Calle gave me the go-ahead to give Jerry a call. When I reached him, Jerry said, "What? Hawaiian songs in Danish?" He thought about it for a minute and replied, "Count me in! I can't miss this!" Later, on Danish television, there was Jodle on Waikiki, singing in Danish with two hula girls dancing.

Jodle also made an album of Mexican songs in Danish. Once again, Calle was looking for an angle to get Jodle into the spotlight, and he suggested that we go to Mexico to finish the album. I called Blondie Calderon, Ray Price's pianist and a native Mexican. Blondie suggested that we might have some troubles getting the work done in Mexico, and he suggested that we go to San Antonio instead. So I arranged for studio time in San Antonio and called my engineer friend Eric Paul to come down from Austin to record the session. We hired a trumpet player and an accordion player to meet us there for the session. When we arrived for the noon session, the only person there was the trumpet player, who told us that they didn't maintain as strict a clock as we did in Nashville. Eventually everyone showed up, and we had a great session. That night, we went down to the River Walk for dinner, and a strolling mariachi band of young girls approached the outdoor restaurant where we were eating. "Do you think they would let me sing?" Jodle asked me. I told him I would ask. The girls agreed, and the customers at that restaurant heard a one-of-a-kind Danish version of "Cielito Lindo."

Jodle was a very dear and special friend, and we had a great many good times together. Sadly, he passed away with a brain tumor in 2004. Denmark is not the same without him.

In 1990, the French auto manufacturer Renault hired us to play a twelve-city tour to celebrate the Jeep's fiftieth anniversary in Europe. The concerts were all free and open to the public, and most of them were held outdoors. The stage consisted of two flatbed truck trailers, outfitted completely with power, sound, and lights to permit us to play in the middle of a field.

On this tour, the United and I met Philippe Kulczak, the agent for the opening band, a group called Wolf Pack. Philippe, who was known as "Guzze," said that he would like to book me for more appearances in France. I was so taken with the French audiences—and the French countryside—that I said that I would love to work there more. Since then, Guzze has booked many tours for me in France, Belgium, and the French-speaking regions of Switzerland. As with Calle, I don't need a contract because Guzze's handshake is better than a contract. He and his wife Francine—who passed away from cancer in early 2010—lived in the Strasbourg area for many years. Our communications have always been tricky because Guzze speaks very little English, and I speak very little French. Luckily, when Francine was around, she could help out because she was fluent in French, German, and English. Nowadays, I get lots of practice reading French thanks to Guzze's emails.

In France, the sets are ninety minutes long, and we never use a set list. The band knows about fifty of my arrangements, so I just call out the next song while the end of the one we just finished is fading out. This helps us keep the shows fresh and prevents us from getting tired of the same sets, and it allows us to respond to the room more effectively. It's always exciting to see how the shows unfold.

Some of the best French shows we played were on so-called "culture tours." The socialistic French government gives money to each little town and village to use for culture, and they are at liberty to use the money in whatever way they see fit. Many communities host small concerts in their *salles de fête*, or activity center. When we started playing these culture tours, our opening act was Vicky Layne, a singer that I had recorded with in Nashville. She left to work with Jill Morris in Germany, and a very talented singer named Annabel joined us. She plays her opening set with just her acoustic guitar, but we always invite her back onstage to sing a song with the full band later on. With all our travel in unfamiliar towns, we sometimes struggled to make sense of the complicated traffic patterns and driving habits of the places we visited. One time, the United and I were playing concerts in Agen and Najac, two towns in the south of France. We were on our way to Najac with Sjœrd Plak driving the lead car and André Sommer following in a second car. Agen was a maze with confusing streets and roundabouts nearly every block. Every time Sjœrd made a turn that seemed wrong, André hollered some Dutch words at him. When I asked him what he was saying, André told me that he was giving Sjœrd a cussing in Dutch. After about five mistakes, André launched into a barrage of English cuss words, really giving it to Sjœrd.

"Oh, when it gets really bad, you change to English," I observed.

"Yes," André replied. "English cuss words are so much more descriptive!"

During one of our French tours in the early 1990s, we met a remarkable Frenchman named Alain Valadon. An electrical engineer who had sold a video game he'd invented to a company in Chicago, Alain had purchased a French estate with a four-hundred-year-old house in the middle of the Burgundy wine region. Alain was a guitar player, and when I met him, he was just learning to play steel guitar. He invited us to come visit him on some of our off days, and I fell in love with the place. Called St. Hilaire, the property has a tower that was built on the property in the 1700s, and the Michelin road maps of France even indicate its location just west of the city of Chalon sur Saône, close to Chagny and Fontaines. The estate sat high on a hill, and every view from it was like a postcard. The house consists of three buildings—the master residence, the guest quarters, and a horse barn that he'd converted into a workshop and storage area—that open onto a courtyard. The property also has a swimming pool with a pool house that has a small stage inside where the musicians that Alain invited to visit could play.

The beauty of St. Hilaire was overshadowed by the hospitality there. Alain's wife, Annie, is absolutely one of the best cooks I have ever known, and she specializes in what might be called "French country" cooking. In their dining room is a long table that could seat at least twenty people, and Alain, a connoisseur of fine wines, loved to entertain there, often holding court during three-hour dinners. We have visited St. Hilaire many times. It is an oasis for us when we tour. We all have become very close to the Valadons: Alain, Annie, their son Willie, and their granddaughter Clara. My visits have been captured musically, too, because it was at St. Hilaire that we wrote some of the songs for my *International Incident* album, including especially the Sjœrd Plak composition "Fontaines," which is a tribute to Alain, Annie, and St. Hilaire.

As an aspiring steel guitarist, Alain idolized Lloyd Green. We arranged to take Lloyd and his wife Dot to visit St. Hilaire several years ago, and Alain found himself immersed in an almost religious experience. Lloyd, a huge history buff, had a great time, too. We also brought Russ and Laney Smallwood Hicks with us one time, much to Alain's delight.

In 2006, after Alain had finally sold the last part of his company and would dedicate the rest of his life to playing music, he died of cancer. We are still friends with Annie and Willie, and the members of the United and I still stop by to visit when we can.

My trips to France have also allowed me to become great friends with Jean-Marc and Anny Versini. Jean-Marc is a fantastic Travis-style guitarist and a gourmet cook, and Anny plays guitar, as well. They play concerts for young schoolchildren, and Jean-Marc has made more than forty albums, most of which are for kids. Jean-Marc has set the works of many classic French poets to music, and he's come to Nashville twice to make country instrumentals. Jean-Marc honored me by playing on my *Duets* album.

With all my travels to France, I decided that it would be helpful to learn some French, so my wife and I enrolled in an adult education course at a local high school. Our first teacher, Dominique, had a great sense of humor and made French a lot of fun. He poked fun at his own language, telling us, "S'il a logique, il n'est pas français"—"If it is logical, it is not French." After studying French for a couple of semesters, I ran into Jimmy C. Newman at the *Opry* and decided to try some of my French out on the great Cajun musician. Clearly, my French was different than his Cajun French because he turned to his wife and said, "Hey, Charlie's learning that Paris French!"

By 1993, it was becoming increasingly difficult to bring the United with me for appearances in Denmark, so Calle introduced me to a band from Sweden called the Tomboola Band. The four-piece group consisted of guitarist Salle Sahlin, steel guitarist Benny Pederson, bassist and singer Kenneth Svenning, and drummer Jonte Svensson. They had enough material to play a six-hour dance, and Kenneth programmed it all on the stage as they played. Kenneth is also one of the strongest singers I have ever heard, and I've had the chance to hear plenty of them! I have performed in seventy-nine Danish cities, most of them with the Tomboola Band. Like the United, the members of the Tomboola Band are some of my very best friends.

Benny lives in a suburb of Malmö, Sweden, called Åkarp. We have had some great parties there, enjoying the best tacos I have ever had. His wife Janna works as a controller for the Swedish national railroad, and, as a railroad buff, I was excited to have an opportunity to visit her at work. The control room had a huge board that wrapped around half of the room to indicate all the trains that were moving around southern Sweden. It looked like a larger-than-life model railroad control.

Through the Tomboola Band, I have met two couples who have become great friends. Nils and Tove Hedeman-Hansen live in the small town of Ørting, near Århus. We have spent a good number of nights with Nils and Tove, always enjoying good conversation and great food. My wife Pat and I have also become great friends with Kim and Lotte Lisbygd, who live in Sorø, which is situated on Sjælland, the biggest island in Denmark. Kim and Lotte have an amazing summer house on the western shore of Sjælland overlooking the massive Storbælt bridge. Pat and I spent a great short holiday there. Kim and Lotte's daughter, Sandra is a fine singer.

In 1989, I began to expand my international touring beyond

Europe, playing the first of many concerts in Japan. Kenji Nagatomi, a dentist from Kyoto who has a great passion for country music, invited me to play some concerts with him and his band, the Tennessee Five, at a club he owns. The Tennessee Five had six members, and every time I asked them about their name, they just laughed. The band started with five members in 1958; Kenji and fiddler Masaru Yasumi celebrated their fiftieth anniversary in 2008. In the early 2000s, Kenji's daughter Mari started singing with the band, and she came to Nashville to record an album, which I produced, and to try to establish a singing career in the United States. She attended Middle Tennessee State University, and now she's pursuing a doctorate in Japan while also working as an interpreter and writing songs.

The Tennessee Five consists of guitarist Shin-ichi Uratani, steel guitarist Yoshiharu Fukada, fiddler Masaru Yasumi, banjoist Teddy Koyama, bassist Masaki Nabeta, and drummer Yasumasa Morita. For a while, Yoshiko Suwa played the keyboard, but she moved away and was replaced by Honey Nakase. Their soundman is Toshiyuki Tokutake, and Shoko Hyodo manages to keep the entire enterprise running, managing the club and coordinating merchandise sales.

Kenji also discovered a great guitarist named Furuhashi Kazuaki—"Kazu," as we call him. One of the finest young guitarists that I've met, Kazu moved to Tokyo and has assembled a great band to back me there. Kazu is a big fan of my friend, guitarist Bob Eggers. I recorded one of Bob's songs called "Julia," a song he wrote for his wife. In 2008, while playing at Kenji's club, Kazu asked if we could play "Julia." I had Mari call Bob and Julia on the cell phone, and they heard us play it live from Japan.

Kenji has arranged some nice surprises for me over the years. One year, there was a man who played the Japanese bamboo flute who played with me on "Shenandoah." Another time, there was a woman who played koto on "The Water Is Wide." In 2009, the mayor of Kyoto presented me with a plaque to commemorate twenty years of my visits to the city. I played a new song that I had written called "Kyoto by Night" while the mayor and singer Dawn Sears danced.

So far, there have been twenty tours in Japan with Kenji. I have made many friends there and have been the beneficiary of much Japanese hospitality. And I've had the chance to bring a lot of Nashville musicians with me for what Kenji called the "Country Dream Festival," including the Jordanaires, Ray Price, George Hamilton IV and George Hamilton V, Skeeter Davis, Jett Williams, and Mandy Barnett, among many others.

When George Hamilton IV and George Hamilton V came to Japan with me in 1992, we met Keiko Walker, a young singer whose mother is Japanese and father is British. She is a beautiful woman who speaks perfect English and has a sparkling personality. Young George V was quite smitten with Keiko, and he was in her company talking to her every chance he had. On the return trip to Nashville, we changed planes in San Francisco. After we cleared customs, we went into a coffee shop in the airport. George IV and George V were going on back to Nashville while my wife and I were going to spend the night and catch a flight back home the next day. I decided to have some fun with George V.

"George," I said, "you know you are a very lucky man."

"What do you mean?" he asked. I told him that Keiko's boyfriend, who was also her bass player, was a black belt in karate and a *kung fu* expert. It was a good thing that he was a good sport. It took a while before George V figured out that I was funning with him.

One of the first years with the "Country Dream" festival in Kyoto, Kenji booked me to play in Osaka with a bluegrass band. The best way to get there was by train, so he sent a young guitarist named Takasi "Tak" Nagai to help me get there. On the train ride down, Tak bragged to me that he was learning English cuss words. I guess that he and André shared a common view that English cuss words were more effective than their own. Tak attended Belmont University in Nashville, moved to New York to teach, got married and moved to Tokyo. He is a fine guitar player.

In the summer of 2001, I made my first trip to the Czech Republic to play at a bluegrass festival held at a castle in Strakonice. When I got off the train in Prague, I was met by a guy named Petr Kuklik, who told me that bluegrass music was very big there. We visited a radio show hosted by banjo and mandolin builder Rosta Capek that aired in primetime on national radio. You have to look long and hard for bluegrass music on most American radio stations, so this came as quite a surprise to me. The following day, we drove some seventy miles to Strakonice. Over two days, fifteen bands played, each one better than the one before. I was amazed by the musicianship that I heard. The last band that played—Robert Křest'an and Druhá Tráva— invited me to sit in with them.

The next summer, Luboš Malina, the leader of Druhá Tráva, called to ask if I could play two festivals with them in August. I was happy to join them because they were such exceptional musicians. Luboš picked me up in Switzerland, and we drove to his home in a small town just north of Prague. He lived on an old farm with horses, cows, pigs, chickens, dogs, cats, and a goose. He told me the goose was the "watch dog."

Luboš—a classically trained clarinetist and cellist who is now also a master of the banjo, saxophone, and Irish whistle—had assembled a new band with four musicians from the Czech Republic and three from Slovakia, and we rehearsed together for two days. The Slovak guys stayed there, and Luboš's wife Marketa showed us exceptional hospitality. The festivals were in Brno and Telc. The band played Irish music, Gypsy music, rock, pop, and bluegrass that sounded like they had all been born in Kentucky. It was truly one of the best bands I have ever heard. I imagine that, if Area Code 615 had stayed together, we could have played music with that kind of variety and facility.

Since 2003, I have visited the Czech Republic several times, often playing with Robert Křest'an and Druhá Tráva. Druhá Tráva is the most popular bluegrass band in the country, and they always draw a huge crowd. In 2004, we recorded a live album—*Live in Brno*— together, and I was fortunate to play on their twentieth-anniversary concert, which was held in Namest nad Oslavou in the same venue where they got their start. The band's personnel has changed over the years, but everyone has been exceptional. In addition to Robert and Luboš Malina, the Druhá Tráva crew has included dobro player Luboš Novotny, guitarist Emil Formánek, bassists Petr Surý and Tomáš

Liška, fiddler Pepa Malina, and drummers David Landštof and Kamil Slezák. Katia Garcia, who appeared as a guest on my *Celtic Bridge* album, also appeared as a guest during my 2013 visit.

In more than four decades of traveling around Europe and Asia, I've had the opportunity to play with many wonderful musicians and to make great friends everywhere I've visited. As session work grew less frequent, these performances gave me a chance to explore new musical territory while seeing the world beyond the walls of a recording studio. I feel very fortunate to have had the opportunity to share my music with welcoming audiences in some of the most beautiful places in the world.

CHAPTER II

—

THE HARMONICA AND ME

I've played many instruments over the course of my career, both on records and in my concert appearances. Overall, I'd say that I'm an average guitar player, an above-average bassist and vibraphonist, a below-average percussionist and keyboardist, and a way-below-average saxophone, trumpet, and tuba player. But, on the harmonica, I have a style that is all mine. It was my first instrument, and, while Nashville has so many amazing players on all the other instruments, the harmonica is the instrument that has allowed me to be a professional musician for nearly sixty years. It's been said that I'm the most-recorded harmonica player in history. I can't confirm or deny it, but it could be possible.

After I learned to play the blues by listening to Jimmy Reed and Little Walter, I never really listened to other harp players. I heard blues harmonica players like Sonny Boy Williamson, Howlin' Wolf, and Slim Harpo, but I didn't study their style. Still today, any time I need inspiration, I listen to *The Best of Little Walter* and *The Best of Muddy Waters* to hear the blues master Little Walter weave his magic. I always hear something new.

Blues harp is what got me into the studio, but I would've had a very short career if that's all I could play. I had to find my own identity as a musician, and, when I found it, I decided to stick with it. Occasionally, a producer will ask me to play through an amplifier to

144

imitate that Jimmy Reed sound, but, most of the time, you're hearing me playing in my style.

When I came to Nashville, I became good friends with Jimmy Riddle and Onie Wheeler, both of whom played with Roy Acuff. Jimmy was a keyboard player, yet played the harmonica upside down with the high notes to the left. I never understood how his brain processed that, but he made it work. Onie was more of a pure country player. He was also an exceptional woodcarver and craftsman. He made me a hand-carved harmonica and a handmade piano, both of which I cherish.

Over the years, I've crossed paths with a number of great harp players. I met Wayne Raney and Lonnie Glosson on *Hee Haw*, and Howard Levy and Steve Baker came to my attention during sessions. Jean-Jacques Milteau and I crossed paths in France, Norton Buffalo on a live show in Chicago, and Don Baker while producing some videos. Lee Oskar and I met at a National Association of Music Merchants convention. There are a number of up-and-coming players whom I've had the pleasure of knowing, as well, including Buddy Greene (who appeared on my duets album), Koichi "Ari" Matsuda, Detlef Grobba, Mike Caldwell, and Jim Hoke. I'm also looking forward to doing projects with P. T. Gazell and "Jelly Roll" Johnson, along with other Nashville players, in the near future.

Mickey Raphael, the long-time harmonica player with Willie Nelson's band, is also a dear friend. One time, my band and I were supposed to open for Willie at the Jimmie Rodgers Memorial Festival in Meridian, Mississippi, but Mickey couldn't make the gig. Willie came to me that afternoon and asked me to sit in with him, and I agreed. When the show came around, I was ready to look for all the spaces in Willie's singing and try to fill them as best as I could. After all, that's what I'd been doing ever since Grady Martin taught me about the importance of the lyrics. Willie, though, didn't give many spaces. He was phrasing far behind the beat sometimes, and when there are spaces, he often fills them with his guitar part. I spent the entire night looking for my space, and I just couldn't find it. It was funny to me, and Willie thought so, too. He'd look back at me and grin! Mickey, who has become a respected session musician in his own right, will be playing a duet with me on my next album.

I have been involved in an organization that has allowed me to meet many great harp players: the Society for the Preservation and Advancement of the Harmonica (SPAH). Based in Troy, Michigan, they have a convention every August that draws about four hundred people who fill the hallways, lounges, and elevators with harp playing. SPAH started out focusing on chromatic harmonica styles like those developed by Larry Adler and Toots Thielemans. They didn't seem to care much for the ten-hole (also known as "diatonic" or "blues" harps), which are typically played in country, blues, and rock music. When I was invited to play at their convention in 1983, I was— as far as I know—the first ten-hole player who had ever been asked to play the main show. It was a great success, and I think we turned some people's heads about the possibilities of the ten-hole harp. I was asked to return in 1989 and 2005, and, in the years that I've been involved, I've seen the interest in ten-hole harp double or triple. In 2013, I played for SPAH's fiftieth anniversary. They even have a blues jam during one night of the convention now. At the same time, SPAH gave me the chance to meet the great chromatic harp players Jerry Murad and Cham-Ber Huang and to develop an appreciation for the instrument's possibilities.

Toots Thielemans is, in my opinion, the finest chromatic harp player in the world. For many, many years, our paths never crossed. Toots played in the house band on *The Jimmy Dean Show*, which filmed in New York. In the late 1960s, the show came to Nashville for two weeks of taping. Sadly, Toots didn't come with them, but I was hired to play the shows. The theme for the show featured Toots, and the part was almost impossible to play without a chromatic harp. When they put the music on my stand, I said, "You've got to be kidding." Jimmy Dean told Toots about my reaction. Later, after the show returned to New York, an artist I had recorded with went up to do the show. They played the record for the band, and Toots was heard to say, "You've got to be kidding." We were a mutual admiration society!

Years later, when I was touring in Europe, I told Klaus Löhmer that I had never met Toots. Klaus told me he had a friend who was good friends with Toots and that he would pass my telephone number along to him. One Sunday, my phone rang, and the voice on the other end of the line said, "Charlie, this is Toots." Talk about a surprise! We talked for a while, and I explained that I would be coming to Europe later in the summer. He invited me to visit him at his home in Belgium. As we prepared to hang up, I said, "It's going to be an honor to meet you."

"Cut out that honor crap," Toots replied. "We're just a couple of old farts trying to boogie!"

On a day off in my tour, I caught the train from Paris to Brussels and hired a taxi to take me to Toots's suburban home. I met his wife, Hugette, who had prepared a wonderful lunch. After lunch, we retired to his music room, where he played the harp and guitar for me and shared several CDs that he wanted me to hear. At eighty-three years old, he was still playing the harmonica as well as he ever did, but he told me that his guitar playing was only at about 80 percent because of a recent stroke. If I could play like that at 80 percent, I would be a very happy camper.

He played me his latest album, which included a song he had written called "Hard to Say Goodbye." It was one of the few songs on the album that fit my style. I told him how much I liked it and said that, if I had the chance to record an album with those kinds of songs, I would love to record it. He smiled and said, "Why don't you try it?" With his guitar accompaniment, I played the harp. It was a very special moment. (I recorded "Hard to Say Goodbye" on my *Over the Rainbow* album.)

Later that evening, we went into the center of Brussels to a restaurant on the walking street. Their specialty was *moules et frites*, or mussels and french fries. Beside the entrance was a small table for three with a sign reading "Reserved for Toots Thielemans." We had lots of mussels, and there was a big bowl on the table that the waiter kept refilling with french fries. Almost every person who walked by knew Toots, and, as they would stop to talk, they would help themselves to some french fries. About 10 p.m., we walked to the train station. As I boarded the train for Paris, Toots said, "The next time you're here, I want you to show me some of that country stuff."

The harmonica was also the catalyst for a great relationship that I developed with a family from Virginia. During the early 1970s, I visited many record stores to promote my records. When we visited in the early 1970s I did a lot of in-store record promotions. In the Norfolk-Newport News area, we played several stores in a single day, and I noticed that one man was at every store. At the last store, he came up to me and introduced himself as Roy Burcher, and he told me that he had purchased my first two albums and was trying to learn to play "country style." Since we were done with the day's visits, I had extra time to talk with him, and we chatted for a while. At the end of the conversation, he invited me to come back to play at the Moose Club in Newport News a couple of months later.

When I brought the Charlie McCoy Band back a few months later, we were welcomed like old friends. Roy's wife, June, fixed a big dinner at their house, and his entire family—brother Bland (a bassist), sons Dale and Skip, and daughters Nancy and Gail—was there. Over the years, we made many trips to that area, and the Burchers became like family. The family came up to Fayetteville for our concerts and visited us in Nashville. Roy joined SPAH and even played there a couple of times. The Burchers are truly wonderful people.

Many people ask me about my harmonicas. Since the very beginning, I have had a long association with Hohner, the old German company that builds the best harmonicas in the business. My relationship with them began early in my session years, thanks to their public relations man, Gil Mathies. During Gil's tenure in the public relations department, they created a Charlie McCoy display for music stores; it featured the Old Standby harps that I played in my early days. Through Gil, I was able to get Hohner to start making harps in twelve keys (to correspond to each of the twelve chromatic pitches) rather than the seven keys that they were manufacturing at the time. When I first started making records, I sometimes had to lay out because the song changed to a key that I didn't have a harp for.

One day, a sixty-five-year-old man named Duane Parker visited my office at Monument. A house painter from upstate New York, he had just moved to Nashville. He explained that he had played the chromatic harp his entire life and didn't think much of the ten-hole harp until he had heard one of my records. He was especially curious about my recording of "Danny Boy," which I had played using two harmonicas. He figured that the only way that I could have recorded it was to take the side off the harmonica and use a razor blade to tune the fifth draw reed up one half step. He then proceeded to demonstrate using one harmonica.

"Is that the way you did it?" he asked.

"No," I replied, "but that's the way I'm going to do it from now on.

This new instrument became known as a "country-tuned" harp, and, through Gil's successor at Hohner, Jack Kavoukian, I was able to call attention to this tuning. Now, Hohner manufactures country-tuned harmonicas for the general public.

My relationship with Hohner has been a special one. They presented me with a sterling silver chromatic harmonica at a National Association of Music Merchants show in Chicago. Hohner has also helped to make me a hero when, in 2012 and 2013, their new artist relations man, Derrick Crowder, gave me thirty harmonicas to give to two of my grandsons' classes.

I've always been more than happy to show other harmonica players some new licks and to be supportive of folks who are just starting to learn to play. But, in the 1990s, I made some of my first serious efforts to formalize my teaching. Pat Conway, an Irishman who represented a British company called Music Sales, called to let me know that they were interested in producing an instructional video with me. He was their producer, and he invited me to come to Ireland to make the video. Although I had been a music education major for a year, I didn't really have much of an idea about how to organize the lessons or what to say. He told me that I shouldn't worry; he would, as he had with dozens of other musicians, handle all those details, even though he wasn't a musician.

I flew to Dublin, and Pat met me at the airport. He had a very heavy accent, and it was hard for me to understand him until after we'd been talking for almost thirty minutes. He asked me questions about my playing and about the ways that I did different things. After about an hour, he said, "Well, we've got enough for two videos now." His plan was for me to talk about a technique, play a song using it, and then play that song with a band. Lucky for me, Downs Thompson was living in Dublin, so I called him to organize a band. The guys he got to play with me—guitarist Jimmy Smyth, bassist Eoghan O'Niell, and drummer Ray Fean—later played with the *Riverdance* tour. I spent quite a bit of time in my hotel room writing tunes to go with the techniques that Pat said we needed to include.

We made the videos in two locations. The first was located in a small coastal town called Laytown in County Meath. Pat borrowed a vacant house and hired a cameraman and a soundman. Unfortunately, a big storm came that day, and the wind was so loud that we had to do a retake in one section. Every time the wind got loud, the two tech guys wanted to take a break to go to the pub. The second location was a performance hall, where Downs and the band joined us to record all the tunes.

We created enough material on that trip to make two videos: *Beginning Country Harp* (which was also published as a book) and *Country Harp Techniques*. A couple of years later, Pat asked me to do two more books for Music Sales. The first was a set of instructions, while the second was a songbook with fifty-seven new harp songs. Fifty-two of them were in the key of G, because most harp players have a harp in the key of C, the harp I use to play in G. We recorded all fifty-seven songs at Wayne Moss's Cinderella Sound. By the end, the band and I were tired of the key of G!

In the internet age, it's a lot easier to get instructional materials into the hands of the people who want to learn just about anything. In the summer of 2010, my French friend Annabel contacted me about a group of guys in Corsica, a beautiful island just southeast of France, who were creating a web platform for music instruction. With some free time in my tour schedule that August, I agreed to travel to Corsica to become an internet harmonica teacher.

When I arrived, I met the team: producer Stephane Chauffriat, engineer Paul Cesari, camera man Paul Miniconi, and bassist Jean Castelli. They had a very interesting concept. A potential student can go to the website, which has lessons for several different instruments. Once students select the instrument that they want to study, they pay a monthly fee for unlimited access to the video lessons. My lessons—which we filmed over four days—allow the students to either play along with me or turn my audio off and play with the backing track.

Although I've published some instructional materials over the past two decades or so, one of the most interesting teaching experiences I've had was a one-on-one lesson. In the winter of 2002, I received an email from Patience Humphrey, a woman living in Cleveland, Ohio. She asked me if I could come to Cleveland to play for her husband's sixtieth birthday party and give him a harmonica lesson while I was there. I agreed, and we worked out all the details.

I have never been to a birthday party like this. They had a sit-down dinner for four hundred of their closest friends, and the entire party was full of pomp and circumstance. A Marine Corps color guard escorted the birthday cake into the room, bagpipers were stationed at the front door, and a ten-piece band played for dancing. Patience's husband, George, was a shy man, but we convinced him to come up on stage with me to play "Orange Blossom Special."

Sometime after the party, George and I met at his mother's plantation in Tallahassee, Florida, for another lesson. George also introduced me to Mike Purvis, a veterinarian in Monticello, Florida, whose brothers, Frank and Wendell, have a band called Encore. I have done several concerts with them in Monticello and the surrounding area.

The harmonica has been very good to me. My mother's willingness to mail in fifty cents and a box top and to put up with my huffing and puffing has translated into a long career that has taken me all over the world. I'm glad she gave me the chance to get started.

REFLECTIONS ON A GOOD LIFE

I've had the great pleasure of making a living in music for nearly sixty years. During that time, I've recorded with some of the leading artists in the country, rock, and pop fields, and I've built a career as a solo recording artist here in the United States and overseas. It's hard to imagine sometimes that I've been able to do most of the things that I set out to do when I first decided to make music my profession. I know that I have been blessed, and I don't take that for granted.

Over the years, I've seen lots of changes in musical style, the music industry, and the city of Nashville. Some of these changes have been for the better, making our lives and our jobs easier, while others, I think, have had a negative effect.

Music is always changing to reflect the tastes and interests of record buyers. Ever since the first country recordings were made in the 1920s, artists have been trying to get their listeners' attention, whether it was Jimmie Rodgers singing blue yodels, the addition of electric lead and steel guitars in the music of Ernest Tubb, or the cosmopolitan country sounds of Charlie Rich, Reba McEntire, or Martina McBride. But no amount of novelty can keep audiences coming back to an artist if the artist doesn't perform with passion.

I witnessed the power of passionate performance many times during my career, but one moment stands out. I was booked to play for the Music Operators of America—the jukebox operators—in Chicago one time during the mid-1970s. The show included artists who played in a variety of musical styles, including some pop acts, the great harp player Norton Buffalo, and, of all things, a polka band called Little Wally Pickle and His Polka Band. I have never been a big fan of polka music, although I've played "Beer Barrel Polka" at a dance or two. As we waited backstage, I could watch Willy's band—which included an accordion, two clarinets, bass, and Little Wally, who played drums standing up—do their thing. They were so passionate about the music and could communicate their excitement to the crowd quite well. To boot, they were excellent musicians who clearly took their craft seriously. By the end of the set, I was patting my foot and wishing for an encore!

I had a similar experience when I was traveling in the Czech Republic with Druhá Tráva. We were playing a festival, and, despite the rain and temperatures around 50 degrees, the audience was there for the duration. The group that played right before us was from Romania, and they played folk music that was full of strange time signatures that I couldn't even snap my fingers to. They sang in Romanian, so we couldn't understand what they were trying to say, but the music had so much feeling and soul that we couldn't ignore it. I hated to see them finish their set because I wanted to hear even more.

When I was a teenager, I was something of a musical snob, but, over the years, I have come to appreciate lots of different kinds of music. Still, there are some forms of music that I just don't care for. I understand why rap and hip-hop were created, but it seems to me like poetry over computers, rhythm without music. Compared to the music that came out of Motown, Memphis, Philadelphia, and Muscle Shoals, rap and hip-hop seem to require very little talent or creativity.

I have similar issues with a lot of contemporary country music. Although I'm still involved in recording, I am no longer in the mainstream. The business is run by young people who have recording budgets that are far larger than we ever could have dreamed of back in the 1960s and 1970s. Most session musicians charge "double scale," or twice as much as the rate set by the musicians' union because they have the artist's money to play with. Sessions drag on much longer than they did in my time as well because musicians play the same parts over and over again in an attempt to create a "perfect" recording. With seemingly unlimited budgets and the technology to play almost anything, musicians tend to get lazy. In the days of the A-Team, we did our best to get it right the first time because the labels kept the budgets slim and expected us to cut as much material as possible in a very short time. At the same time, I know that there are a lot of great session musicians who have pride in their work and who are as dedicated to their craft as we were.

The development of digital recording technology has also had an impact on the sounds of contemporary productions. Computers give us an unlimited number of tracks, and many producers use those tracks to build layer after layer of musical material. As a consequence, there is always something going on in the background of the song. There's never any space between the lyrics. Listen to Merle Haggard's recording of "Today, I Started Loving You Again," and all you'll hear is a strumming acoustic guitar, a few runs on the low strings, and a great singer delivering great lyrics. I tried listening to a new hit album by one of the more recent country stars on a long drive back from a gig in south Alabama, and, after nineteen songs, the production left me exhausted, despite stellar singing and lyrics.

Although technology has come a long way, I think that we may have taken a step backwards in the ways that we use it. One example is when producers decide to use drum loops on a recording. Rather than having one of Nashville's great drummers come into the studio and lay down a solid drum part, they program the computer to play a repeated pattern that just lays down a basic beat. A live drummer can respond to what's going on in the music, but a computer can only do what it's programmed to do. I think that takes some of the soul out of a lot of contemporary music.

Nowadays, the record business has become even more about marketing than ever before. A new artist today must be "video-friendly" and look good on camera. Combine that with modern recording technologies that allow artists to retune their vocals or even add a word or a single letter to their performance, and we have many artists who pass the camera test but aren't really musicians.

Our current situation reminds me of an old comedy record by Stan Freberg called "The Old Payola Roll Blues." These record producers had recorded a track, and they were heard to say, "Well, we have almost everything we need, rhythm section, horns, background vocals, all we need is a teenage idol." They go outside to find one and ask a good-looking teenaged boy if he can sing. When he replies that he can't, the producer says, "Great, come on in and stand behind that microphone." The kid, surveying the studio, sees a stick and asks, "What are you going to do with that sharp stick?" The producer asks the engineer to roll tape, and, in the middle of the song, we hear the kid let out a scream. "Great, kid," the producer says. "It's a hit!"

Television has been an important part of marketing artists and their music, and, in the United States, we watch more television than just about anyone else in the world. Television sales have helped some artists make great inroads with their audiences. Christy Lane, for instance, had one of the best-selling albums of all time with *One Day at a Time* thanks to her exposure on television. And, of course, the people who performed on the old Perry Como, Dean Martin, and Ed Sullivan shows delivered memorable live performances that still hold up today. And I'm proud to say that our *Hee Haw* performances were high quality and always live.

Unfortunately, as television has become more and more important to the way that records are sold, the record labels have demanded a level of musical perfection from their artists that ticket-buying audiences don't expect. It's not uncommon for artists to sing to prerecorded backing tracks on national television, even when they have a live band onstage. Those musicians are often just pantomiming, despite the fact that the staff band is often made up of the same musicians who played on the record in the first place. It's been my experience that, if someone's favorite artist performs a favorite song, the audience is happy, and it doesn't matter if it sounds exactly like the record.

Another downside to television's increasing importance in the record business is the music video. Music videos are the worst thing that ever happened to our business. Great performances of great songs can communicate deep meanings, and any person with a hint of intelligence can hear great lyrics and imagine a picture that is much better than anything that a television producer can create. As a marketing tool, music videos might be very effective, but they also don't leave much room for anyone who isn't young and good-looking. In the video age, it would be hard for someone like Willie Nelson, Johnny Cash, Ernest Tubb, or Kris Kristofferson to get signed today.

I have seen a lot of artists come and go during my time in Nashville. It takes a lot of ego to get up in front of a group of people and ask them to listen to you sing or play. It takes even more to ask them to pay for that privilege. Artists have to believe that they have something to offer, and that has led some amazingly talented artists to shoot their careers in the foot by acting inappropriately around people, both inside and outside the business. The old adage remains true: "You meet the same people on the way up that you later meet on the way down."

With success comes the adoration of the fans. The fans really ask very little. They buy records and concert tickets, and the only thing they ask for free is perhaps an autograph. I have heard artists say, "I gave them everything I had on stage, so there will be no autographs." There are certainly times when I don't necessarily wish to sign an autograph, such as when I'm in the middle of a big bite of food at a restaurant, but for the most part, I'm more than happy to oblige.

In my mind, it is such a privilege to play or sing for a living. It beats the heck out of digging ditches.

Just as the music industry has changed over the last six decades, so, too, has the city of Nashville. When I first moved here, Nashville was a typical southern city with a courthouse square and lots of good restaurants serving "meat and three," where the vegetables were fresh and cooked with lots of grease. You couldn't buy liquor by the drink in Nashville, except in Printer's Alley, where they served every night. (When I played in the Alley with the Escorts, there would be a raid from time to time; the police would come in, look around, and then leave!)

During the 1960s, Nashville was becoming known as "Music City," which led a lot of people to wonder about the name. There were just a few live music venues in town, mostly in Printer's Alley and Lower Broad, where a lot of locals felt uneasy. Now, we have many great music venues where people can hear great musicians every night of the week. Personally, I love to visit the Station Inn to hear great bluegrass and western swing and the Bluebird Café, where many of the city's best songwriters come to play. We also have one of the finest symphony orchestras in the United States. This is a town where musical energy is always present. You never know when your waitress at a restaurant might be the next big star or be just minutes away from writing a hit song.

The city really began to change during the 1990s, when city officials began to clean up the downtown area. At one time, locals didn't feel comfortable walking downtown after dark, but now, Nashville's downtown is a happening place. These changes brought the new Country Music Hall of Fame facility, the Schermerhorn Symphony Center, the Musicians' Hall of Fame, and lots of new music venues, hotels, and restaurants. With fine universities and colleges, hospitals, and the music industry all here in Nashville, it's a great place to live.

I've been a huge sports fan since I was a little kid, so I was thrilled to see two national sports teams move to Nashville in the late 1990s. Nashville has been home to a minor league baseball team—the Nashville Sounds—for many years, but the introduction of the National Football League's Tennessee Titans and the National Hockey League's Nashville Predators really improved our sports options in Music City.

My first love was baseball. When I was a kid, my mother and I would sit on a blanket out in the yard with a pitcher of Kool-Aid and listen to the Mutual Radio Network's "Game of the Day." It was a lot like the great Lionel Cartwright record, "I Watched It All (On My Radio)," which captures how the announcers painted a perfect picture of what was happening on the field. Through those experiences, I became a huge St. Louis Cardinals fan, and my favorite player was Stan "The Man" Musial. If you had told me that I'd be able to meet him and even play the harmonica with him (let alone on national television!), I wouldn't have believed it.

I've had the opportunity to watch a lot of great baseball games over the years, including six World Series games, two MLB All-Star Games, and the game when Hank Aaron beat Babe Ruth's home run record. My love of baseball remained with me until the player strikes of the early 1990s. My interest in the sport waned as players refused to accept a salary cap, pushing some of the small-market, low-income teams out of the running before the season even begins. Minor league and college baseball, however, still bring me a lot of joy. The AAA Nashville Sounds are great fun because the guys are top-notch players, but they're not earning the superstar salaries of the majors and bringing the egos that come with them. And the Vanderbilt University baseball program has been fun to watch over the years.

Football has also been an important part of my life, from high school ball to college and professional games. I tend to pull for the college teams that prioritize academic standards and use the players' grades to determine who gets a scholarship, schools like Vanderbilt, Duke, Notre Dame, Northwestern, Army, Navy, and Air Force. Most of the headlines concerning athletes from these schools are about their gameplay and not about their legal troubles. I also love the Tennessee Titans, and it seems like most of the city feels the same way because every home game has been a sellout since they moved to town. It really bothers me, though, that NFL teams pay so much money for untried rookies. I think they should receive a standard salary (perhaps one that reflects their draft position) and then renegotiate for the mother lode if they have a great rookie season. NFL fans are always excited when their team drafts a high-profile college player no matter what the cost, but those costs trickle down to the ticket holders.

Over the years, I've been fortunate to attend Super Bowls II and III—my dad bought the Super Bowl III tickets directly from the Orange Bowl ticket office just one week before the game—and I was lucky to be in the crowd for the so-called "Music City Miracle" when the Titans defeated the Buffalo Bills in 2000.

Most people would probably be surprised to learn that I'm also a hockey fanatic and have been since the 1960s. In 1963, Nashville built its Municipal Auditorium, and they brought in a hockey team called the Nashville Dixie Flyers, a club in the Eastern Hockey League. This was bush league hockey at its best, just like in the movie *Slap Shot*. The team traveled in a rickety old bus that broke down all the time and had only intermittent heat. One time, on a road trip in the north, they played seven games in eight nights in the dead of winter with no heat on the bus. A musician might say, "We have tours that are that tough, as well. What's the big deal?" The difference is that a musician's audience comes to the shows to love you; the out-of-town hockey fans hate you, and their players are always trying to hit you.

When my son was five years old, he started playing ice hockey, and I was drafted to coach. When one is dealing with kids who are five and six years old, coaching is little more than making sure that the kids get equal playing time. It's amazing to watch young kids learn to skate because they have no fear and don't get embarrassed when they fall. And when they do fall—which happens often when they're getting started—they never get hurt because they are so relaxed. Although it wasn't required for coaches, I decided to learn to skate. I finally got to the point where I wouldn't fall, and I learned one important lesson: When you go to public skating, stay away from the side boards. If you go out in the middle, there are people who can skate, and they won't run in to you.

I found one musician who was a huge hockey fan: Ray Edenton. Each February for two or three years, we traveled to the Baltimore-Philadelphia area to take in as many hockey games as possible. Since there were five hockey teams in the area, it was pretty easy to stay entertained. One "hockey crazies" weekend, we saw the NHL's Philadelphia Flyers on Thursday, took the train to Baltimore to see the AHL's Baltimore Skip Jacks on Friday, returned to Philadelphia on Saturday for an afternoon Flyers game before driving to Hershey, Pennsylvania, to see the AHL's Hershey Bears, and then watched the EHL's Jersey Devils in Cherry Hill, New Jersey, and the WHA's Philadelphia Blazers on Sunday. We were definitely fanatics!

In 1972, the NHL came to Atlanta. Ray and I went completely off the deep end and bought season tickets for the new Atlanta Flames. We would finish a 10 a.m. session and drive like maniacs to get to Atlanta in time for the opening face-off. When the game was over, we sped back home so we could make our morning session, listening to the CB radio to keep the "smokies"—police—off our tail. It was probably good for our health that, after seven years, the Flames moved to Calgary. It must have been good for the Flames, too, because they won the Stanley Cup just a few years later. In Atlanta, there were nights when the team seemed to be just going through the motions, but, then again, they didn't really have the fan support that they received in Canada, where hockey is a national pastime.

In 1998, a millionaire from Milwaukee named Craig Leopold got an expansion team in the NHL, and he brought it to Nashville, where they could play in a brand-new sparkling seventeen-thousand-seat arena. A group of musicians got together and went down to pick out our season ticket seats. Of course, Ray and I were right there in the middle of the crowd. The Nashville Predators have given me so much pleasure. They're a hard-working, blue-collar team that always shows up and gives 100 percent, unlike the old Atlanta Flames.

I have had the good fortune to attend two Olympics: 1976 in Montreal and 1996 in Atlanta. In 1996, we attended the women's gold medal team handball game at the Olympics. I was introduced to the sport in Denmark, where it was invented. Played on a basketball court, it resembles soccer because there is a goalie who guards the goal from the other six players on the court. The game is fast and furious! At the 1996 Olympics, the Danish team won the gold medal in an exciting overtime game against South Korea. After we returned to Nashville, I made a copy of my ticket and faxed it—without a word—to Calle, my Danish agent. Shortly after I faxed it, the phone rang. It was Calle, asking, "Were you there? Our whole country stayed up very late in the night to watch it."

As much as I have enjoyed watching sports over the years, I've also had a great time coaching and playing some, too. In the late 1960s, Buddy Harman told me that he was interested in starting a bowling league for music business folks to get together on a Sunday night. We initially thought about having a men's league, but we realized that our wives stayed at home all week while we were in the studio. We formed a mixed league with teams that had two men and two women. The initial response was great, and we started with sixty-four people. The league continued for forty years before it disbanded, having provided entertainment, exercise, and social time for more than two hundred people over the years. My wife, Pat, and I had to drop out in 1998 because we were going to live in Florida for the winter.

Over the course of those four decades, there were some great highlights. One time, a studio violinist named Alan Umstead bowled a perfect game, which is not something that you get to see very often. And on two occasions, the cowboy star Roy Rogers came out to bowl as a substitute. The first time, another league was finishing their games, and I could see that word was getting around the bowling alley that Roy Rogers was in the house. Roy was "ghermed" badly by the folks in the earlier league. The second time he came to bowl with us, we had him come in at the last minute so the experience could be more peaceful for him. By the way, Roy was a 185-average bowler.

Sports and music have a lot in common with one another. Just as an average team can beat a team of superstars when they work together, a band with limited talent can often outshine a band of amazing musicians when they cooperate.

Nashville has been my home since 1960, but, beginning in 1998, Pat and I have been spending the winter months in Florida. When I was a kid in Miami, we joked about the "snowbirds" who came to Florida to escape the cold northern winters, but, with my studio work slowing, we decided that it might be nice to spend some time in the Sunshine State. That winter, we bought a condo in Fort Myers, where we've spent every winter for nearly twenty years. When I arrived in January 1999 with a Ford Explorer loaded down with clothes, computers, a guitar, and the frame of a rollaway bed, I'm sure that my new next-door neighbor, Georgette McGauley, thought the Beverly Hillbillies were moving in next door. And during our first week or so there, I had serious doubts about whether the move was the right one; everyone in our neighborhood seemed to be ten or fifteen years older than we were. Fortunately, as we started meeting people, we realized that these were active seniors who played golf and tennis and swam regularly. Now our snowbird stays are filled with card games, cookouts, and all sorts of social gatherings, and our friends in Florida have become such a special part of our lives.

Nowadays, I still play several shows each year, and I play several sessions each month. I've returned to writing songs from time to time, and I'm finding that, with additional practice, the songs come easier each time. I have also played a role in telling the story of Nashville's music industry thanks to a Swedish promoter named Bruno Tillander, who organizes trips to New Orleans, Memphis, and Nashville for European tourists. They start in New Orleans, where they get to meet Fats Domino, see Bourbon Street and Preservation Hall, and take in some of New Orleans's great restaurants. On the bus trip from New Orleans to Memphis, they meet James Burton in Natchez and hear some Delta blues music in Clarksdale, Mississippi. In Memphis, they visit Graceland, Beale Street, Sun Records, Stax, and sometimes meet the sibling of an artist like Jerry Lee Lewis. Then they stop in Jackson, Tennessee, to visit the Rockabilly Hall of Fame before traveling to Nashville, where they meet up with me. I introduce them to the Country Music Hall of Fame, the Musicians' Hall of Fame, and RCA Studio B. The next day, we take them on a tour of Music Row and the homes of some of Nashville's biggest stars before stopping at the *Grand Ole Opry*, where an *Opry* artist surprises them with a special mini-concert. I have great fun on these tours, and the tourists are always surprised when I can speak Danish or pull out my harp to play a bit of "Stone Fox Chase" for the British visitors.

Pat and I have also become very deeply involved in our church community. Despite being a spiritual person with a belief in God, I hadn't felt at home in a church since high school. That changed on Easter Sunday of 2000, when Pat and I visited Bellevue Community Church in the Nashville suburbs. We had heard great things about the music, which was led by Lionel Cartwright, a former Nashville recording artist whom I had met on the television show *I-40 Paradise*, and we were not disappointed. (Sadly, the record business dropped the ball with him, and he never became the superstar that he should've been.) And when we heard the minister, Dr. David Foster, speak, we felt that he was someone who understood us and our needs. We became members of Bellevue Community Church, and volunteered our time there. Pat worked in the office, and I played music in the services from time to time. When, in 2006, the church decided to fire Dr. Foster, we followed him to his new church, The Gathering. Ken and Barbie Isham became the music leaders, and now I play every Sunday when I'm in town with a great band composed of drummer Ted Tretiak, guitarists Leigh Reynolds and Ken and Jim Long, fiddler and vocalist Loretta Brank, keyboardists Dave Innis (of Restless Heart) and Zack Forbes, and a rotating cast of bassists that includes Robert Kerns, who currently plays with Sheryl Crow. Sadly, Dr. Foster passed away in his sleep in April 2012, but the church is still going strong.

Without a doubt, I have had the great fortune to have a wonderful family that has taught me so much. My grandmother, Esther Kelley, lived in the coal mine camps for most of her life and, with six children to care for, found a way to survive despite all the work stoppages that were common in those days. She was a devoutly religious woman who played the piano at two churches each Sunday. My mother, Opal Kelley Thrift, was never hindered by the fact that she was a coal miner's daughter. She survived three rough marriages, giving my brother and me a set of values that we never forgot even when it must have been hard for her. She became interested in etiquette and read Emily Post to teach herself how to be at home in any situation, whether it was in the company of coal miners or heads of state. Always a mother, when she was diagnosed with cancer at Duke University Hospital, the only thing she could talk about was whether I had been taking the medicine that I had been prescribed for a bad cold. My first wife, Susan Bennett Mayo, raised our two children practically single-handedly because I was doing four hundred or more sessions each year when the kids were young. She is always the first person to come to someone's aid, and, now a minister's wife, she supports a very lucky congregation.

My wife, Pat Maguire McCoy, loves me even when I don't understand why. Of course, I have to believe her because I know that she always sees the truth and tells it like it is, no matter how hard the truth might be to hear. She is one of the most organized people I have ever met. I always thought that I was fairly organized for a musician, but I'm a bumbling idiot in comparison to her. During her nineteen years at the musicians' union, she handled all the musician payments for recordings, television, and radio, doing it all by hand. Today, it is done by four people using computers! Pat is also quick to lend a hand, and she is constantly volunteering, whether for the Nashville Humane Society, Hands On Nashville, or our church. I feel very fortunate to have found my soul mate in her.

My greatest productions are my two kids, Ginger McCoy Jordan and Charles Ray McCoy Jr. Ginger has had an amazing career as a labor and delivery nurse at Nashville's Baptist Hospital, the busiest labor and delivery hospital in Tennessee. She graduated with her RN from Belmont University in Nashville and a B.S. in nursing from the University of Tennessee—Memphis. She's currently working on her master's degree. Ginger is raising three fine kids: Hannah, Abby, and Austin Jordan. Hannah—who played flute on *A Celtic Bridge*—graduated from Tennessee Tech University with a degree in elementary education and is teaching second grade in Gallatin, Tennessee. Abby designed the album covers for my *Over the Rainbow, Smooth Sailing,* and *Celtic Dreams* albums and is a student at the University of Arkansas. Austin Jordan is quite an athlete, playing on his high school football team. Ginger is not only a great nurse and mother, but she has a strong Christian faith that helped her win her fight with breast cancer.

Charlie McCoy Jr. graduated from Tennessee Tech University with a degree in computer science. He works for a Houston-based company that has sent him around the world to help clients solve computer problems. Some of his destinations have been India, Sweden, Switzerland, England, and Scotland. He is very talented playing guitar, bass, and keyboards, and he is the worship leader for his church. An active cyclist, he has explored many miles of the Swamp Rabbit Trail in Greenville, South Carolina. He is the father of two great kids: Caroline and Bennett. Caroline plays piano, violin, and guitar and is a student at the College of Charleston. Bennett, like his cousin Austin, is very athletic and very excited about baseball.

My life has been filled with so many blessings. I have been able to make a living doing the thing that I love most. I have had the opportunity to spend much of my time in the company of some of the most talented people on earth. I've made friends all over the world. And I have a loving family that continues to bring me joy every day. In August 2010, a French reporter asked me what I thought the keys to happiness were. I told him that I didn't know about other people, but for me it was *"Le bon Dieu, la bonne femme, la bonne famille, le bon santé, la bonne musique, et les bons amis"* [A good God, a good wife, a good family, good health, good music, and good friends]. With those simple but important things in my life, I know that I lived a good life.

A NOTE ON SOURCES

Travis D. Stimeling

Charlie first approached me to take a look at a manuscript that he'd been working on during an interview that I conducted with him on July 30, 2014. After our initial meeting, he forwarded the manuscript—totaling more than 100,000 words—to me. I read it eagerly, anxious to learn everything that I could about Charlie's remarkable career. As I read it, though, it became clear that, although the facts of Charlie's life and career were inherently interesting to me as a longtime fan and scholar of country music, significant revision would be necessary to trace a narrative through the book. After several phone conversations and email exchanges, Charlie agreed to let me work on the book. Much of the material in this book originated in that first manuscript, while some additional passages are drawn from Charlie's responses to questions that I sent him via email. The discussion of Charlie's performance with Willie Nelson at the Jimmie Rodgers Memorial Festival came from the interview that I conducted with him in July 2014.

Additional sources were used to confirm dates, spellings, and chart positions. Songwriting credits were confirmed using Broadcast Music, Inc.'s online repertoire database (www.repertoire.bmi.com), while chart positions were confirmed using Academic Rights Press's Music Industry Data database and Joel Whitburn's *Top Country Singles, 1944–2001* (Menomoneee Falls, WI: Record Research, Inc., 2002). Additional discographical information was drawn from www.discogs.com, the Charlie McCoy discography at www.rocky-52.net, and *Prague Frank's LP Discography* (www.lpdiscography.com). Additional dates were confirmed using the Internet Movie Database (www.imdb.com) and Wikipedia (www.wikipedia.org). Michael Krogsgaard's "Bob Dylan: The Recording Sessions, Part Two" (available online at www.punkhart. com/dylan/sessions-2.html), proved to be particularly helpful in organizing the timeline for Charlie's sessions with Dylan.

The Encyclopedia of Country Music, 2nd ed. (New York: Oxford University Press, 2012) provided important biographical background on several figures discussed in the book, as did Peter Cooper's obituary for Jimmy C. Newman (published in *The Tennesseean*, June 22, 2014), Dave Laing's obituary for Shelby Singleton (published in *The Guardian*, October 12, 2009), and an unsigned obituary for Marijohn Wilkin (published at www.CMT.com, October 28, 2006). Mel Tillis's early popularity was confirmed in "The Billboard 11th Annual Disc Jockey Poll" (*Billboard* [November 17, 1958], 20).

Information on Hewgley's Music Store was drawn from their company history, published on their website (www.hewgleysmusic.com/ about). Information about Nashville's recording scene was confirmed using RCA Studio B's website (www.studiob.org), as well as a 1970 *Billboard* magazine essay ("Nashville Studios—At Full Schedule," *Billboard* [October 17, 1970], CM-48). Additional background on Woodland Studios was gathered from "Is East Nashville Becoming a Recording Studio Mecca?" (*Nashville Skyline* [October 14, 2006], www.nashvilleskyline.org/legacy/music/is-east-nashville-becoming-a-recording-studio-mecca). The early history of music video and cable television is traced in Rob Tannenbaum and Craig Marks's *I Want My MTV: The Uncensored History of the Music Video Revolution* (New York: Dutton, 2011), and information about the television program *Yesteryear* was taken from a press release dated August 18, 1994 (archived at www.the freelibrary.com / EDDY + RAVEN + TO CO-HOST + 'YESTERYEAR' -a015718282).

Descriptions of Charlie's West Virginia homes, Oak Hill and Fayetteville, were drawn from the Federal Writers' Project's *West Virginia:*

A Guide to the Mountain State ([New York: Oxford University Press, 1941], 398-99). Additional information about Mme. Renée Longy was drawn from the Longy School of Music (www.longy.edu/about/history) and Humphrey Burton's *Leonard Bernstein* ([New York: Doubleday, 1994)], 67-68). The history of the Frost School of Music at the University of Miami is discussed in their institutional history (published at www.miami.edu/frost/index.php/frost/about_us/frost_school_history); additional information is found in Laura Capell's finding aid for the Dr. John Bitter Collection in the University of Miami's Special Collections (http://proust.library.miami.edu/findingaids/?p=collections/findingaid&id=580).

Toronto's Yonge Street music scene is very well documented. Juliette Jagger's "Historical Venue Spotlight: Le Coq d'Or" (*Noisey: Music by Vice*, http://noisey.vice.com/en_ca/read/historic-venue-spotlight-le-coq-dor) provided useful information about one of the scene's most important venues, as did Ryerson University's 2012 essay "A Historical Corner: Yonge and Gould's Musical Past" (http://news.library.ryerson.ca/musiconyonge/a-historical-corner-page-4/). Michael Dougherty's *National Post* essay, "Remembering Yonge Street's Musical Roots" (published March 19, 2011, http://news.nationalpost.com/posted-toronto/remembering-yonge-streets-musical-roots), and Alan Parker's 2011 feature on the *Toronto Sun*'s "Nosey Parker" blog (published May 5, 2011, http://blogs.canoe.com/parker/tag/edison-hotel) also proved useful. Additional information was found in director Bruce McDonald's *Yonge Street: Toronto Rock & Roll Stories* (David Brady Productions, 2011), Craig Harris's book *The Band: Pioneers of Americana Music* ([Lanham, MD: Rowman & Littlefield, 2014], 39-64), and a biographical statement published on Levon Helm's website (www.levonhelm.com/biography.htm).

To better understand Charlie's work with Bob Dylan, I consulted Sean Wilentz's excellent essay, "Mystic Nights: The Making of *Blonde on Blonde* in Nashville" (*The Oxford American*, no. 58 [2007]), as well as his insightful liner notes for the boxed set *The Cutting Edge, 1965–1966: The Bootleg Series, Vol. 12* (Sony Legacy, 2015). A visit to Bob Dylan's office in New York allowed me to listen to the complete session tapes from the *Blonde on Blonde* sessions. Finally, Al Kooper's *Backstage Passes & Backstabbing Bastards: Memoirs of a Rock 'n' Roll Survivor* (updated ed. [Milwaukee: Hal Leonard, 2008], 67) provided an alternate perspective on the Blonde on Blonde sessions, although, as Charlie points out, he did not, as Kooper asserts, play bass and trumpet simultaneously on any of the recordings from those sessions.

Finally, one of the most valuable resources in this process has been the remarkable archive of music that Charlie has left for us all to enjoy. Spending time listening to the music of someone who was already one of my favorite musicians has allowed me to deepen my appreciation of his work and to broaden my understanding of the complex pop music landscape of the past sixty years.

—

THE NASHVILLE NUMBER SYSTEM

Charlie McCoy

One day on a session, Wayne Moss asked me, "Do you understand what Neal Matthews of the Jordanaires is writing down when we start learning a song?"

"Yes, it's music shorthand," I replied. "I studied it in college."

"Could you explain it to me?" he asked.

"I'll try," I said. I explained to Wayne how the numbers corresponded with the root note of the chords and the steps of the scale. Instead of saying the old Italian do, re, mi, fa, sol, la, and ti, we say, 1, 2, 3, 4, 5, 6, 7.

Wayne tried it out and proved to be a quick study. Soon he was using it for every session, checking with me to make sure that he'd gotten everything right. Before long, Harold Bradley wanted to learn, too, and lots of other session musicians picked it up after him. Now, it's the standard way that we write charts in Nashville, and I've even seen it used in Europe and Japan.

There have been three books on the subject. Neal Matthews wrote the first one, and there were two other written by guitar player Chaz Williams. On his first book, Chaz asked some of Nashville's session players to write charts on five country standards to show the subtle differences in the ways that we each notate the song. In his second book, Chaz included a compact disc of some of his original songs and had several of us write charts for them. Any time I'm asked about books on the Nashville Number System, I always recommend Chaz's.

The Nashville Number System is built on knowledge of how the musical scale works. There are three important things that you need to know about scales:

1. Each musical scale consists of eight notes, and the notes in them are labeled with the letters from A through G.
2. There are whole tones between each letter *except* between B and C *and* E and F, which are each separated by a half tone.
3. All major scales use the same pattern of notes:
    * Between steps 1 and 2: whole tone
    * Between steps 2 and 3: whole tone
    * Between steps 3 and 4: half tone
    * Between steps 4 and 5: whole tone
    * Between steps 5 and 6: whole tone
    * Between steps 6 and 7: whole tone
    * Between steps 7 and 8: half tone

As an example, the C major scale looks like this:

Do	Re	Mi	Fa	Sol	La	Ti	Do
C	D	E	F	G	A	B	C
1	2	3	4	5	6	7	8

Similarly, the G major scale looks like this:

Do	Re	Mi	Fa	Sol	La	Ti	Do
G	A	B	C	D	E	F#	G
1	2	3	4	5	6	7	8

In the Nashville Number System, we use the numbers to indicate which note of the scale each chord is built on. For instance, a 1 chord in the key of C major is built on C, and a 5 chord is built on G. Here's how we notate chords:

1. The chord: When we see a number standing alone, we are playing the major chord with its bass note as "Do" or "1" of the key.

2. Bass notes: If the chord has no other number indicated below it, we assume that we play the 1 chord with a 1 bass note. If the chord looks like a fraction (1/3), then the chord uses 3 (or mi) as the bass note.

3. Rhythm: If a song is in 4/4 time, the 1 that stands alone gets four beats. Likewise, if the song is in 3/4 time, the 1 gets three beats. If a bar of music has more than one chord, it is called a split bar. There are several ways to indicate these. Some people use a slash (1/4). Others use a box, like this: 1/4 . In 4/4 time, each chord would get two beats. In 3/4 time, we must indicate under the measure how many beats each chord gets.

4. Repeat signs work just like they do in standard musical notation. Similarly, D.S. (*dal segno*) tells us to go back to a special sign and repeat from there, while D.C. (*da capo*) tells us to return to the beginning of the tune and repeat from there.

Here is an example of the Nashville Number System at work. This is how I would chart the popular hymn "Amazing Grace."

"Amazing Grace"

3/4 time

1 1 4 1 1 1 5 5

1 1 4 1 6m 1/5 1 5

—

CHARLIE MCCOY ALBUM DISCOGRAPHY

HARMONICA ABBREVIATIONS

std   Standard ten-hole harmonica
ct   Country-tuned harmonica (fifth draw reed raised 1/2 tone)
dbl   third blow reed and fifth draw reed raised 1/2 tone
chr   Chromatic harmonica
vp   Hohner "Vest Pocket" harmonica sounding one octave higher than standard ten-hole harmonica
bs   Hohner bass harmonica
poly   Hohner polyphonic harmonica
v   Harmonica with "valves" on the blow reeds

....

1968   The World of Charlie McCoy   Monument SLP-18097

....

"Jump Back Baby" (C) .... F-std
"Gimmie Some Lovin'" (E) .... A-vp
"Hey Baby" (G) .... C-std
"Candy Man" (G) .... C-std
"Turn on Your Lovelight" (F) .... Bb-std
"Harpoon Man" (B) .... E-std
"Fingertips" (Bb) .... Bb-chr, Eb-std
"Up Tight" (Bb) .... Eb-std
"Ode to Billy Joe" (D) .... G-vp, G-std, bs, poly
"Shot Gun" (F) .... Bb-std
"Juke" (E) .... A-std
"Good Vibrations" (Bb, D, A, D) .... Bb-chr, D-chr, A-chr, bs

Harmonica and lead vocals: Charlie McCoy
Guitars: Mac Gayden, Wayne Moss
Piano: Bill Aikins, David Briggs
Organ: Bergen White
Trumpet: Benny McDonald, Bob Phillips, Don Sheffield
Saxophone: Wayne Butler, Jerry Tuttle
Trombone: Wayne Butler
Bass: Wayne Moss, Bergen White, Chip Young
Drums/percussion: Kenneth Buttrey, Jim Isbell
Background vocals: Mac Gayden, Ricki Page, Bergen White
Recorded at Cinderella Studio and Fred Foster Sound Studio
Engineers: Brent Maher, Wayne Moss, Tommy Strong, Neil Wilburn

| 1969 | The Real McCoy | Monument SLP-18121 |

"Orange Blossom Special" (C, F) .... F-std, Bb-std

"The Only Daddy That'll Walk the Line" (E) .... A-std, D-std, E-std

"Today I Started Loving You Again" (F#)[4] .... B-std

"Jackson" (C) .... F-std

"Hangin' On" (E) .... A-std, A-vp

"The Real McCoy" (B) .... E-std

"Son of a Preacher Man" (E) .... A-std

"Build Me Up, Buttercup" (C, D, E) .... F-std, G-vp, A-vp

"Harper Valley PTA" (A, Bb, B) .... D-std, Eb-std, E-std

"Hooked on a Feeling" (A) .... D-std

"The Games People Play" (A) .... D-std

"The Look of Love" (B, C, C#) .... E-std, F-std, F#-std

Harmonica: Charlie McCoy
Guitars: Harold Bradley, Ray Edenton, Mac Gayden, Wayne Moss, Pete Wade
Keyboards: David Briggs, Bill Pursell, Hargus "Pig" Robbins, Jerry Smith, Bergen White
Steel guitar: Weldon Myrick
Dobro: Josh Graves, Wayne Moss
Trumpet: Benny McDonald, Eddie Tinch
Saxophone: Wayne Butler, Jerry Tuttle
Trombone: Wayne Butler
Bass: Junior Huskey, Norbert Putnam, Joe Zinkan
Drums/percussion: Kenneth Buttrey, Buddy Harman, Jim Isbell, Bergen White
Background vocals: Delores Edgin, Carol Montgomery, Bergen White
Recorded at Bradley's Barn, Music City Recorders
Engineers: Tommy Strong, Charlie Tallent

1972   The Real McCoy   Monument Z-31329

"Orange Blossom Special" (C, F) .... F-std, Bb-std
"The Only Daddy That'll Walk the Line" (E) .... A-std, D-std,
                                                          E-std
"Today I Started Loving You Again" (F#) .... B-std
"Jackson" (C) .... F-std
"Hangin' On" (E) .... A-std, A-vp
"The Real McCoy" (B) .... E-std
"Lovin' Her Was Easier" (A) .... D-std
"Easy Lovin'" (Bb) .... Eb-std
"How Can I Unlove You" (C) .... F-std
"Help Me Make It Through the Night" (E) .... A-std, D-std
"Country Roads" (C) .... F-std

Harmonica: Charlie McCoy
Guitars: Jim Colvard, Ray Edenton, Mac Gayden, Wayne Moss, Bobby Thompson,
*   Pete Wade, Chip Young*
Banjo: Bobby Thompson
Steel guitar: Weldon Myrick
Dobro: Josh Graves
Piano: Hargus "Pig" Robbins, Jerry Smith
Organ: David Briggs, Dr. John Harris
Bass: Junior Huskey, Don Smith, Henry Strzelecki, Joe Zinkan
Drums/percussion: Kenneth Buttrey, Jim Isbell
Vibes: Bergen White
Background vocals: Dennis Linde, Bergen White
Recorded at Cinderella Studio, Bradley's Barn, Jack Clement Recording Studio,
*   Monument Recording Studio*
Engineers: Wayne Moss, Charlie Tallent, Mort Thomasson

....

| 1972 | Charlie McCoy | Monument KZ-31910 |

....

"Me & Bobbi McGee" (C, D) .... F-std, G-vp
"I'm So Lonesome I Could Cry" (F#, G)[5] .... B-std, C-std
"Delta Dawn" (A) .... D-std
"The First Time Ever I Saw Your Face" (Ab) .... Db-std
"I Can't Stop Loving You" (D) .... G-std, G-vp
"Grade A" (A) .... D-std
"I Really Don't Want to Know" (Eb)[6] .... Ab-std
"Woman, Sensuous Woman" (D, Eb) .... G-std, Ab-std
"To Get to You" (E, F) .... A-std, Bb-std
"Danny Boy" (F, F#) .... Bb-std, F-std, B-std, F#-std
"Rocky Top" (A) .... D-std

Harmonica: Charlie McCoy
Guitars: Jim Colvard, Ray Edenton, Mac Gayden, Grady Martin, Don Smith,
    Bobby Thompson, Pete Wade, Chip Young
Banjo: Bobby Thompson
Steel guitar: Curly Chalker, Lloyd Green, Russ Hicks, Weldon Myrick
Dobro: Josh Graves
Piano: David Briggs, Hargus "Pig" Robbins, Jerry Smith
Organ/synthesizer: Dr. John Harris
Bass: Bob Moore, Don Smith, Henry Strzelecki, Joe Zinkan
Drums/percussion/vibes: Kenneth Buttrey, Jim Isbell, Kenny Malone
Background vocals: Dennis Linde, Wayne Moss, Bergen White
Recorded at Cinderella Studio and Monument Recording
Engineers: Wayne Moss, Mort Thomasson

1973 Good Time Charlie	Monument KZ-32215

"Good Time Charlie's Got the Blues" (G)	C-std
"San Antone" (A)	D-std
"Soul Song" (G, Ab)	C-std, Db-std
"Something" (C, A)	F-std, D-std
"Minor Miner" (F#m, A)	D-std
"Don't Touch Me" (D)	G-std
"John Henry" (A)	D-std
"'Till I Get It Right" (Ab)	Db-std
"Louisiana Man" (A, D)	D-std, G-vp
"Shenandoah" (Db, D)[7]	Db-std, D-std
"Orange Blossom Special" (C, F)[8]	F-std, Bb-std

Harmonica: Charlie McCoy
Guitar: Jimmy Capps, Jim Colvard, Bobby Dyson, Ray Edenton, Grady Martin,
*   Billy Sanford, Jerry Shook, Bobby Thompson, Pete Wade, Chip Young*
Banjo: Bobby Thompson
Dobro: Josh Graves
Steel guitar: Stu Basore, Pete Drake, Russ Hicks, Weldon Myrick, Hal Rugg
Fiddle: Tommy Jackson, Shorty Lavender, Lisa Silver, Buddy Spicher
Piano: Hargus "Pig" Robbins, Jerry Smith, Jerry Whitehurst
Concertina: Doug Kershaw
Bass: Joe Allen, Bobby Dyson, Billy Linneman, Bob Moore, Don Smith, Joe Zinkan
Drums/percussion: Jerry Carrigan, Buddy Harman, Jim Isbell, Kenny Malone,
*   Farrell Morris*
Harp: Mary Alice Hoepfinger
Strings: Goodlettsville String Sextet (Lloyd Green, Dr. John Harris, Russ Hicks,
*   Tommy Jackson, Shorty Lavender, Weldon Myrick, Bill Pursell, Lisa Silver,*
*   Buddy Spicher)*
Backing vocals: Dennis Linde, Wayne Moss, Bergen White
Recorded at Cinderella Studio
Engineers: Tom Knox, Wayne Moss, Paul Richmond, Paul Skala
Harp arrangement on "Shenandoah": Bill Pursell

1973   The Fastest Harp in the South   Monument KZ-32749

"Silver Wings" (E)   ....   A-std
"Why Me, Lord?" (A)   ....   A-std, D-std
"Paper Roses" (G)   ....   G-chr
"You Are the Sunshine of My Life" (B, G#, C)   ....   E-std, Db-std,
F-std
"Almost Persuaded" (G, A)   ....   C-std, D-std
"The Fastest Harp in the South" (B)   ....   E-std
"Release Me" (D, Eb)[9]   ....   G-std, Ab-std
"Rollin' in My Sweet Baby's Arms" (B)   ....   E-std
"Behind Closed Doors" (D, Eb)   ....   G-std, Ab-std
"Faded Love/Maiden's Prayer" (D, A, F)   ....   D-std, G-std,
Bb-std
"Ruby (Are You Mad?)" (G, A, B, C#, Eb)   ....   C-std, D-std,
E-std, F#-std, Ab-vp

Harmonica: Charlie McCoy
Guitar: Tommy Allsup, Harold Bradley, Jimmy Capps, Jim Colvard, Dave Doran,
Grady Martin, Wayne Moss, Fred Newell, Pete Wade
Banjo: Bobby Thompson
Dobro: Josh Graves
Steel guitar: Stu Basore, Curly Chalker, Pete Drake, Lloyd Green, Russ Hicks,
Weldon Myrick, Hal Rugg
Keyboard: David Briggs, Chuck Cochran, Dr. John Harris, Ron Oates, Hargus
"Pig" Robbins, Buddy Skipper, Jerry Whitehurst
Bass: Joe Allen, Billy Linneman, Bob Moore, Don Smith, Henry Strzelecki, Joe
Zinkan
Drums: Kenneth Buttrey, Buddy Harman, Jim Isbell, Kenny Malone
Percussion: Farrell Morris
Background vocals: Joe Babcock, Lea Jane Berinati, Dottie Dillard, Delores Edgin,
Louis Nunley, Wendy Suits, Jeanine Walker, Bergen White, Hurshel
Wiginton, Gil Wright
Recorded at Cinderella Studio
Engineers: Wayne Moss, M. C. Rather, Paul Richmond, Paul Skala, Jerry Tuttle

1974   The Nashville Hit Man   Monument KZ-32922

"Silver Threads and Golden Needles" (G)[10] .... C-std
"Help Me" (Eb) .... Ab-std
"Fireball Mail" (C#) .... F#-std
"You Win Again" (F) .... Bb-std
"Keep on Harpin'" (A) .... D-std
"I Can't Help It" (E, F) .... A-std, Bb-std
"T. D.'s Boogie Woogie" (F)[11] .... F-chr, Bb-std
"The Way We Were" (A) .... A-chr
"Heart Over Mind" (A) .... D-std
"Ruby" (F) .... F-std
"Let Me Be There" (A) .... D-std

Harmonica: Charlie McCoy
Guitars: Tommy Allsup, Harold Bradley, Jim Colvard, Terry Dearmore, Ray
   Edenton, Bobby Dyson, Dave Kirby, Fred Newell, Leon Rhodes, Billy
   Sanford, Dale Sellers, Bobby Thompson, Jimmy Wilkerson, Chip Young
Banjo: Bobby Thompson
Steel guitar: Russ Hicks, Weldon Myrick, Hal Rugg, Jim Vest
Dobro: Josh Graves, Russ Hicks
Fiddle: Johnny Gimble, Buddy Spicher
Keyboards/bells: Larry Butler, John Propst, Hargus "Pig" Robbins, Buddy Skipper,
   Jerry Smith
Bass: Johnny Johnson, Billy Linneman, Wayne Moss, Don Smith, Joe Zinkan
Drums/percussion: Kenneth Buttrey, Si Edwards, Jim Isbell, Kenny Malone, Farrell
   Morris, Jerry White
Clarinet: Buddy Skipper
Strings: Byron Bach, Brenton Banks, George Binkley, Marvin Chantry, Carl
   Gorodetzky, Lenny Haight, Sheldon Kurland, Martha McCrory, Steve
   Smith, Gary VanOsdale, Stephanie Woolf
Background vocals: Russ Hicks, Carol Montgomery, Buddy Skipper, Wendy Suits,
   Bergen White
Recorded at Cinderella Studio, Starday Studio
Engineers: Wayne Moss, Paul Skala, Mike Stone
String arrangements: Charlie McCoy, Bill McElhiney

1974 Christmas	Monument KZ-33176

"Jingle Bells" (G, Bb, D, G) .... C-std
"White Christmas" (Bb) .... Bb-chr
"Christmas Time's A-Comin'" (G) .... C-std
"Blue Christmas" (E) .... A-std
"Christmas Cheer" (C, F, G, Gm) .... bs, C-chr
"The Christmas Song" (C, Bb, B) .... C-chr, Bb-chr
"Silent Night" (Bb, Db) .... Bb-std, Db-std
"Angels We Have Heard on High" (D, Bb, D) .... D-chr
"Away in a Manger" (G, Eb, F#) .... G-chr, F-chr
"Oh, Holy Night" (Db) .... C-chr
"The First Noel" (G, C) .... G-chr, C-chr

Harmonica/lead vocals: Charlie McCoy
F-hole guitar: Harold Bradley
Electric guitar: Jerry Shook, Pete Wade, Jimmy Wilkerson
Rhythm guitar: Harold Bradley, Russ Hicks, Glenn Keener, Fred Newell, Bobby Thompson
Banjo: Bobby Thompson
Slide dobro: Josh Graves
Steel dobro: Lloyd Green, Russ Hicks
Mandolin: Harold Bradley, Jerry Shook, Pete Wade
Fiddle: Tommy Jackson
Piano: Beegie Adair, Tony Migliore, John Propst, Bill Pursell
Electric piano/celeste: Bill Pursell
Pipe organ: Buryl Red
Bass: Johnny Johnson, Bob Moore, Jack Williams, Joe Zinkan
Bass guitar: Russ Hicks
Drums: Willie Ackerman, Kenneth Buttrey, Jerry Carrigan, Buddy Harman, Jim Isbell, Jerry White
Sleigh bells: Jerry Carrigan, Jim Isbell
Bell tree: Farrell Morris, Buryl Red
Orchestra bells: Beegie Adair, Tony Migliore, Farrell Morris
Vibes: Beegie Adair, Farrell Morris
Chimes/crotales: Farrell Morris
Harp: Mary Alice Hoepfinger, Ann Wall
Violin: Brenton Banks, Carl Gorodetzky, Lennie Haight, Sheldon Kurland, Steve Smith, Christian Teal, Stephanie Woolf
Viola: Marvin Chantry, Gary VanOsdale
Cello: Byron Bach, David Vanderkooi
Recorded at Cinderella Studio, Woodland Sound Studio
Engineers: David McKinley, Wayne Moss, Paul Skala

....

1975   Charlie, My Boy   Monument KZ-33384

....

"Old Joe Clark" (A) .... D-std
"The 12th of Never" (F) .... Bb-std
"City Lights" (A, D) .... D-std
"I Honestly Love You" (F) .... Bb-std
"New River Gorge" (C) .... F-std
"Please Don't Tell How the Story Ends" (Eb) .... Ab-std
"Stand Up and Holler for the Union" (F, F#) .... Bb-std, B-std
"Makin' Believe" (E, F) .... A-std, Bb-std
"Back Home in Indiana" (Bb) .... Eb-std
"Sweet Memories" (A) .... D-std
"Juke" (A) .... D-std

Harmonica/lead vocals: Charlie McCoy
Guitar: Tommy Allsup, Harold Bradley, Jim Colvard, Terry Dearmore, Dave
    Doran, Ray Edenton, Grady Martin, Wayne Moss, Fred Newell, Billy
    Sanford, Bobby Thompson, Jimmy Wilkerson, Chip Young, Reggie Young
Banjo: Fred Newell, Bobby Thompson
Steel guitar: Pete Drake, Lloyd Green, Russ Hicks, John Hughey, Weldon Myrick
Dobro: Josh Graves
Fiddle: Jimmy Buchanan, Shorty Lavender
Keyboards: David Briggs, Larry Butler, Bobby Emmons, Warren Hartman, John
    Propst, Hargus "Pig" Robbins, Buddy Skipper, Bobby Wood
Bass: Bobby Dyson, Johnny Johnson, Mike Leech, Wayne Moss, Don Smith, Henry
    Strzelecki
Drums/percussion: Hayward Bishop, Kenneth Buttrey, Si Edwards, Jim Isbell,
    Kenny Malone, Farrell Morris, Jerry White
Horns: Wayne Butler, Ralph Childs, Russ Hicks, Buddy Skipper
Strings: Byron Bach, Brenton Banks, George Binkley, Marvin Chantry, Roy
    Christensen, Virginia Christensen, Carl Gorodetzky, Lennie Haight,
    Sheldon Kurland, Martha McCrory, Steve Smith, Gary VanOsdale,
    Stephanie Woolf
Background vocals: Lea Jane Berinati, Tom Brannon, Terry Dearmore, Russ Hicks,
    Wayne Moss, Jimmy Nall, The Nashville Edition, Buddy Skipper, Sharon
    Vaughn, Duane West
Recorded at Cinderella Studio, Bradley's Barn, Starday Studio
Engineers: Joe Mills, Wayne Moss, Paul Skala, Mike Stone
Arrangers: Archie Bleyer, Charlie McCoy, Bill Pursell

1975   Harpin' the Blues

"After Hours" (G)   ....   N/A
"Lovesick Blues" (F)   ....   Bb-std
"I Heard That Lonesome Whistle Blow" (D)   ....   G-std "Basin
Street Blues" (F, Ab)   ....   Bb-ct, Db-std
"A Tribute to Little Walter" (E)   ....   A-std
"Columbus Stockade Blues" (G, Ab)   ....   C-std, Db-std
"T for Texas" (E)   ....   A-std
"Blues Stay Away from Me" (G, Ab)   ....   C-std, Db-std
"St. Louis Blues" (G, Gm)   ....   C-std
"Night Life" (D)   ....   G-vp, D-std
"Workin' Man's Blues" (B)   ....   E-std

Harmonica/lead vocal: Charlie McCoy
Guitar: Phil Baugh, Harold Bradley, Steve Chapman, Jim Colvard, Wayne Moss,
*   Dale Sellers, Bobby Thompson*
Slide guitar: Mac Gayden
Steel guitar: Curly Chalker, Paul Franklin, Russ Hicks, Weldon Myrick
Dobro: Josh Graves
Fiddle: Kenny Baker, Buddy Spicher
Bass: Lightnin' Chance, Terry Dearmore, Bobby Dyson, Johnny Johnson, Bob
*   Moore, Don Smith*
Drums/percussion: Kenny Buttrey, Si Edwards, Jim Isbell, Farrell Morris, Jerry
*   White*
Vibes: Kenny Malone, Farrell Morris
Trumpet: Al Hirt, Don Sheffield
Clarinet: Pete Fountain, Buddy Skipper
Saxophone: Billy Puett
Trombone: Bruce Waterman
Background vocals: The Nashville Sounds
Recorded at Cinderella Studio, Sea-Saint Studio
Engineers: Roberta Grace, Tom Knox, Wayne Moss
Horn arrangements: Bill Justis, Bill Pursell

....

| 1976 | Play It Again, Charlie | Monument MC-6630 |

....

"Wabash Cannonball" (B, D)[12] .... E-std
"Tuff" (Bb) .... Eb-std, G#-vp
"Muleskinner Blues" (E) .... A-std
"Theme from A Summer Place" (A, C) .... A-chr, C-chr
"Pots and Pans" (F#) .... F#-std, B-std
"We Sure Can Love Each Other" (A) .... D-std
"Summit Ridge Drive" (C)[13] .... F-std
"Missing You" (Ab) .... Db-std
"Ode to Billy Jo" (D) .... G-vp, G, bs, poly
"Stephen Foster/Nashville Style" (D, G, Eb, E, C) .... D-std, C-std,
Eb-std, C-chr
"Play It Again, Charlie" (Eb, E) .... Ab-std, A-std

Harmonica: Charlie McCoy
Guitar: Phil Baugh, Harold Bradley, Jimmy Capps, Barry Chance, Steve Chapman,
Jim Colvard, Steve Davis, Terry Dearmore, Ray Edenton, Steve Gibson, Russ
Hicks, Dave Kirby, Wayne Moss, Fred Newell, Bobby Thompson
Banjo: Harold Bradley, Bobby Thompson
Steel guitar: Stu Basore, Pete Drake, Buddy Emmons, Paul Franklin, Lloyd Green,
Russ Hicks, Weldon Myrick
Slide guitar: Mac Gayden
Dobro: Josh Graves, Russ Hicks
Fiddle: Shorty Lavender
Keyboards: Warren Hartman, Shane Keister, Bill Pursell, Hargus "Pig" Robbins,
Buddy Skipper, Jerry Smith, Jerry Whitehurst
Bass: Terry Dearmore, Billy Linneman, Bob Moore, Wayne Moss, Don Smith,
Henry Strzelecki
Drums/percussion: Kenneth Buttrey, Si Edwards, Buddy Harman, Jim Isbell,
Farrell Morris
Harp: Mary Alice Hoepfinger
Clarinet: Buddy Skipper
Strings: Byron Bach, Brenton Banks, George Binkley, Marvin Chantry, Carl
Gorodetzky, Lenny Haight, Sheldon Kurland, Martha McCrory, Steve
Smith, Gary VanOsdale, Stephanie Woolf
Background vocals: The Holladay Sisters, The Nashville Sounds, The Lea Jane
Singers, The Nashville Edition
Guest vocal: Jimmy Nall

....

| 1977   Country Cookin' | Monument MG-7612 |

....

"Country Cookin'" (E)	.... A-std
"The Last Letter" (E)	.... A-ct
"Crazy Arms" (F)	.... Bb-std
"Evergreen" (G)	.... C-ct
"Squeezin's" (B)	.... E-std
"Together Again" (F, F#)	.... Bb-std, B-std
"Amazing Grace" (Ab)	.... Db-std
"Cotton Eyed Joe" (A, D, G, A)	.... D-std, C-std
"We Could" (E)	.... A-ct
"18th-Century Rosewood Clock" (G)	.... C-ct
"Foggy River" (G)	.... C-std

Harmonica/lead vocals: Charlie McCoy
Guitar: Phil Baugh, Pete Bordonali, Harold Bradley, Barry Chance, Steve
* Chapman, Johnny Christopher, Terry Dearmore, Ray Edenton, Bob Eggers,*
* Steve Gibson, Russ Hicks, Wayne Moss, Bobby Thompson*
Banjo: Buddy Blackmon, Bobby Thompson
Steel guitar: Buddy Emmons, Lloyd Green, Russ Hicks, Weldon Myrick
Dobro: Josh Graves, Lloyd Green
Mandolin: Pete Bordonali
Fiddle: Johnny Gimble, Charlie Justice, Tommy Williams
Keyboards: Randy Goodrum, Shane Keister, Hargus "Pig" Robbins, Jerry Smith
Bass: Mike McBride, Bob Moore, Norbert Putnam, Steve Schaffer, Don Smith
Drums/percussion: Kenneth Buttrey, Si Edwards, Buddy Harman, Jim Isbell,
* Farrell Morris*
Strings: George Binkley, John Catchings, Marvin Chantry, Roy Christensen, Carl
* Gorodetzky, Lenny Haight, Shelly Kurland, Steve Smith, Chris Teal, Sam*
* Terranova, Gary VanOsdale*
Background vocals: Tom Brannon, Bobby Harden, Alan Moore, Duane West
Recorded at Cinderella Studio
Engineers: John Moss, Wayne Moss
String arrangements: Bill Pursell

··

1977   Stone Fox Chase   Monument MNT-81866

··

"Stone Fox Chase"
"Me and Bobby McGee"
"Release Me (And Let Me Love Again)"
"I Can't Stop Loving You"
"Fireball Mail"
"Today I Started Loving You Again"
"Delta Dawn"
"Let Me Be There"
"Louisiana Man"
"Behind Closed Doors"
"Silver Threads and Golden Needles"
"Help Me Make It Through the Night"
"Lovesick Blues"
"I Can't Help It (If I'm Still in Love with You)"
"I Honestly Love You"
"Rollin' in My Sweet Baby's Arms"

1978   Greatest Hits   Monument MG-7622

"Today I Started Loving You Again" (F#) .... B-std

"Wabash Cannonball" (B, D, B) .... E-std, G-vp

"Release Me" (D, Eb) .... G-std, Ab-std

"I Really Don't Want to Know" (Eb) .... Ab-std

"Silver Threads and Golden Needles" (G) .... C-std

"I'm So Lonesome I Could Cry" (F#, G) .... B-std, C-std

"T. D.'s Boogie Woogie" (F) .... Bb-std, F-chr

"I Can't Help It" (E, F) .... A-std, Bb-std

"Shenandoah" (Db, D) .... Db-std, D-std

"Orange Blossom Special" (C, F) .... F-std, Bb-std

Harmonica: Charlie McCoy
Guitar: Jimmy Capps, Jim Colvard, Ray Edenton, Mac Gayden, Grady Martin,
*   Wayne Moss, Billy Sanford, Dale Sellers, Jerry Shook, Bobby Thompson,*
*   Pete Wade, Chip Young*
Banjo: Bobby Thompson
Dobro: Josh Graves
Steel guitar: Curly Chalker, Paul Franklin, Lloyd Green, Russ Hicks, Weldon
*   Myrick, Hal Rugg*
Fiddle: Johnny Gimble, Tommy Jackson, Shorty Lavender, Lisa Silver, Buddy
*   Spicher*
Piano: David Briggs, Warren Hartman, Hargus "Pig" Robbins, Buddy Skipper,
*   Jerry Smith*
Concertina: Doug Kershaw
Drums/percussion: Kenny Buttrey, Jerry Carrigan, Buddy Harman, Jim Isbell,
*   Kenny Malone, Farrell Morris*
Clarinet: Buddy Skipper
Harp: Mary Alice Hoepfinger
Background vocals: The Holladay Sisters, Dennis Linde, The Nashville Edition,
*   Bergen White*
Recorded at Bradley's Barn, Cinderella Studio, Monument
Engineers: Wayne Moss, Charlie Tallent
Harp arrangement: Bill Pursell

....

| 1979 | Appalachian Fever | | Monument MG-7632 |

....

"Fair and Tender Ladies" (A, C)[14] .... D-std
"Midnight Flyer" (A) .... D-std
"Ramblin' Music Man" (C) .... N/A
"West Virginia Mountain Melody" (D) .... D-std
"Cripple Creek" (G) .... C-std
"Red Haired Boy" (B) .... C-std
"Drifting Lovers" (G, A)[15] .... C-std, D-std
"Ruby (Are You Mad?)" (A) .... D-std
"In the Pines" (G, C) .... C-std
"Carolina Morning" (B) .... E-std
"Appalachian Fever" (E) .... E-std

Harmonica/lead vocals/all instruments on "Fair and Tender Ladies" and "In the Pines": Charlie McCoy
Acoustic guitar: Bob Eggers, Wayne Moss
Electric guitar/slide acoustic guitar: Barry Chance
Banjo: Buddy Blackmon
Dobro: Josh Graves, Russ Hicks
Steel guitar: Russ Hicks
Fiddle: Buddy Spicher
Bass: Barry Chance, Wayne Moss
Drums: Si Edwards, John Moss
Recorded at Cinderella Studio
Engineers: John Moss, Wayne Moss

| 1986 | One for the Road | Asphodel FH-0001 |

"Scotland" (A) .... D-std

"Georgia on My Mind" (G) .... C-ct

"In the Mood" (Ab) .... Db-ct

"Last Date" (E) .... A-ct

"Red Haired Boy" (B) .... E-std

"Real Love" (C#, D) .... F#-std

"I Believe You" (A) .... N/A

"Gospel Medley" (C, G, D, Eb) .... N/A

"Shenandoah" (Db, D) .... Db-std, D-std

"Orange Blossom Special" (C, F) .... F-std, Bb-std

Harmonica/lead vocals: Charlie McCoy
Vocals: Laney Smallwood Hicks
Electric guitar/vocals: Vip Vipperman
Steel guitar/vocals: Russ Hicks
Bass/vocals: David Hicks
Recorded at Cinderella Studio
Engineer: Wayne Moss

....

| 1988 | Charlie McCoy's 13th | Step One SOR-0038 |

....

Released in Denmark as Harmonica Jones *(World Wide 050987, 1987)*

"Harmonica Jones" (B) .... E-ct
"You Were Always on My Mind" (E) .... A-ct
"You Can't Get Off with Your Shoes On" (A) .... D-std
"Shenandoah" (Db, D) .... Db-std, D-std
"Orange Blossom Special" (C, F) .... F-std, Bb-std
"Take the New River" (E) .... A-ct
"I'm So Lonesome I Could Cry" (G, Ab) .... C-std, Db-std
"One O'Clock Jump" (G, Eb, F, G) .... C-std
"Funky Country Living" (A) .... D-std
"Today I Started Loving You Again" (E) .... A-std

Harmonica/vibes: Charlie McCoy
Acoustic guitar: Buddy Blackmon
Electric guitar: Jerry Kimbrough, Vip Vipperman
Steel guitar: Russ Hicks
Piano: Rodger Morris
Bass: David Hicks
Drums: Jerry Kroon
Percussion: Si Edwards
Recorded at Masterlink Studio
Engineers: Wayne Moss, Glenn Rieuf

1988   Another Side of Charlie McCoy   **World Wide Music**
                                                  WWM-040987

Released in the United States as Beam Me Up, Charlie
(Step One Records SOR-0048, 1989)

"Southern Comfort" (A, F#, G, G#) .... D-std, B-std
"Funky Country Living" (A) .... D-std
"Fingertips" (C) .... C-chr, F-std
"You Can't Get Off with Your Shoes On" (A) .... D-std
"You've Got It All Over Him" (Db, D, Eb)* .... F#-std, G-vp,
                                                               G#-vp
"The Friendship Song" (D, Eb, E)* .... N/A
"Birdland" (G) .... C-std, C-ct
"Katy Hill" (G) .... C-ct
"Funky Country Music" (G) .... C-std
"She Knows How to Treat Me Right" (A) .... A-std, D-std
"Take the New River" (E) .... A-ct
"If There Were Only Time for Love" (D, E)* .... N/A
"Invitation to the Blues" (G, Ab, A)* .... C-std
"Little Maggie" (A) .... D-std
* *Not included on* Beam Me Up, Charlie

Harmonica/lead vocals: Charlie McCoy
*Guest vocals: Laney Smallwood Hicks**
Guitar: Buddy Blackmon, Vip Vipperman
Banjo: Buddy Blackmon
Steel guitar: Russ Hicks
Piano: Rodger Morris, Hargus "Pig" Robbins, Buddy Skipper
Bass: David Hicks
Background vocals: David Hicks, Laney Smallwood Hicks, Russ Hicks, Vip
     Vipperman
Drums: Si Edwards, Jerry Kroon, Kenny Malone
Recorded at Masterlink
Engineer: Wayne Moss, Glenn Rieuf

1989	Candelight, Wine, and Charlie	World Wide Music
		WWM-180189

Released in Denmark

"Blue Spanish Eyes" (C, D)	C-chr
"Yesterday" (F, G)	C-chr
"Fool on the Hill" (C, F)	C-chr
"Step Inside Love" (G, Ab)	C-chr
"Leavin' on a Jet Plane" (G)	C-std
"Love Me Tender" (C, D)	C-chr, F-std
"Green, Green Grass of Home" (G, A)	C-std, D-std
"The Sloop John B" (G)	C-std, C-chr, bs
"Pretty Magic" (Dm)	Bb-ct
"Windmills of Your Mind" (Em)	C-chr
"The Streets of London" (Bb, C)	Eb-ct, F-ct
"He Ain't Heavy" (G)	C-chr

Harmonica/vibes/piano/acoustic guitar/trumpet/flugelhorn: Charlie McCoy
Electric guitar: Vip Vipperman
Acoustic guitar: Charlie McCoy Jr.
Steel guitar: Russ Hicks
Keyboards/percussion/arranger: Phil Barrett
Bass: David Hicks
Drums: Si Edwards
Recorded at Cinderella Studio, Puk Studio
Engineers: Phil Barrett, Wayne Moss

1990	International Incident	Cezane I96242-244

Released in France

"The Funky Duck" (A)	D-std
"Price-less Shuffle" (G)	C-ct
"Lark in the Morning" (D)	G-ct
"Let's Get Started" (C)	F-std
"Send in the Krowns" (E)	A-ct
"For Jim" (G)	C-ct
"Crawdaddy Stomp" (A)	D-std
"Get Funktry" (E)	A-ct
"Chicano Waltz" (Bb)	Eb-ct
"Kro-Hoppin'" (B)	E-ct
"January 25" (G)	C-ct
"Fontaines" (G)	C-ct

Harmonica: Charlie McCoy
Guitar: Sjœrd Plak
Banjo/steel guitar: Jean-Yves Lozac'h
Fiddle: Downs Thompson
Keyboard: André Sommer
Bass: Tijmen Zinkhaan
Drums: Hans Molenaar
Recorded at Bananas Studio
Engineer: Jos Haagmans

....

| 1991 | Out on a Limb | Step One SOR-0067 |

....

"Whiskey Before Breakfast" (G) .... C-ct
"You Don't Know Me" (Eb, E) .... Ab-ct, A-ct
"I Hope It Ain't a Train" (E) .... A-std
"Cayman Moon" (Eb) .... Ab-std
"You've Still Got a Place in My Heart" (Bb, B) .... Eb-std, E-std
"Out on a Limb" (A) .... D-ct
"Smokey Places" (E) .... N/A
"The Other Woman" (A) .... D-ct
"Dutch Treat" (E) .... A-ct
"Lasso the Moon" (G, Ab) .... C-ct, Db-ct
"Saved by the Belle" (A) .... D-ct
"Julia" (G) .... C-ct

Harmonica/lead vocal/gut-string guitar/vibes: Charlie McCoy
Acoustic guitar: Buddy Blackmon, Wayne Moss, Vip Vipperman
Gut-string guitar: Bob Eggers
Electric guitar: Brent Mason, Sjœrd Plak, Vip Vipperman
Banjo: Buddy Blackmon, Jean-Yves Lozac'h
Steel guitar: Russ Hicks, Jean-Yves Lozac'h
Keyboards: Bobby Ogdin, Hargus "Pig" Robbins, André Sommer, Keith Stegall
Drums: Si Edwards, Hans Molenaar
Percussion: Si Edwards, Farrell Morris
Vibes: Ginger McCoy Jordan
Background vocals: Laney Smallwood Hicks, Russ Hicks, The Jordanaires (Gordon
    Stoker, Neal Matthews, Louis Nunley, Duane West)
Recorded at Balladsound Studio, Cinderella Studio, Oak Valley Studio
Engineers: Edward Boellaard, Kevin McManus, Wayne Moss

| 1992 | International Airport | Music Choice 21800156 |

Released in Germany

"Take It Easy" (F) .... Bb-ct
"International Airport" (C, C#) .... F-ct, F#-ct
"Irgendwo" (Em) .... C-std
"Sie war jung und frei" (A) .... D-ct
"Renovier deine Seele" (D) .... G-ct
"Ich wünsch' dir Hals- und Beinbruch" (E) .... E-std, A-ct
"Hall, guten Morgen Deutschland" (E) .... A-ct
"Junger Adler" (A) .... D-ct
"Sie und er und ich" (E) .... A-ct
"Jeden Montag freu'n uns aufs Wochenende" (G) .... C-std
"Freunde" (G) .... G-std, C-std
"Nutz die Zeit" (A) .... D-ct

Harmonica: Charlie McCoy
Guitar: Bill Hullett
Steel guitar: Russ Hicks
Fiddle: Hoot Hester
Piano: Buddy Skipper
Bass: Larry Paxton
Drums: Jerry Kroon
Background vocals: The Jordanaires
Recorded at Masterlink
Engineer: Glenn Rieuf

....

1994   Choo, Choo, Ch'Boogie   International POCD-006

....

Released in Denmark

"Choo, Choo, Ch'Boogie" (A, B) .... D-ct, E-ct

"Swamp Thing" (A) .... D-std

"A Little Bit of Soap" (D) .... G-ct

"Rock My World (Little Country Girl)" (E) .... A-ct

"Scotland" (A) .... D-std

"Honky Tonk Attitude" (G) .... C-ct

"No One Will Ever Know" (E) .... A-ct

"Barefootin'" (D) .... N/A

"Chattanooga Choo Choo" (F, Bb) .... Bb-ct, Eb-ct

"Love Bug" (A) .... D-ct

"My Special Angel" (Eb, F#) .... Ab-ct, B-ct

"Sugarfoot Rag" (A) .... D-std

"The Way You Do the Things You Do" (G, Ab) .... C-std, Db-std

"I.C. 3" (B) .... E-ct

"Under the Boardwalk" (F) .... Bb-ct

"Den Toppede Høne" (G) C .... ct

Harmonica/lead vocals/bass/acoustic guitar/marimba/vibes: Charlie McCoy
Acoustic guitar: Sjœrd Plak, Vip Vipperman
Electric guitar: Sjœrd Plak, Salle Sahlin, Vip Vipperman
Slide guitar: Vip Vipperman
Banjo: Jean-Yves Lozac'h
Steel guitar: Russ Hicks, Jean-Yves Lozac'h, Benny Pedersen
Fiddle/mandolin: Downs Thompson
Piano: Bobby Ogdin, André Sommer
Bass: David Hicks, Kenneth Svenning, Tijmen Zinkhaan
Drums: Jerry Kroon, Kenny Malone, Hans Molenaar, Jonte Svensson
Background vocals: The Jordanaires
Recorded at Cinderella Studio, Country Sound Studio, Euro-Sound Studio,
*   Masterlink Studio, Puk Studio*
Engineers: Jos Haagmans, Chad Hailey, Peter Iversen, Glenn Rieuf, Jørgen
*   Sørensen*

| 1995 | Charlie Live in Paris | PSB PSB-850 |

Released in France

"Scotland" (A) .... D-std
"I'm So Lonesome I Could Cry" (G, Ab) .... C-std, Db-std
"One O'Clock Jump" (G) .... C-std
"Cold, Cold Heart" (E) .... A-ct
"Lark in the Morning" (D) .... G-ct
"I Heard It Through the Grapevine" (Cm) .... N/A
"John Henry" (A) .... D-std
"You Don't Know Me" (Eb, E) .... Ab-ct, A-ct
"Wabash Cannonball" (B) .... E-std
"Georgia on My Mind" (G) .... C-ct
"Whiskey Before Breakfast" (G) .... C-ct
"Boogie Woogie" (F) .... Bb-std
"Barefootin'" (D) .... N/A
"The Funky Duck" (A) .... D-std
"For Jim" (G) .... C-ct
"Stand by Me" (A) .... N/A
"Shenandoah" (Db, D) .... Db-std, D-std
"Orange Blossom Special" (C, F) .... F-std, Bb-std

Harmonica/lead vocals: Charlie McCoy
Guitar: Sjœrd Plak
Banjo/steel guitar: Jean-Yves Lozac'h
Fiddle: Downs Thompson
Piano: Luc Bertin
Bass: Tijmen Zinkhaan
Drums: Hans Molenaar
Recorded in a "Peakson" Truck Mobil System
Engineers: Jean-Marie Geraud, Julien Omnes, Philippe Omnes

....

| 1995 | American Roots | Koka Media KOK-2101 |

....

Released in France

"Daisy Rag" (G)	N/A
"Melody Ranch" (G)	C-std
"Hot Rod Fever" (E)	N/A
"Angelene the Baker" (D)	G-ct
"Take the A Train" (E)	A-std
"Mud Bug" (C)	F-ct
"My West Virginia Home" (E)	A-std
"Karin's Dream" (G)	C-std, bs
"Rosita" (D)	N/A
"Wicklow Mountain" (D)	G-ct
"Even the Dog Has the Blues" (C)	N/A
"Bayou LaFayette" (G)	C-ct, E-std
"Pioneer Medley" (D, C, E, D)	N/A
"Ain't That the Blues" (D)	G-std
"Loose Shoes" (G)	C-ct
"McCloud's Reel" (G)	C-ct
"Bourbon Street March" (E)	N/A

Harmonica: Charlie McCoy
Guitar: Sjœrd Plak, Rens Van der Zalm
Accordion/Irish whistle/mandolin: Rens Van der Zalm
Steel guitar/banjo: Jean-Yves Lozac'h
Fiddle: Downs Thompson
Bass: Tijmen Zinkhaan
Drums: Si Edwards
Recorded at unknown studio, Nijmegan, Holland
Engineer: Unknown

1998   Le Legende Country   Versailles VER 491305

Released in France; all tracks previously released

"Orange Blossom Special" (C, F) .... F-std, Bb-std
"Wabash Cannonball" (B, D, B) .... E-std, G-vp
"Today, I Started Loving You Again" (F#) .... B-std
"Release Me" (D, Eb) .... G-std, Ab-std
"I Really Don't Want to Know" (Eb) .... Ab-std, Ab-vp
"Silver Threads and Golden Needles" (G) .... C-std
"I'm So Lonesome I Could Cry" (F#, G) .... B-std, C-std
"Boogie Woogie" (F) .... Bb-std, F-chr
"I Can't Help It" (E, F) .... A-std, Bb-std
"Shenandoah" (Db, D) .... Db-std, D-std
"Kro Hoppin'" (B) .... E-ct
"Let's Get Started" (C) .... F-std
"Send in the Krowns" (E) .... A-ct
"Mess in the Mountains" (G) .... C-std
"Melody Ranch" (G) .... C-std
"Take the A Train" (E) .... A-std
"Karin's Dream" (G) .... C-std, bs
"Bayou Lafayette" (G) .... C-ct, E-std
"Loose Shoes" (G) .... C-ct
"Funky Duck" (A) .... D-std

| 1998 | Precious Memories | Revival RR 5719-2 |

Released in the United Kingdom

"What a Friend We Have in Jesus" (Ab, B, Ab) .... B-std
"That Old Rugged Cross" (E) .... A-ct-v
"Wayfaring Stranger" (F#m) .... D-std
"Don't Worry 'Bout Nothin'" (G, E, G) .... C-std, A-std
"In the Garden" (G, E, G) .... C-ct, A-ct
"Just a Closer Walk with Thee" (F, A, Bb, Eb) .... Bb-ct-v, D-ct, Ab-ct-v
"Precious Memories" (D, G) .... G-std, C-std
"I'll Fly Away" (C, G, C) .... F-std
"Peace in the Valley" (F) .... Bb-ct
"I Love to Tell the Story" (Ab, Db, Gb) .... Db-std, Gb-std, B-std
"Amazing Grace" (C) .... F-std
"The Lord's Prayer" (F) .... Bb-std
"If There Were Only Time for Love" (F, G) .... N/A

Harmonica/lead vocals/harmony vocals/vibes: Charle McCoy
Additional lead vocals: Laney Smallwood Hicks ("In the Garden"), The Jordanaires ("I'll Fly Away"), The Music City Tonight Singers ("Don't Worry 'Bout Nothin'"), Lulu Roman ("Wayfaring Stranger")
Guitar: Vip Vipperman
Steel guitar/harmony vocals: Russ Hicks
Dobro: Wanda Vick
Fiddle: Downs Thompson, Wanda Vick
Piano/keyboards: Rodger Morris, Buddy Skipper
Clarinet: Buddy Skipper
Bass: David Hicks, Larry Paxton
Drums: Gene Chrisman, Kenny Malone, Bob Mater
Percussion: John Decker
Background vocals: The Jordanaires, The Music City Tonight Singers

2003   Classic Country   **Green Hill GHD-55338**

"On the Road Again" (E, G) .... A-ct
"Crazy" (Bb, B) .... Eb-ct, E-ct
"Today I Started Loving You Again" (F#) .... B-std
"Orange Blossom Special" (C, F) .... F-std, Bb-std
"Don't It Make My Brown Eyes Blue" (F) .... Bb-ct
"Tennessee Waltz" (Eb, B, C, Eb) .... Ab-ct
"Walkin' After Midnight" (G, Ab) .... C-std, F-std, Db-std
"You Needed Me" (Ab) .... Db-std
"John Henry" (A) .... D-std
"Here Comes My Baby Back Again" (D, Bb, Eb) .... A-ct, Eb-ct,
                                                                         Ab-ct
"Looking for Love" (E) .... A-std
"I'm So Lonesome I Could Cry" (G, Ab) .... C-std, Db-std
"San Antonio Rose" (E, F) .... A-ct, E-ct, Bb-ct, F-ct
"Shenandoah" (Db, D) .... Db-std, D-std

Harmonica/vibes: Charlie McCoy
Acoustic guitar: Andy Reiss, Wanda Vick, Vip Vipperman
Lead guitar: Bill Hullett, Andy Reiss, Pete Wade
Banjo/dobro/strings: Wanda Vick
Steel guitar: Russ Hicks
Fiddle/strings: Craig Duncan
Piano/keyboards: Beegie Adair, Tony Migliore, Bobby Ogdin
Bass: Tim Smith
Drums: Bob Mater
Recorded at Masterlink Studios
Engineer: Bil VornDick

2004   Czech Mates: Live in Brno   Universal (Czech) 986 625-9

Released in the Czech Republic

"Scotland" (A) .... D-std
"Texas, When I Die" (G) .... C-ct
"Midnight Flyer" (A) .... D-std
"I'm So Lonesome I Could Cry" (G) .... C-std
"Take the New River" (E) .... A-ct
"Choo, Choo, Ch'Boogie" (A, B) .... D-ct, E-ct
"Cripple Creek" (G) .... C-std
"Ruby (Are You Mad?)" (A) .... D-std
"John Henry" (A) .... D-std
"Wayfaring Stranger" (Em) .... C-std
"Kdo to obchazi muj dum" (E) .... A-std
"In the Pines" (G) .... C-std
"Rollin' in My Sweet Baby's Arms" (A) .... D-std
"Chattanooga Choo-choo" (F, Bb) .... Bb-ct, Eb-ct
"Orange Blossom Special" (C, F) .... F-std, Bb-std
"Amazing Grace" (C) .... F-std

Harmonica/lead vocals: Charlie McCoy
Vocals: Katia Garcia
Guitar: Robert Křest'an, Martin Ledvina
Banjo/Irish whistle: Luboš Malina
Dobro: Luboš Novotny
Fiddle: Stanislav Palúch
Bass: Petr Vavfik
Drums: Peter Solarik
Recorded live in Brno, Czech Republic
Engineer: Jiri Mašek

2004   Bouchon   CMC 0405

Released in France

"Scotland" (A) .... D-std
"Texas, When I Die" (G) .... C-ct
"Thinking with My Heart" (A) .... D-std
"You Were Always on My Mind" (E) .... A-ct
"Sugarfoot Rag" (A) .... D-std
"Six Days on the Road" (C) .... F-std
"Funky Country Living" (A) .... D-std
"The Devil Went Down to Georgia" (Dm) .... N/A
"Crazy" (Bb) .... Eb-ct
"You Can't Get Off with Your Shoes On" (A) .... D-std
"Hot Rod Fever" (E) .... N/A
"Bayou LaFayette" (G) .... C-ct, E-std
"Big Boss Man" (A) .... D-std
"Hey Elvis" (C) .... F-std
"Under the Boardwalk" (F) .... Bb-ct
"Choo, Choo, Ch'Boogie" (A, B) .... D-std, E-std
"Stand by Me" (A) .... N/A
"Orange Blossom 'Very' Special" (C, F, E, A) .... F-std, Bb-std
"Amazing Grace" (C) .... F-std

Harmonica/lead vocals: Charlie McCoy
Guitar/background vocals: Sjœrd Plak
Electric guitar/fiddle/background vocals: Danny Vriet
Steel guitar: Jean-Yves Lozac'h
Bass: Tijmen Zinkhaan
Drums: Hans Molenaar
Recorded in Nancy, France
Engineer: Tijmen Zinkhaan

....

2007   A Celtic Bridge   Flying Harp (no catalog number)

....

"The Water Is Wide" (E) .... A-ct

"Irish Aire" (C, F, Bb) .... F-dbl, Eb-dbl

"Klan's Song" (F) .... Bb-ct

"Mary and the Soldier" (D) .... G-ct

"Victoria's Dream" (Em) .... C-ct

"Drums of Donegal" (Dm, D) .... Bb-ct, G-ct

"When Paddy Went to Dublin" (D) .... G-ct

"Irish Waltz" (G) .... C-ct

"The Girl I Left Behind/Speedy Return" (D, E) .... G-ct, A-ct

"Irish Reel Medley" (G) .... C-ct

"If You Cared for Me" (A) .... D-ct

"An Aire for Patricia" (F) .... Bb-ct

"Lost and Found" (G) .... C-ct

"The Bridges of My Heart" (E) .... A-ct

"Carrickfergus" (G) .... C-dbl

"John Henry Jones" (Em) .... C-ct

"An Irish Pedigree" (D .... D-std

Harmonica/lead vocals/bass/acoustic guitar/four-string banjo/vibes: Charlie McCoy
Guest vocal: Katia Garcia, Laney Smallwood Hicks, Johnny Logan
Acoustic guitar: Peter Cairney, Bob Eggers, Russ Hicks, Bill Hullett, Petr Kosumbersky, Johnny Logan, Larry Paxton, Rens Van der Zalm, Wanda Vick, Vip Vipperman
Steel guitar: Russ Hicks
Fiddle: Downs Thompson, Rens Van der Zalm, Wanda Vick
Mandolin: Rens Van der Zalm
Five-string banjo: Luboš Malina
Celtic harp: Sean Barry
Piano: Lionel Cartwright
Keyboard/violin/viola: Kristin Wilkinson
Accordion: Jeff Taylor, Rens Van der Zalm
Flute: Burt Dickerson, Hannah Jordan
Whistle: Luboš Malina, Jeff Taylor, Rens Van der Zalm
Strings: Wanda Vick, Kristin Wilkinson
Bass: Mark Burchfield, Larry Paxton
Percussion: Sam Bacco, Larry Paxton
Background vocals: Larry Paxton, Vip Vipperman

2007   Charlie's Christmas Angels   **Hithouse HP 2007I7**

Released in Denmark

"Sleigh Ride" (C, E, D, A) .... F-ct, A-ct, G-ct, D-ct
"Silver Bells" (F, C#, F#) .... Bb-ct, F#-ct, B-ct
"White Christmas" (Bb) .... Eb-ct
"Winter Wonderland" (G, B, D, Ab) .... C-ct, Db-ct
"Have Yourself a Merry Little Christmas" (Eb, F#) .... Ab-dbl,
Eb-std
"Blue Christmas" (A, Bb) .... D-ct, Eb-ct
"Christmas in County Kerry" (G) .... C-ct
"Hangin' around the Mistletoe" (D) .... G-ct
"The Christmas Song" (Bb) .... C-chr
"Oh Beautiful Star of Bethlehem" (C) .... F-ct
"Il Est Né/Mary's Boy Child" (C, D, Bb) .. bs, chr, F-std, G-ct, Bb-ct
"Oh Come All Ye Faithful" (D, Eb) .... G-ct, Ab-ct
"Bethlehem Medley" (Bb, G, F) .... chr, C-ct, Bb-ct
"It Wasn't His Child" (B) .... F#-ct
"Baby King" (Ebm) .... B-std
"Go Tell It on the Mountain/Silent Night" (C, Bb, F) .... F-std,
Bb-std

Harmonica/lead vocals/bass/vibes/bells: Charlie McCoy
Guest vocal: Charlie McCoy Jr.
Acoustic guitar: Gary Burnette, Hoot Hester, Kerry Marx, Vip Vipperman
Electric guitar: Gary Burnette, Kerry Marx
Steel guitar: Russ Hicks
Fiddle: Hoot Hester, Downs Thompson
Mandolin: Hoot Hester
Flute/whistle: James Fenton
Piano/keyboards: Bob Patin
Drums/percussion: Tommy Wells
Background vocals: Lindsay Hicks, The Jordanaires, Ginger McCoy Jordan
Charlie's grandchildren: Abby Jordan, Austin Jordan, Caroline McCoy, Hannah Jordan
Les enfants français: Agathe Bonnet, Morane Lozac'h
Charlie's Christmas Angels: The Country Sisters, Donna Fargo, Laney Smallwood Hicks, Moore and Moore, Tamra Rosanes, Jett Williams, Wenche

....

2008   Over the Rainbow   **Diamondisc 001**

....

"Just the Way You Are" (F) .... Bb-ct
"Cry Me a River" (Ab) .... Db-ct, F-std
"Lover's Key" (G) .... C-ct
"My Funny Valentine" (Eb) .... Ab-std
"Wind Beneath My Wings" (F, G) .... Bb-dbl, C-ct
"The Nearness of You" (Bb) .... Eb-dbl
"Somewhere Over the Rainbow" (Eb) .... Ab-dbl
"How Insensitive" (Dm) .... Bb-ct
"You Belong to Me" (Ab, Bb) .... Db-ct, Eb-ct
"Maybe You'll Be There" (Bb) .... Eb-ct
"Meditation" (G) .... C-ct
"Hard to Say Goodbye" (Eb) .... Ab-ct

Harmonica/vibes, lead vocal: Charlie McCoy
Acoustic guitar: Mark Casstevens, Don Potter
Electric guitar: David Hungate, Andy Reiss
Piano: Beegie Adair
Alto flute: Rufus Long
Clarinet: Buddy Skipper
Soprano saxophone: Sam Levine
Tenor saxophone: Denis Solee
Flugelhorn: George Tidwell
Trombone: Barry Green
Bass: Roger Spencer
Drums: Chris Brown
Guest vocal: Laney Smallwood Hicks
Recorded at Skaggs' Place
Engineers: Lee Groitzsch, Eric Paul

2009   Classic Country Hymns   CMD/Spring House 211572

"Precious Memories" (A) .... D-std
"Will the Circle Be Unbroken" (D, G, C, F) .... G-std, Bb-std
"Wayfaring Stranger" (Gm) .... Eb-std
"How Great Thou Art" (F) .... Bb-dbl
"Unclouded Day" (C, F) .... F-std, Bb-std
"It Is Well with My Soul" (F, Bb, Eb) .... Bb-dbl
"Love Lifted Me" (D) .... G-ct
"Softly and Tenderly" (Bb, G, Bb) .... Eb-dbl
"I Saw the Light" (G, C, F, Bb) .... C-std, Eb-dbl
"Sweet Hour of Prayer" (Eb, F) .... Ab-dbl, Bb-dbl
"Just a Closer Walk with Thee" (C, D, C) .... Low F-std, F-ct
"Whispering Hope" (E, A) .... A-ct
"In the Sweet By and By" (E, G) .... A-dbl, C-dbl
"I Believe" (A, Bb, B) .... D-dbl, Eb-std

Harmonica/vibes/tin whistle: Charlie McCoy
Acoustic guitar: Pat Flynn, Hoot Hester, Bruce Watkins, Vip Vipperman
Electric guitar: Jimmy Capps, Greg Galbraith, Bill Hullett
Steel guitar: Sonny Garrish, Lloyd Green, Russ Hicks, Tommy White
Fiddle: Craig Duncan, Hoot Hester, Wanda Vick
Mandolin: Wanda Vick
Hammered dulcimer: Craig Duncan
Piano: John Hobbs, Clayton Ivey, Hargus "Pig" Robbins
Bass: Wayne Moss, Craig Nelson, Larry Paxton
Recorded at Ronnie's Place
Engineer: Bil VornDick

2010 Duets (Volume I)	Flying Harp (no catalog number)

"Harp Playin' Fools" (E) .... A-std
"Monday at the Bakery" (G, Bb) .... C-std, Eb-std
"A Georgia Goodbye" (C) .... Low F-ct, F-ct
"Sweet Morgan's Blues" (Em) .... C-ct
"Just Doing Nothing with You" (G) .... N/A
"Uptown" (E) .... A-std
"Fanny Man Blues" (A) .... D-std
"Faubin Cross Blues" (D, E) .... G-ct, A-ct, High G-std
"Blues in the Basement" (B, E) .... E-std, A-std
"Goodbye World, Goodbye" (C) .... F-ct
"Snake Bite" (Bb) .... Eb-std
"Pretty Magic" (Dm) .... Bb-ct
"Julia" (G) .... C-ct

Harmonica/lead vocals/vibes: Charlie McCoy
Duet partners: Bob Eggers, Buddy Green, Laney Smallwood Hicks, Jim Isbell,
  Richard Kiser, Jean-Yves Lozac'h, Wayne Moss, Sjœrd Plak, Fab Tranzer,
  Nils Tuxen, Jean-Marc Versini, Vip Vipperman, Danny Vriet
Piano: Hargus "Pig" Robbins
Organ: Christophe Cravero
Keyboards: Bobby Ogdin, Vip Vipperman
Steel guitar: Russ Hicks
Bass: Franck Bedez, David Hicks, Tony Kent, Vip Vipperman
Drums: Todd Cooper, Si Edwards, Jim Isbell, Loic Pontieux
Congas: Roy Schneider
Recorded at Cinderella Studio, Oak Valley Studio, Subterrainia, Vipperman
  House, Flat 5 Studio, Chelsea Studio South, The Bakery, Tuxen Huset, Chez
  Cracero, Chez Lozac'h, La Chapelle en Serval, Chez Versini
Engineers: Martin Bakker, Christophe Cravero, Jean-Yves Lozac'h, Wayne Moss,
  Kevin McManus, Tom Ohmsen, Rob Stennett, Greg Timko, Nils Tuxen,
  Jean-Marc Versini, Vip Vipperman

2011	Lonesome Whistle: A Tribute to Hank Williams	Catbone Music/ Diamonddisc 0720

"Heard That Lonesome Whistle Blow" (E) .... A-std

"Lovesick Blues" (F) .... Bb-std

"So Lonesome I Could Cry" (G, Ab) .... C-std, Db-std

"Your Cheatin' Heart" (G) .... C-ct

"Cold, Cold Heart" (E) .... A-ct

"Mind Your Own Business" (F) .... Bb-std

"I Can't Help It (If I'm Still in Love with You)" (E, F) .... A-std, Bb-std

"I Saw the Light" (A) .... D-ct

"Long, Gone, Lonesome Blues" (D) .... G-std

"Jambalaya (On the Bayou)" (D, G) .... G-ct, C-ct

"You Win Again" (E) .... A-std

"The Hank Williams Song" (D) .... G-std

Harmonica/vibes/lead vocals: Charlie McCoy
Guest vocals: Roy Clark, Ricky Skaggs, Hank Williams, Jett Williams
Acoustic guitar: Leigh Reynolds, Michael Spriggs, Hank Williams
Electric guitar: Jimmy Capps, Roy Clark, Bill Hullett, Sammy Pruett
Steel guitar: Russ Hicks, Mike Johnson, Weldon Myrick
Dobro: Rob Ickes
Electric sitar: Harold Bradley
Mandolin: Ricky Skaggs
Fiddle: Loretta Brank, Hoot Hester, Jerry Rivers, Kenny Sears
Piano: Dirk Johnson, Rodger Morris, Hargus "Pig" Robbins
Bass guitar: Harold Bradley, Russ Hicks
Bass: Dennis Crouch, Dave Martin, Cedric Rainwater
Drums: Bob Mater, Tommy Wells
Background vocals: Lea Jane Berinati, Margie Cates, Cedric Rainwater, Jerry Rivers
Recorded at Skaggs' Place Studio
Engineers: Lee Groitzsch, Eric Paul

....

2012   On the Road Again   No label information available

....

"Wayfaring Stranger" (C)   .... F-std
"On the Road Again" (E)   .... A-ct
"Welcome to My World" (F)   .... Bb-ct
"Yakety Axe" (G, C)   .... C-ct, F-ct
"Ashoken Farewell" (D, G)   .... G-dbl
"Oh, Lonesome Me" (E)   .... A-ct
"The Water Is Wide" (E, A)   .... A-ct
"Freight Train" (F, C)   .... F-std
"Unchained Melody" (C)   .... Low F-dbl
"I've Got That Old Time Religion" (G, C)   .... F-dbl
"Last Date" (C)   .... Low F-ct
"Orange Blossom Special" (C, F)   .... F-std, Bb-std

Harmonica/bass/vibes: Charlie McCoy
Guitar: Richard Kiser
Piano: Jason Coleman
Drums: Bob Mater
Recorded at Watershed Studio
Engineer: Chris Barnes

2013   Smooth Sailing   Flying Harp (no catalog number)

"Smooth Sailing" (Bb) .... Eb-ct
"Blue Bayou" (A) .... D-ct
"I Love New Orleans Music" (C, D, Bb, C) .... F-std
"I Told You So" (D) .... G-ct
"One Woman" (G) .... C-std
"Ashoken Farewell" (D, G) .... G-ct
"Fanny Mae" (F) .... Bb-std
"Rainy Night in Georgia" (F) .... Bb-std
"Concrete Jungle" .... N/A
"From a Distance" (G) .... C-ct
"Sticks and Stones" (Eb) .... Ab-ct
"Kyoto by Night" (E) .... A-ct
"Leona" (E, F#) .... A-ct, B-ct

Harmonica/lead vocals/vibes/bass/keyboard/trumpet/tuba: Charlie McCoy
Duet partners: Laney Smallwood Hicks, Roddy Smith
Guest soloists: Jason Coleman, Richard Kiser
Guitar: Buddy Blackmon, Bill Hullett, Richard Kiser, Chris Leuzinger, Brent Mason, Roddy Smith, Vip Vipperman, Biff Watson
Steel guitar: Mike Douchette, Russ Hicks, Tim Wright
Fiddle: Loretta Brank, Glen Duncan
Banjo: Glen Duncan, Tim Wright
Accordion: Joey Miskulin
Piano: Jason Coleman, Dave Innis, Hargus "Pig" Robbins, Buddy Skipper, Bobby Wood
Trumpet: Steve Herman
Saxophone: Jim Hoke, Buddy Skipper
Clarinet/flute: Jim Hoke
Trombone: Roger Bissell
Bass: David Hicks, Wayne Moss, Larry Paxton, Tim Smith
Drums: Gene Chrisman, Si Edwards, Paul Leim, Bob Mater, Hans Molenaar, Ted Tretiak, Tommy Wells
Percussion: Farrell Morris
Strings: Nashville String Machine
Background vocals: Lori Brooks, Ellen Dockery, Marabeth Quin, Lisa Silver, Stephanie Hall Wedan
Recorded at Battery Studios, Cinderella Studio, Skaggs' Place, Sound Emporium, Subterrennia, Watershed
Engineers: Chris Barnes, Lee Groitzsch, Jon Hensey, Robert Lucas, Kevin McManus, Wayne Moss, Eric Paul, Brandon Shattuck, Rob Stennett
String arrangement: Bergen White
Horn arrangements: Jim Hoke, Buddy Skipper

| 2015 | Celtic Dreams | Flying Harp (no catalog number) |

"Alten Moor" (Bb) .... Bb-dbl
"Irish Jig Medley" (G, D, Em) .... C-ct, G-ct, C-ct
"Only Our Rivers Run Free" (Ab) .... Db-ct
"Sailor's Jig" (G) .... C-ct
"Going to America" (D, G) .... G-std, C-std
"The Holyoaks" (D) .... G-dbl
"Mountain Laurel" (A, B) .... D-std, E-std
"Lonesome Eyes" (D) .... G-ct
"Chasin' Bart, Girdy and Willie" (G) .... C-ct
"Flowers of Edinburgh" (D) .... G-ct
"McKenna Brigh" (G) .... C-ct
"Blues for Aiden" (Dm) .... Bb-ct
"Kid on the Mountain" (Em) .... C-ct
"Risky Whiskey" (D) .... G-ct
"'Tis a Fine Thing You're Doin'" (F, G) .... Bb-ct, C-ct
"La Fete de L'Orient" (F) .... Bb-ct
"Kelley's Reel" (E) .... A-ct
"The Rats Are Winning the Race" (E, F) .... A-std, Bb-std
"Leather Britches" (G) .... C-ct
"You're Gonna Have to Choose" (D, E) .... G-ct, A-ct
"Cluney's Dance" (F) .... Bb-ct
"Women of Ireland" (C) .... F-ct
"Learmonth's Jig" (A) .... D-ct
"Dublin D.A.R.T." (A) .... D-std, A-std

Harmonica/lead vocals/harmony vocals/bass/vibes/guitar/four-string banjo:
Charlie McCoy
Guitar: Marian Bradfield, Peter Cairney, Gil Draper, Hoot Hester, Bill Hullett, Ken
Isham, Jim Long, Pavel Malina, Michael Spriggs, Vip Vipperman
Mandolin/bouzouki: Wanda Vick
Fiddle: Chad Beauchaine, Hoot Hester, Pepa Malina, Laura McGhee, Downs
Thompson, Wanda Vick, Kristin Wilkinson, Jonathan Yudkin
Four-string banjo: Ken Isham
Piano/keyboard: Jason Coleman, Downs Thompson, Kristin Wilkinson, Ross
Wilson

Accordion: Jeff Taylor
Irish whistle: Jason Herrera, Luboš Malina, Jeff Taylor
Flute: Burt Dickerson
Bass: Spady Brannan, Mark Burchfield, Larry Crew, Hoot Hester, Byron House,
*   Larry Paxton, Pavel Peroutka, Tijmen Zinkhaan*
Cello: Jenny Young
Bodhran: Sam Bacco
Drums: Liam Bradley, Chris Brooks, Bob Mater
Guest harmonica: Donald Black
Guest vocals: Marian Bradfield, Laney Smallwood Hicks, Betsey Long
Background vocals: Lindsay Hicks Gipe, Holly Hicks Singleton, Chris Brooks,
*   Larry Crew, Ken Isham, Jim Long, Barry Murphy, Eric Paul, Jeff Taylor*
Recorded at Chelsea South, Chem 19, Clearmix, Cool NIC2KA, House of Hester,
*   House of Hullett, House of Spriggs, House of Thompson, Inch by Inch,*
*   Laurel Theatre, Signal Path, Skaggs' Place, Watershed, Stateley Paxton*
*   Mansion*
Engineers: Chris Barnes, Will Connell, Lee Groitzsch, Lou Gross, Hoot Hester, Bill
*   Hullett, Jiri Mašek, Dave McCauley, Brian Murphy, Eric Paul, Michael*
*   Spriggs, Greg Timko, Downs Thompson, Kristin Wilkinson, Tijmen*
*   Zinkhaan*

NOTES

1. *Billboard* 70, no. 45 (November 17, 1958), 20.
2. The session logs published by Michael Krogsgaard indicate that a total of 61.5 hours were booked for the sessions, but this figure does not account for meal breaks ("Bob Dylan: The Recording Sessions, Part Two," http://www.punkhart.com/dylan/sessions-2.html.
3. Published session logs indicate that a total of 12.5 hours were booked for the *John Wesley Harding Sessions*, but, as before, meal breaks are not included in this documentation (Krogsgaard, "Bob Dylan: The Recording Sessions, Part Two," http://www.punkhart.com/dylan/sessions-2.html).
4. Reached number 16 on the *Billboard* Hot Country Singles chart.
5. Reached number 23 on the *Billboard* Hot Country Singles chart.
6. Reached number 19 on the *Billboard* Hot Country Singles chart.
7. Reached number 33 on the *Billboard* Hot Country Singles chart.
8. Reached number 26 on the *Billboard* Hot Country Singles chart.
9. Reached number 33 on the *Billboard* Hot Country Singles chart.
10. Reached number 68 on the *Billboard* Hot Country Singles chart.
11. Reached number 22 on the *Billboard* Hot Country Singles chart.
12. Reached number 97 on the *Billboard* Hot Country Singles chart.
13. Reached number 98 on the *Billboard* Hot Country Singles chart.
14. Reached number 30 on the *Billboard* Hot Country Singles chart.
15. Reached number 96 on the *Billboard* Hot Country Singles chart.

ABOUT THE AUTHORS

Over the course of his nearly six-decade career as a session musician, harmonica virtuoso and multi-instrumentalist Charlie McCoy has appeared on thousands of country, pop, and rock recordings. A member of the Country Music Hall of Fame, the Musicians Hall of Fame, and the West Virginia Music Hall of Fame, McCoy also led the famous "Million-Dollar Band" on the syndicated country music program *Hee Haw* for more than two decades.

Travis D. Stimeling is assistant professor of music history at West Virginia University, where he also directs the WVU Bluegrass and Old-Time Bands. His previous books include *Cosmic Cowboys and New Hicks: The Countercultural Sounds of Austin's Progressive Country Music* and *The Country Music Reader*.

INDEX

A

Aaron, Hank, 159
Absalom, Howard, 91
Absalom, John, 5
Ackerman, Willie, 62, 112, 183
Acuff, Roy, 111, 145
Adair, Beegie, 183, 203, 208
Adler, Larry, 146
The Agendas, Charlie McCoy &,
     10–11, 19
Agenda Records, 10–11
Aikins, Bill, 87–89, 91–92, 176
Alaimo, Steve, 10
Alexander, Arthur, 64–65
Alexander, Lamar, 115
Allen, Joe, 180, 181
Allsup, Tommy, 181, 182, 184
Alpert, Herb, and the Tijuana
     Brass, 79
American Bandstand (television
     program), 12, 48
American Federation of Musicians,
     26, 43, 55, 155, 165
Anglin, Jack, 76
Ann-Margret, *x*, 46–47, 50–51
Anita Kerr Singers, 24, 56, 67

Area Code 615, 93–95, 124, 129, 142
Arnold, Eddy, 2, 74
The Arthur Godfrey Show
     (television program), 45
Atkins, Chet, 23, 50, 59, 61, 62, 70,
     78, 104, 117
Autry, Gene, *ix*, 3–4,

B

Babcock, Joe, 67, 112, 181
Bacco, Sam, 207, 215
Bach, Byron, 182, 183, 184, 186
Baez, Joan, 80, 82
Baker, Don, 145
Baker, Kathy, 116
Baker, Kenny, 185
Baker, Steve, 145
The Bakery, 210
Bakker, Martin, 210
Ball, Noel, 64–65
Balladsound Studio, 196
Bananas Studio, 195
Band, The, 35
Banks, Brenton, 182, 183, 184, 186
Barclay, Eddy, 125
Bare, Bobby, 57, 59, 61

Barefoot Jerry, 95–96, 104, 105
Barnes, Chris, 212, 213
Barnett, Mandy, 141
Barrett, Phil, 194
Barry, Sean, 206
Baseball, 3, 105–6, 158–59
Basore, Stu, 180, 181, 186
Battery Studios, 213
Baugh, Phil, 185, 186, 187
Beach Boys, The, 96
Beatles, The, 70, 93
Bedez, Franck, 210
Bellevue Community Church,
    163–64
Benson, Jo Jo, 63
Benton, Barbi, 116
Benton, Brook, 63
Berinati, Lea Jane, 67, 119, 124, 181,
    184, 211
Bernstein, Leonard, 29
Berry, Chuck, 14, 15, 20, 22, 45
Bertin, Luc, 199
Beverly Hillbillies, The (television
    program), 76
Biel, Koos, 130
Bilbrey, Keith, 122
Binkley, George, 182, 184, 186, 187
Birge, Jodle, 128, 130–31, 133, 134–36
Birth Idoffs, 132–33
Bishop, Art, 39–40
Bissell, Roger, 213
Bitter, John, 30
Black, Donald, 215
Black, Larry, 122
Blackmon, Buddy, 96, 104, 107, 118,
    120, 187, 190, 192, 193, 196, 213
Bleyer, Archie, 45–46, 50, 88, 184
Boellaard, Edward, 196
Bonnet, Agathe, 207
Bordonali, Pete, 187
Bowling, 162
Braddock, Bobby, 27
Bradfield, Marian, 215

Bradford, Marian, 214
Bradley, Bobby, 68
Bradley, Charlie, 68
Bradley, Harold, 24, 46, 51, 52, 56, 58,
    79, 171, 177, 181–187, 211
Bradley, Liam, 215
Bradley, Lou, 68
Bradley, Owen, 23, 44, 51, 54, 59–60,
    62, 65, 75, 77
Bradley's Barn, 68, 76, 104, 177, 178,
    184, 189
Bradshaw, Terry, 115
Brank, Loretta, 164, 211, 213
Brannan, Spady, 215
Brannon, Tom, 67, 184, 187
Briggs, David, 62, 93, 124, 176, 177,
    178, 179, 181, 184, 189
Brooks, Chris, 215
Brooks, Garth, 120
Brooks, Lori, 213
The Browns, 59
The Buckaroos, 112
Buffalo, Norton, 145, 154
Burcher, Roy, 148
Burchfield, Mark, 206, 215
Burgess, Wilma, 60
Burnette, Gary, 121, 207
Burns, Jethro, 116
Butler, Carl, 25, 63
Buter, Larry, 182, 184
Butler, Pearl, 63
Butler, Wayne, 81, 92, 176, 177
Buttrey, Kenny, 62, 71, 81, 82, 87, 91,
    93, 96, 124, 176, 177, 178, 179, 181,
    182, 183, 184, 185, 186, 187, 189
Byrds, The, 82
Byrd, Jerry, 63, 135

C
Cadence Records, 45–50
Caire, Clay, 121
Cairney, Peter, 206, 214
Calderon, Blondie, 135

Caldwell, Mike, 145
Caldwell, Walter, 105
Campbell, Archie, 111
Campbell, Pat, 87
Cannon, Freddy, 91
Capek, Rosta, 142
Capitol Records, 65, 95, 97–100
Capps, Jimmy, 122, 180, 181, 186, 189,
   209, 211
Cargill, Henson, 63
Carrigan, Jerry, 62, 72, 180, 183, 189
Carter, Carlene, 74
Carter, Fred, Jr., 62, 78
Carter (Cash), June, 74
Cartwright, Lionel, 158, 164, 206
Cash, Johnny, 63, 64, 73–74, 94, 97,
   127, 157
Casstevens, Mark, 208
Castelli, Jean, 151
Catchings, John, 187
CBS (television network), 109
Cedarwood Publishing, 22, 42–3, 50
Centurymen, The, 66
Cesari, Paul, 151
Chalker, Curly, 100–101, 112, 115, 179,
   181, 185, 189
Chance, Barry, 96, 104, 114, 186, 187,
   190
Chance, Helen, 67
Chance, Lightnin', 56, 185
Chantry, Marvin, 181– 184, 186, 187
La Chapelle en Serval, 210
Chapman, Steve, 185, 186, 187
Charisse, Cyd, 78
Charles, Ray, 109
Chase, Charlie, 121
Chauffriat, Stephane, 151
Checker, Chubby, 121
Chelsea Studio South, 210, 215
Chem 19, 215
Chez Lozac'h, 210
Chez Versini, 210
Childs, Ralph, 184

Chordettes, The, 45
Chrisman, Gene, 202, 213
Christensen, Roy, 184, 187
Christensen, Virginia, 184
Christofferson, Terry, 112
Christopher, Johnny, 187
Cinderella Sound, 68, 95, 124, 150,
   176, 178, 179, 180–185, 187, 189–191,
   194, 196, 198, 210, 213
Clark, Dick, 11, 48
Clark Race Show, The (television
   program), 48
Clark, Roy, 109, 115, 116, 117, 119, 211
Clausi, John, 121
Clearmix, 215
Clement, Jack, 68; recording studio.
   See Cowboy Arms Hotel and
   Recording Spa
Cline, Patsy, 60, 71, 74
Club 17, 26–27
Cochran, Chuck, 181
Coffeen, Selby, 68
Cohen, Leonard, 64, 82–83
Coleman, Jason, 212
Colt, MacKenzie, 116
Columbia Records, 21, 25, 62, 63–64,
   67, 68, 73, 75, 76, 80, 97–102, 107, 126
Colvard, Jim, 96, 124, 125, 178, 179,
   180, 181, 182, 184, 185, 186, 189
Combine Music, 107
Cool NIC2KA, 215
Le Coq d'Or, 35
Cooper, George, 43, 55
Cooper, Todd, 210
Como, Perry, 61, 77, 156
Conn, Mervyn, 127–28, 130
Connell, Will, 215
Conway, Pat, 149–50
Country Dream Festival, 141–2
Country Music Hall of Fame, x, 27,
   108, 158, 163,
Country Showdown (television
   program), 120

Country Sisters, The, 207
Country Sound Studio, 198
Cowboy Arms Hotel and Recording
    Spa, 68, 178
Cramer, Floyd, 24, 46, 51, 52, 56, 59,
    71, 104, 116,
Cravero, Christophe, 210
Crew, Larry, 215
Crook, Lorianne, 121
Crouch, Dennis, 211
Crow, Sheryl, 164
Crowder, Derrick, 149
Cyrus, Billy Ray, 120
Cyrus, Miley, 120

D
Dade County Armory, 19
Dade County Home Show, 7
Damone, Vic, 78, 115
Daniels, Charlie, 82, 96
Danny and the Juniors, 14
Davis, Danny, 116
Davis, Jimmie, 77
Davis, Skeeter, 59, 75, 141
Davis, Steve, 96, 186
Davis, Tex, 98–100, 107, 124
Day, Jimmy, 37
Dean, James, 9
Dean, Jimmy, 60, 120, 146
Dearmore, Terry, 96, 182, 184–186, 187
Decca Records, 21, 22, 23, 62,
Decker, John, 202
Dennis, Quitman, 89–90, 91
Denny, Jim, 22–23, 42, 45, 50
DeSola, Margaret, 16–17
d'Estaing, Valéry Giscard, 127
Dickerson, Burt, 206, 215
Dicky Doo and the Don't's, 14–15, 48
Diddley, Bo, 121
Dillard, Charlie, 98–9
Dillard, Dottie, 24, 56, 67, 181
Dinning (Edgin), Dolores, 67, 112,
    177, 178, 181

Dixon, Willie, 89
Dockery, Ellen, 213
Dollinger, Bud, 47–9
Domino, Fats, 8, 163
Doran, Dave, 96, 181, 184
Dot Records, 64
Douchette, Mike, 213
Dowell, Joe, 63
Drake, Pete, 62, 82, 180, 181, 184, 186
Draper, Gil, 214
Druhá Tráva, 142–43, 154
Duncan, Craig, 203, 209
Duncan, Glen, 213
Dylan, Bob, x, 64, 67, 73, 80–82
Dyson, Bobby, 180, 182, 184, 185

E
Eddy, Duane, 32
Edenton, Ray, 24, 46, 51, 56, 79, 160,
    177, 178, 179, 180, 182, 184, 186, 187,
    189
Edgin, Dolores. See Dinning (Edgin),
    Dolores
Edison Hotel, 35
Edwards, Si, 96, 104, 118, 182, 184, 185,
    186, 187, 190, 192, 193, 194, 196, 200,
    210, 213
Eggers, Bob, 140, 187, 190, 196, 206,
    210
Eichelberger, Gene, 68
Ellison, John, ix
Emery, Ralph, 121, 122
Emmons, Bobby, 184
Emmons, Buddy, 37, 127, 186, 187
The Escorts, Charlie McCoy &, 76,
    80, 81, 88–93, 96, 158
Euro-Sound Studio, 198
Evans, Dale, 115
Everly Brothers, 45, 60

F
Fargo, Donna, 207

Fayetteville, WV, ix–x, 2–5, 91, 105–6, 120, 148
Fean, Ray, 150
Felts, Narvel, 35
Ferguson, Bob, 65
Ferguson, Johnny, 33–36
Fernandez, Jean, 124–25
Fillmore West, 94
Flat 5 Studio, 210
Flatt & Scruggs, 64, 76
Flores, Rosie, 37
Flynn, Pat, 209
Football, 159–160
Forbes, Zack, 164
Ford, Shannon, 119
Formánek, Emil, 143
Foster, David, 164
Foster, Fred, 51–52, 62–63, 88–9, 92, 96, 98, 99, 105, 107, 117
Fountain, Pete, 106–7, 185
Francis, Connie, 14, 60, 61
Franklin, Paul, 185, 186, 189
Freberg, Stan, 156
Fred Foster Sound Studio, 176
Frick, Bob, 7
Fricke, Janie, 67
Fukada, Yoshiharu, 140
Fye, Charlie, 10

G
Galbraith, Greg, 209
Garcia, Katia, 143
Garfunkel, Art. See Simon & Garfunkel
Garland, Hank, 46, 51, 56
Garrish, Sonny, 209
Gathering, The,164
Gatlin Brothers, The, 63
Gayden, Mac, 92, 93, 96, 176, 177, 178, 179, 185, 186, 189,
Gayle, Crystal, 105, 127
Gaylord, Ed. See Gaylord Entertainment

Gaylord Entertainment, 110, 118–9
Gazell, P. T., 145
Geraud, Jean-Marie, 199
Gibson, Steve, 186, 187
Gifford, Frank, 116
Gifford, Kathy Lee (Johnson), 116
Gill, Vince, 88–89
Gilley, Mickey, 120
Gillotti, Angelo, 13
Gimble, Johnny, 116, 127, 182, 187, 189
Glosson, Lonnie, 115, 145
Goldsboro, Bobby, 65–66
Goodman, Diana, 116
Goodrum, Randy, 187
Gordon, Marianne, 116
Gorodetzky, Carl, 182, 183, 184, 186, 187
Grace, Roberta, 185
Grammer, Billy, 63, 88
Grand Ole Opry, 37, 38, 39, 55, 60, 62, 75, 87, 95, 104, 118, 122, 139, 163
Grant, Milt, 49
Graves, Uncle Josh, 77, 107, 177, 178, 179, 180, 181, 182, 183, 184, 185, 186, 187, 189, 190
Gray, Wayne, 21, 38
Grateful Dead, The, 94
Green, Barry, 208
Green, Bob, 10, 49
Green, Buddy, 145, 210
Green, Lloyd, 62, 127, 138, 179, 180, 181, 183, 184, 186, 187, 189, 209
Greene, Buddy, 145
Greene, Jack, 60
Grizzard, Ed, 75
Grobba, Detlef, 145
Groitzsch, Lee, 208, 211, 213, 215
Gross, Lou, 215
Guitar, Hawaiian, 7–8, 135

H
Haagmans, Jos, 195, 198
Haggard, Merle, 65, 155

Haight, Lenny, 182, 183, 184, 186, 187
Hailey, Chad, 68, 198
Haley, Bill, 35
Haley, Rick, 8
Hall, Bill, 65
Hall, Rick, 62, 64
Hall (Wedan), Stephanie, 121, 213
Hall, Tom T., 63, 106
Hallman, Victoria, 116
Hamilton, George, IV, 141
Hamilton, George, V, 141
Hanson, Dennis, ix
Harman, Buddy, 24, 51, 52, 56, 79, 162, 177, 180, 181, 183, 186, 187, 189
Harmonica, bass, 78; chromatic, 146, 148–49; country-tuned, 149; first, 2–3; Hohner, 148–49; rhythm and blues influences, 11; ten-hole, 146, 149
Harpo, Slim, 11, 144
Harris, John, 95, 96, 178, 179, 180, 181
Hart, Freddie, 67
Hartford, John, 115
Hartman, Jan, 130, 132
Hartman, Warren, 96, 184, 186, 189
Hawkins, Hoyt, 56, 67
Hazelwood, Lee, 78
Hazen, Lee, 68
Heart Warming Records, 85
Hedeman-Hansen, Nils, 139
Hedeman-Hansen, Tove, 139
Hee Haw (television program), x, 67, 109–19, 122, 128, 145, 156
Hee Haw Honeys, The (television program), 116
Helms, Bobby, 60, 67
Hensey, Jon, 213
Herman, Steve, 213
Herrera, Jason, 215
Hester, Hoot, 120, 121, 197, 207, 209, 211, 214, 215
Hickman, Elmer, 1–2

Hicks, David, 118, 120, 191, 192, 193, 194, 198, 202, 210, 213
Hicks (Gipe), Lindsay, 207, 215
Hicks (Singleton), Holly, 215
Hicks, Russ, 76, 96, 104, 118, 119, 120, 124, 125, 179, 180, 181, 182, 183, 184, 185, 186, 187, 189, 190, 191, 192, 193, 194, 196, 197, 198, 202, 203, 206, 207, 209, 210, 211, 213
Hill, Benny, 71
Hirt, Al, 106, 185
Hobbs, John, 209
Hockey, Ice, 160–1
Hoepfinger, Mary Alice, 180, 183, 186, 189
Hohner. *See* Harmonica, Hohner
Hoke, Jim, 145
Holladay, Ginger, 124
Holladay, Mary, 124, 125
Holladay Sisters, The, 124, 186, 189
Hooper, Paul, 8, 17
Horner, Yvette, 126–7
House, Byron, 215
House of Hester, 215
House of Hullett, 215
House of Spriggs, 215
House of Thompson, 215
Houston, David, 64
Howlin' Wolf, 144
Huang, Cham-Ber, 146
Hudson, Ed, 68, 83
Hughey, John, 184
Hullett, Bill, 121, 197, 203, 206, 209, 211, 213, 214, 215
Humbard, Maude-Amie, 85
Humbard, Rex, 85
Humphrey, Patience, 151
Hungate, David, 208
Huskey, Junior, 56, 177, 178
Husky, Ferlin, 65
Hutton, Gunilla, 116, 118
Hyodo, Shoko, 140

I

I-40 Paradise (television program), 164
Ickes, Rob, 211
Inch by Inch, 215
Innis, Dave, 164
Isbell, Dottie, 10
Isbell, Jim, 9–10, 35, 47, 87, 176, 177, 178, 179, 180, 181, 182, 183, 184, 185, 186, 187, 189, 210
Isbell, Susan, 10
Isham, Barbie, 164
Isham, Ken, 164, 214
Iversen, Peter, 198
Ivey, Clayton, 209
Ivy, Mark, 121

J

Jackson, Stonewall, 38, 40, 42, 45, 46
Jackson, Tommy, 180, 183, 189
Jackson, Wanda, 37
James, Sonny, 65, 75
Jarrett, Hugh, 56, 67
Jefferson Airplane, 94
Jimmie Dean Show, The (television program), 146
Jo, Damita, 79
Jordan, Abby, 165
Jordan, Austin, 165
Jordan, Hannah, 165, 206
Johnson, Bill, 20, 21, 39, 40
Johnson, Dirk, 211
Johnston, "Jelly Roll," 145
Johnston, Bob, 57, 63, 64, 78, 80–4
Jones, Frank, 63
Jones, George, x, 21, 27
Jones, Grandpa, 111, 115, 118
Jones, Quincy, 79
Jordan, Vic, 119
Jordanaires, The, 25, 56, 58, 66–7, 124, 131, 141, 171, 196, 197, 198, 202, 207
Justice, Charlie, 21, 187
Justis, Bill, 66, 79, 185

K

Kavoukian, Jack, 149
Kazuaki, Furuhashi, 140
Kealoha, Elon, 7–8
Keener, Glenn, 183
Keister, Shane, 186, 187
Kelley, Keith, 4
Kelley, Esther, 84–85, 164
Kelley (Thrift), Opal Winona, 1–5, 164
Kennedy, Jerry, 62, 63, 79
Kent, Tony, 210
Kerns, Robert, 164
Kerr, Anita, 24, 56, 65, 67
Kershaw, Doug, 180, 189
Kimbrough, Jerry, 192
King, B. B., 49
King, Ben E., 57
King, Brent, 68
King, Jana, 121
King, Sherry, 104
Kingston Trio, 32
Kirby, Dave, 182, 186
Kirk, Rahsaan Roland, 79
Kirkham, Doug, 46
Kirkham, Millie, 56, 67
Kiser, Richard, ix, 210, 212, 213
Knox, Tom, 180, 185
Kooper, Al, 81
Kosumbersky, Petr, 206
Koyama, Teddy, 140
Křesťan, Robert, 142–43, 204
Kristofferson, Kris, 88, 89, 157
Kroon, Jerry, 120, 192, 193, 197, 198
Kuklik, Petr, 142
Kulczak, Philippe "Guzze," 136
Kurland, Sheldon, 182, 183, 184, 186, 187

L

La Rosa, Julius, 45
Ladd, Les, 68
Landštof, David, 143

Lane, Christy, 156
Larry's Country Diner (television program), 122
LaSorda, Tommy, 115
Lauper, Cyndi, 37
Laurel Theatre, 215
Lavender, Shorty, 180, 184, 186, 189
Law, Don, 25, 62, 63, 73
Lea Jane Singers, The, 67, 186
Learmouth, William A. "Buddy," 4
LeCroix, Roy, 13
Ledvina, Martin, 204
Lee, Brenda, 23–5, 44, 60, 65, 67, 71, 75
Leech, Mike, 184
Leim, Paul, 213
Leuzinger, Chris, 213
Levine, Sam, 208
Levy, Steve, 145
Lewis, Jerry Lee, 35–6, 63, 163
Liles, Sandy, 110
Lindsay, George, 111
Linde, Dennis, 178, 179, 180, 189
Linneman, Billy, 121, 180, 181, 182, 186
Lisbygd, Kim, 140
Lisbygd, Lotte, 140
Liška, Tomáš, 143
Little Richard, 105
Little Wally Pickle and His Polka Band, 154
Little Walter, 11, 44, 144
Live with Regis and Kathy Lee (television program), 116
Lively, Buddy, 5
Locklin, Hank, 59
Logan, Johnny, 206
Löhmer, Klaus, 147
London, Larrie, 16
Long, Betsey, 215
Long, Ken, 164
Long, Jim, 164
Long, John, 113, 115
Long, Rufus 208

Longy-Miquelle, Renée, 28–31, 33, 34, 41, 58
Loudermilk, John D., 33
Louvin Brothers, The, 65
Lovullo, Sam, 109, 111, 119
Lozac'h, Jean-Yves, 130–31, 195, 196, 198, 199, 200, 205, 210
Lozac'h, Morane, 207
Lucas, Robert, 213
Ludder, Doris, 16
Lynn, Loretta, 60, 76

M
MacKenzie, Bob, 85
Maher, Brent, 176
Malina, Luboš, 142–43, 204, 206, 215
Malina, Pavel, 214
Malina, Pepa, 143, 214
Malloy, Jim, 68, 78
Malone, Kenny, 96, 179, 180, 181, 182, 184, 185, 189, 193, 198, 202
Mancini, Henry, 61
Mandrell, Barbara, 105–6
Mandrell, Irlene, 116
Manhattan Transfer, 82
Marx, Kerry, 207
Martin, Dave, 211
Martin, Dean, 156
Martin, Grady, 24, 44–45, 54–55, 56, 71, 77, 80, 145, 179, 180, 181, 184, 189
Martin, Rodge, 57
Martin, Tony, 78
Martino, Al, 78
Mašek, Jiri, 204, 215
Mason, Brent, 196, 213
Masterlink Studio, 192, 193, 197, 198, 203
Mater, Bob, 121, 202, 203, 211, 212, 213, 215
Mathies, Gil, 148
Matsuda, Koichi "Ari," 145
Matthews, Neal, 25, 56, 57–59, 67, 171, 196,

Mayo, Susan (Bennett), 164–65
Mazer, Elliott, 93
McBride, Martina, 120, 153
McBride, Mike, 187
McCartney, Paul, 82
McCauley, Dave, 215
McCoy, Bennett, 166
McCoy, Caroline, 166
McCoy, Charles Ray, Jr., 165–66
McCoy, Pat Maguire, 165
McCoy, Ray Hampton, 1, 2, 5, 9,
    11–14, 26, 30, 31, 32, 33, 34, 36, 45,
    47, 70, 91, 116, 159
McCoy (Jordan), Ginger, 165
McCrory, Martha, 182, 184, 186
McDonald, Benny, 92, 176, 177
McDonald, Country Joe, and the
    Fish, 94
McElhiney, Bill, 65, 182
McEntire, Reba, 153
McKinley, David, 68, 183
McKinley, Dawn, 116
McManus, Kevin, 196, 210, 213
Meader, Vaughn, 50
Mercury Records, 63, 66, 68, 107
Mersey, Bob, 64
Metters, Gil "Chick," 36
Migliore, Tony, 119, 120, 183, 203
Miller, Jimmy, 87, 89
Miller, Jody, 101–2
Miller, Roger, 63
Mills, Joe, 68, 184
Milteau, Jean-Jacques, 125–26, 145
Miniconi, Paul, 151
Minor, Marsha, 112
Miskulin, Joey, 213
Mitchell, Eddy, 123–26, 128
Moby Grape, 94
Moeller, Lucky, 44
Molenaar, Hans, 130, 195, 196, 198,
    199, 205, 213
Montgomery, Bob, 65
Montgomery, Carol, 177, 182

Monument Records, 51–52, 62–63, 68,
    88–89, 96–98, 99, 107, 117, 124, 128,
    149
Moonshine Cloggers, The, 118
Moore and Moore, 207
Moore, Alan, 187
Moore, Bob, 24, 25, 51, 56, 79, 179, 180,
    181, 183, 185, 186, 187
Moore, Mary Tyler, 107
Morita, Yasumasa, 140
Morris, Farrell, 180, 181, 182, 183, 184,
    185, 186, 187, 189, 196, 213
Morris, Jill, 137
Morris, Rodger, 121, 192, 193, 202, 211
Moss, John, 96, 187, 190
Moss, Wayne, 58, 62, 68, 81, 82, 87, 91,
    93, 96, 124, 150, 171, 176, 177, 178,
    179, 180, 181, 182, 183, 184, 185, 186,
    187, 189, 190, 191, 192, 193, 194, 196,
    209, 210, 213
Mouskouri, Nana, 79, 130
MTM Records, 107
Mullins, Cam, 65
Murad, Jerry, 146
Murphy, Brian, 215
Murphy, Barry, 215
Musial, Stan, x, 115, 159
Music City Tonight (television
    program), 121–22
The *Music City Tonight* Singers, 202
Music Operators of America, 153–54
Music Sales, 149–50
Music videos, 157
Myrick, Weldon, 62, 93, 104, 177, 178,
    179, 180, 181, 182, 184, 185, 186, 187,
    189

N
Nabeta, Masaki ,140
Nagai, Takasi "Tak," 141–42
Nagatomi, Kenji, 140–42
Nagatomi, Mari, 140
Nakase, Honey, 140

Nall, Jimmy, 184, 186
Nashville Edition, The, 67, 112, 116, 118, 184, 186, 189
Nashville Network, The (television network), 120–22
Nashville Now (television program), 120–21
Nashville Number system, 57–59, 171–73
Nashville Palace, The (television program), 119–20
Nashville Sounds, The (baseball team), 158–9
Nashville Sounds, The (vocal group), 67, 185, 186
Nashville String Machine, The, 213
Nashville Symphony Orchestra, 62
National Association of Music Merchants (NAMM), 145, 149
Nelson, Craig, 209
Nelson, Ken, 65, 97–99
Nelson, Willie, 145–46
Newell, Fred, 96, 121, 181, 182, 183, 184, 186
Newman, Jimmy C., 37–38, 40, 42, 139
Newton, Wayne, 118
Nielsen, Bodle, 133
Nielsen, Calle, 128, 133–35, 136, 139
Nielsen, Chris, 133
Nielsen, Christina, 133
Nielsen, Mike, 133
Nielsen, Nigge, 133
Nielsen, Patrick, 133
Norris, Becky, 116
Norris, Lindy, 116
Novotny, Luboš, 143
Nunley, Louis, 24, 56, 67, 181, 196

O

Oak Hill, WV, ix, 1–2
Oak Valley Studio, 196, 210
Ogdin, Bobby, 120, 196, 198, 203, 210

Ohmsen, Tom, 210
Old Grey Whistle Test, The (television program), 94
Old South Jamboree, 19–21, 22, 26, 27, 36, 38, 39
Olympics, 161
Omnes, Julien, 199
Omnes, Philippe, 199
O'Niell, Eoghan, 150
Opryland, 113, 118, 119
Orbison, Roy, 51–53, 63, 65, 71
The Osborne Brothers, 77
Osborne, Bobby. *See* The Osborne Brothers
Osborne, Sonny. *See* The Osborne Brothers
Owens, Buck, 65, 109, 112

P

Pachuki, Al, 68
Page, Patti, 60, 61, 64, 80
Page, Ricki, 67, 176
Palúch, Stanislav, 204
Parker, Duane, 149
Parman, Cliff, 66
Parton, Dolly, 63, 88
Patin, Bob, 207
Paul, Eric, 68, 135, 208, 211, 213, 215
Paxton, Kip, 119
Paxton, Larry, 121, 197, 202, 206, 209, 213, 215
Paycheck, Johnny, 21, 64
Pearl, Minnie, 111
Pederson, Benny, 139
Pederson, Janna, 139
Penrod, Guy, 121
Perkins, Carl, 8
Perkins, Reggie, 13
Peroutka, Pavel, 215
Peter, Paul, and Mary, 82
Petersen, Kirsten, 130
Phillips, Bob, 176
Phillips, Bill, 21

Phillips, Sam, 71, 88
Pierce, Webb, 21
Plak, Sjœrd, 132, 137, 138, 195, 196, 198,
    199, 200, 205, 210
Plantation Records, 63
Polydor Records, 93, 95
Pontieux, Loic, 210
Pop Goes the Country (television
    program), 121
Potter, Don, 208
Presley, Elvis, 8, 25, 52, 56, 60, 67,
    71–73, 78, 124
Price, Ray, 37, 65, 135, 141
Pride, Charley, 75
Propst, John, 182, 183, 184
Pruett, Sammy, 211
Puett, Billy, 185
Puk Studio, 194, 198
Pursell, Bill, 66, 106, 177, 180, 183,
    184, 185, 186, 187, 189
Putnam, Norbert, 62, 93, 177, 187

Q
Quadrafonic Sound Studios, 68
Quin, Marabeth, 213
Quonset Hut, The, 23, 25, 55, 68, 76,
    126

R
Raeger, Eddie, 39
Rainwater, Cedric, 211
Randolph, Boots, 24, 25, 52–53, 62,
    66, 71, 73, 79, 88, 104, 116
Raney, Wayne, 115, 145
Raphael, Mickey, 145–46
Rather, M. C., 181
Rawlings, Dave, 68
RCA Victor, 23, 50, 51, 55, 59, 62, 67,
    68, 71, 75, 76, 78, 117, 163
Red, Buryl, 66, 106, 183
Red Coats, The, 10–11
Reed, Jerry, 57, 62
Reed, Jimmy, 11, 44, 75, 144–45

Reiss, Andy, 203, 208
Restless Heart, 164
Reynolds, Jody, 14
Reynolds, Leigh, 164
Reynolds, Ron "Snake," 68
Reeves, Jim, 60, 74
RFD-TV (television network), 122
Rhodes, Curly, 46
Rhodes, Leon, 112, 182
Rich, Charlie, 64, 67, 153
Rich, Don, 112
Richard, Cliff, 61
Richards, Earl, 37
Richey, George, 97, 98, 109, 111
Richmond, Paul, 180, 181
Riddle, Jimmy, 145
Rieuf, Glenn, 68, 192, 193, 197, 198
Riley, Jeannie C., 63
Rimes, LeAnn, 120
Ripley, Alice, 116
Ritter, Tex, 21
Rivers, Jerry, 211
Rivers, Johnny, 44
Robbins, Hargus "Pig," 56, 65, 71, 79,
    81, 82, 83, 127, 177, 178, 179, 180, 181,
    182, 184, 186, 187, 189, 193, 196, 209,
    210, 211, 213
Robbins, Marty, 60, 63
Robertson, Robbie, 81
Robinson, Smokey, and the Miracles,
    48
The Rockin' Maniacs, 13–14
Rodgers, Jimmie, 145, 153, 163
Rodman, Judy, 67
Rodriguez, Luis, 12
Rogers, Roy, ix, 3, 115, 162
Rohan, Brian, 94
Roman, Lulu, 111, 116, 202
Ronnie's Place, 209
Ronstadt, Linda, 82, 94
Roosevelt, Franklin Delano, 1
Rosanes, Tamra, 207

Rowan and Martin's Laugh-In
(television program), 109
Rowe, Misty, 116, 118
RTL (radio station), 127
Rugg, Hal, 60, 62, 180, 181, 182, 189
Russell, Leon, 82
Ruth, Babe, 159
Ryman Auditorium, 37

S
Sahlin, Salle, 139, 198
Saive, Harold, 8
Sanford, Billy, 62, 180, 182, 184, 189
Sasser, Larry, 121
Schaffer, Steve, 187
Schneider, Roy, 210
Scott, Peggy 63
Scruggs, Earl, 76, 104
Sears, Dawn, 141
Sears, Kenny, 211
Seely, Jeannie, 63
Seitz, Chuck, 68
Self, Ronnie, 24
Sellers, Dale, 112, 118, 124, 125, 182, 185, 189
Seventeen (magazine), 46
Shattuck, Brandon, 213
Sheffield, Don, 176, 185
Shelton, Blake, 27
Sherrill, Billy (engineer), 68
Sherrill, Billy (producer), 63–64, 67
Shook, Jerry, 180, 183, 189
Signal Path, 215
Silver, Lisa, 180, 189, 213
Simon & Garfunkel, 78
Simon, Paul, 78–79
Sinatra, Frank, 78
Sinatra, Nancy, 78
Singleton, Shelby, 63, 79
Sinks, Earl. *See* Richards, Earl
Skaggs' Place, 208, 211, 213, 215
Skaggs, Ricky, 211
Skala, Paul, 180, 181, 182, 183, 184

Skipper, Buddy, 96, 121–22, 181, 182, 184, 185, 186, 189, 193, 197, 202, 208, 213
Slezák, Kamil, 143
Slichter, Jimmy, 7–8
Smallwood (Hicks), Laney, 105, 114, 118, 119, 129, 138, 191, 193, 196, 202, 206, 207, 208, 210, 213, 215
Smash Records, 63
Smith, Cal, 60
Smith, Carl, 40, 63
Smith, Connie, 65, 74
Smith, Don, 178, 179, 180, 181, 182, 184, 185, 186, 187
Smith, Roddy, 213
Smith, Snuffy, 33–34, 37, 47
Smith, Steve, 182, 183, 184, 186, 187
Smith, Tim, 203, 213
Smith, Velma, 56
Smyth, Jimmy, 150
Society for the Preservation and Advancement of the Harmonica (SPAH), 146
Solarik, Peter, 204
Solee, Denis, 121, 208
Sommer, André, 130, 137, 195, 196, 198
Sons of Champlin, 94
Sony Records, 107
Sørensen, Jørgen, 198
Sound Emporium, 213
South, Joe, 62
Sovine, Red, 38–41, 42, 45
Sparkman, Tom, 68
Sparxxx, Bubba, 94
Spencer, Roger, 208
Spicher, Buddy, 62, 93, 94, 107, 180, 182, 185, 189, 190
Spriggs, Michael, 211, 215
St. Louis Cardinals, 158–9
St. Marie, Buffy, 80, 82
Starr, Ringo, 82
Stateley Paxton Mansion, 215
Statler Brothers, The, 63, 105–6

Stampley, Joe, 64
Stennett, Rob, 210, 213
Stevens, Ray, 57, 62, 63, 66, 79
Stevenson, Kenny, 10, 32
Stewart, Wynn, 65
Stoker, Gordon, 56, 67, 196
Stokes, Donna, 116
Stone, Henry, 10–11
Stone, Mike, 182, 184
Stoneman, Ronnie, 111, 115
Street, Mel, 105
Strong, Tommy, 68, 176, 177
Strzelecki, Henry, 62, 71, 81, 82, 112, 118, 178, 179, 181, 184, 186
Sturdivant, John, 76, 89, 92
Subterrennia, 213
Suits, Wendy, 67, 112, 181, 182
Sullivan, Ed, 156
Sullivan, Larry, 111, 112
Sun Records, 71, 73, 163
Surý, Petr, 143
Suwa, Yoshiko, 140
Svenning, Kenneth, 139, 198
Svensson, Jonte, 139, 198
Swahn, Yan, 128
Swan, Billy, 63
The Sweethearts of the Rodeo, The, 120

T

Tallent, Charlie, 68, 177, 178, 189
Tapp, Gordie, 111, 115, 118
Taylor, Jeff, 206, 215
Teal, Christian, 183
Terranova, Sam, 187
Texas Troubadours. See Tubb, Ernest
That Good Ole Nashville Music (television program), 121
Thaxton, "Happy" Harold, 20–3, 25, 26
Thielemans, Toots, 146–48
Thomasson, Mort, 68, 178, 179
Thompson, Bobby, 93, 96, 112, 115, 118, 178, 179, 180, 181, 182, 183, 184, 185, 186, 187, 189
Thompson, Downs, 119, 130, 132, 150, 195, 198, 199, 200, 202, 206, 207, 214–15
Thompson, Linda, 116
Thrift, Robert J., Jr., 4–5
Tidwell, George, 121, 208
Tillander, Bruno, 163
Tillis, Mel, 21–23, 42, 105
Tillotson, Johnny, 45, 49
Timko, Greg, 210, 215
Tinch, Eddie, 92, 177
Todd, Lisa, 116
Tokutake, Toshiyuki, 140
Tomblin, Earl Ray, ix
Tomboola Band, 139
Tootsie's Orchid Lounge, 37
Tranzer, Fab, 210
Tretiak, Ted, 164
Tropicopa, 12–13
Tubb, Ernest, 37, 153, 157
Tucker, Tanya, 64
Tuttle, Jerry, 35, 92, 176, 177, 181
Tuxen Huset, 210
Tuxen, Nils, 128, 130–1, 132, 210
Tweedy, Don 66
Twitty, Conway, 60, 127

U

Umstead, Alan, 162
United Artists, 65
United Steels of Europe, The, 130–32
University of Miami, 26–32, 61
Uratani, Shin-ichi, 140
Urban Cowboy (film), 120

V

Valadon, Alain, 137–8
Valadon, Annie, 138
Valadon, Willie, 138
Valadon, Clara, 138
Van der Zalm, Rens, 200, 206

Van Dyke, Leroy, 63
Vanderkooi, David, 183
Vandervort, Bill, 68
Vannelli, Gino, 82
VanOsdale, Gary, 182, 183, 184, 186,
    187
Vaughn, Sharon, 67, 184
Versini, Anny, 138
Versini, Jean-Marc, 138–39
Vibraphone, xi, 59, 61, 66, 67, 75, 78,
    121
Vick, Wanda, 121, 202, 203, 206, 209,
    214
Villadsen, Mogens, 128
Vincent, Gene, 98
Vineyard, Shirley, 16–17, 28
Vinton, Bobby, 77–78
Vipperman House, 210
Vipperman, Vip, 96, 104, 118, 119, 120,
    191, 192, 193, 194, 196, 198, 202, 203,
    206, 207, 209, 210, 213, 214
VornDick, Bil, 68, 203, 209
Vriet, Danny, 205, 210

W

Wade, Pete, 62, 177, 178, 179, 180, 181,
    183, 189, 203
Wall, Ann, 183
Walker, Bill, 121
Walker, Jeanine, 181
Walker, Keiko, 141
Walker, Ray, 56, 67
Walker, Wayne, 42
Waterman, Bruce, 185
Watershed Studio, 212
Watson, Biff, 213
Watson, Doc, 77
Webster, Chase, 64
Welch, Gillian, 68
Welch, Lenny, 49
Wells, Kitty, 21, 75–6
Wells, Tommy, 213
Wembley Festival, 127–28

Wenche, 207
West, Duane, 67, 184, 187, 196
West Virginia Music Hall of Fame,
    ix, 6, 41
West Virginia University, 6
Westberry, Kent, 9, 21, 32–4, 36–8,
    42–3, 47, 50
Wheeler, Billy Edd, 78
Wheeler, Onie, 145
Where the Action Is, 11
White, Bergen, 66, 92, 106, 176, 177,
    178, 179, 180, 181, 182, 189, 213
White, Jerry, 182, 183, 184, 185
White, Tommy, 121, 209
Whitehurst, Jerry, 112, 121, 180, 181,
    186
Wiginton, Hurshel, 67, 112, 181
Wilburn, Neil, 67, 68, 83, 176
Wilde, Claude, 126
Wilkerson, Jimmy, 182, 183, 184
Wilkinson, Kristin, 206, 214–5
Williams, Andy, 45, 50
Williams, Bobby, and the Night
    Lifters, 87–88
Williams, Chaz, 171–72
Williams, Don, 105
Williams, Hank, 1, 33, 75, 211
Williams, Jack, 141, 183, 207
Williams, Jett, 211
Williams, Mason, 93–4
Williams, Tommy, 112, 115, 187
Williamson, Sonny Boy, 11, 144
Wilkin, Marijohn, 36, 38, 42, 46, 50,
    168
Wilson, Ross, 214
Winfrey, Ernie, 68
Wise, Chubby, 73
Witherspoon, John, 74
Witherspoon, Reese, 74
Witt, Johnny, 105
WCKY (radio station), 115
WJJD (radio station), 99–100
WLAC (radio station), 11–12

WOAY (radio station), 1–2
Wolf Pack, 136
Woolf, Stephanie, 182, 183, 184, 186
Wood, Bobby, 184, 213
Wood, Randy, 64–65
Woodland Studios, 68, 183
Wright, Bobby, 76
Wright, Gil, 24, 56, 67, 181
Wright, Johnny, 21, 75–6, 104
Wright, Tim, 213
Wynette, Tammy, 21, 64, 105, 111, 127

X
XERF (radio station), 115

Y
Yarborough, Chuck, 13
Yasumi, Masaru, 140

Yelvington, Jim, 9, 10, 19
Yesteryear (television program), 121
Young, Chip, 62, 68, 73, 176, 178, 179, 180, 182, 184, 189
Young, Donnie. *See* Paycheck, Johnny
Young, Jenny, 215
Young, Reggie, 184
Yudkin, Jonathan, 214

Z
Zinkhaan, Tijmen, 132, 195, 198, 199, 200, 205, 215
Zinkan, Joe, 25, 56, 177, 178, 179, 180, 181, 182, 183